HEAL
THE WOUNDS OF
CHILDHOOD

A psychologist's journey and discoveries from wretched beginnings to a thriving life

DON ST JOHN, PH.D.

Healing the Wounds of Childhood

Copyright © 2016 Don St John, Ph.D.

Printed in the United States of America

All rights reserved. No part of this book may be reproduced or transmitted in any form or by any means, electronic or mechanical, including photocopying, recording, or by any information storage and retrieval system, without permission in writing from the publisher.

Paths of Connection
www.pathsofconnection.com

Cover Design: Judy Haas
http://www.troutart.com

Formatting: Debora Lewis
arenapublishing.org

ISBN-13:9780997130102

Dedication

This book is dedicated to all of you who intuitively know that "being normal" is so far from who you can truly be.

It is dedicated to all of you, who know you carry scars of early wounding, who know your childhood was less than perfect, who may struggle with health, relationship or well-being issues; it is dedicated to all of you, who want to understand fully how you may have been affected; and, how you can best heal, grow and thrive.

I dedicate it as well to all the psychotherapists and counselors who want to understand where the body fits into healing and growth; and, to all the "body people"—from physicians, somatic therapists, acupuncturists and bodyworkers who want to understand how upbringing and relationships influence the bodies they work with.

ACCLAIM FOR
HEALING THE WOUNDS OF CHILDHOOD

This authoritative and comprehensive exploration of healing and wellness is also a riveting page-turner, full of practical advice and personal stories, including from the author's own traumatic childhood. It offers a remarkable and uncommon integration of brain science, mainstream psychology, and cutting edge ideas and practices. Effective, hopeful, and profound, this is a gem.

> Rick Hanson, Ph.D., author of *Buddha's Brain* and *Hardwiring Happiness: The New Brain Science of Contentment, Calm, and Confidence*

Don St. John's book is a huge accomplishment, a miraculous personal journey intertwined with the miraculous evolution of many disciplines seeking to understand mind and human heart to help people heal. Despite the pervasiveness of trauma, amply manifested in the author's own "wretched" beginnings, his theme is that love is ever abundant— if we learn how to receive it, how to take it in so that we can thrive. Read this book to learn about the evolution of science and the field of psychotherapy. Read this book to learn about one's man journey from trauma to love-ability. And read this book to get some wonderful sage, truly tried-and-true advice about how you too can apply these lessons to make your self's journey sweeter and richer.

> Dr. Diana Fosha, Developer of AEDP and author of *The Healing Power of Affect* and *The Healing Power of Emotion: Affective Neuroscience, Development and Clinical Practice*, edited with Daniel Siegel and Marion Solomon

We are very pleased to recommend Don's book to all of you. "Healing the Wounds of Childhood" is really two different offerings. First of all it is a very personal anecdotal document that lays out the very raw wounds of his life and how he dealt with them. In opening his very personal process to us, he also has given to his readers a clear and intimate view of a wide range of therapeutic disciplines. Thirdly he is able to tie it all together with a combination of wisdom, clarity and always a sense of presence in relationship to the material and to the reader. The wounds of our life are made to be healed by our efforts rather than being drowned in the sense of victimhood that so easily can run our life. Don's writing is a gift to those of us who do our best to travel the path of consciousness and to those of us who are looking for how to begin the journey.

Hal Stone, PhD and Sidra Stone, PhD, authors of *Embracing Our Selves: The Voice Dialogue Manual; Embracing Each Other: How to Make All your Relationships Work for You; Embracing the Inner Critic: Turning Self Criticism into a Creative Asset*; and *The Shadow King: The Invisible Force that Holds Women Back*; and *Partnering: A New Kind of Relationship.*

In this book Don St. John draws on his personal experience to develop a model of integration which is both simple and profoundly effective. He begins by looking at the values that are really important to our development as a person. He illustrates his points by describing experiences from his personal and his professional development with the sort of sensitivity that can result from deep wounding. After a thorough tour of all the physiological as well as the psychological elements of a healthy life, he delivers an intelligent and coherent pathway to integrate all the various aspects of our lives and to literally incorporate the lessons from both our positive and our "negative" experiences. It is a pathway in that it includes for each aspect some practical steps to integrate that aspect. An inspired and inspiring work of synthesis, I think it is brilliant!

Joseph Heller, Author—*BodyWise* and Founder, Hellerwork Structural Integration.

ACKNOWLEDGMENTS

This book would never have been written without the love and support of my wife, partner and dearest friend, Diane. I don't mean that just in the sense of the enormous generosity of time and energy that she has contributed. Indeed, she has tirelessly read each version of the manuscript, and has been among my sharpest critics—editing, suggesting and urging for more clarity. Of course, this in itself has been hugely helpful. More importantly however, I have been able to write this book because she is the person, who along with me, forged something neither one of us knew in the past—a strong, enduring, intimate marriage that seems to improve with every passing year. Without this I would not have the ground, the moral standing, to speak of a thriving life.

I want to thank our very dear friend Elizabeth Anne Sutcliffe for her courageous feedback and support. Courageous because a year ago, I thought the manuscript was near completion. I brought it to Hawaii for some final tweaking. After spending a few hours reading it, she and my wife both, facing my incredulous ire, told me in no uncertain terms that it was too cumbersome and needed to return to the drawing board. As I write this now, I know I have a different book here. Thank you, Elizabeth.

My editor Sarah Aschenbach did a remarkable job. On one hand she made numerous line by line changes in my grammar and sentence structure. On the other, when I read her edition, it didn't seem as if she made any changes at all. It was my voice through and through. Thank you Sarah.

My assistant, Jenny Mauro, has been constant with her creative and administrative input.

Joseph Heller has been both mentor and friend, for over forty years. Many years ago he predicted that I would write this type of book.

I owe a great deal to Emilie Conrad, a mentor who taught me something about what it means to be alive in this body. I so wish she were still among us to read what I have written. She always expressed sincere interest in how this project was progressing.

Thank you to my oldest and dear friends Jerry and Nancy Noloboff, who throughout this writing expressed their love and support.

And to my brother, Rocky. I have loved you since the day you were born.

And to Debbie, Matt, Elias and Ruth, I thank you from the depths of my heart for being such a great family.

CONTENTS

INTRODUCTION

"Love is the only emotion that expands intelligence."
~ Humberto Maturana

In this book, I share my personal story with you and my discoveries about what our bodies, our "selves," and our relationships need in order to heal from the wounds of life, especially those we sustain in childhood. I wouldn't wish my beginnings on anyone. There was only one possible way for me to survive the brutality I endured and that was to shut myself down. Essentially, I was incapable of feeling. I was numb. Yes, my story is extreme, but it required me to leave no stone unturned to discover how to restore my humanity. I wanted to be able to really enjoy a long-term intimate sexual relationship with one person, to be able to tune into another's emotional experience and empathize, to feel good and free in my body and spirit, to stand before groups and speak without fear, to age with vitality and grace, to look forward to adventures. I acquired all of these abilities during adulthood. As a young man embarking upon adulthood, I would have received an F in those subjects.

I hope that your story is not as extreme as mine, yet I have learned that most people have had their share of wounding. This wounding conspires with the speed of our culture and with ignorance regarding what we need and how we are affected by not receiving it. At best, it prevents us from reaching our full potential.

In the past few years, a huge number of books have been written about trauma.[1] This interest has become especially acute given the number of soldiers returning from Iraq and Afghanistan in the past dozen years. The cost to society and the suffering of these individuals are enormous, making understanding trauma vitally important work. A common conclusion drawn by these books is that the body must be included in the healing process in some way. There is recognition that the functioning of the nervous system of these wounded veterans has been impaired and that treatment must go beyond simple talk therapy.

I am in full support of this direction. However, I do have one problem with the emphasis on those who have been seriously traumatized. By presuming that those who experienced severe wounding, such as from the battlefield, are traumatized or "sick," and those who did not experience such calamities are "normal," we are looking through lenses that are too narrow. I believe a wider set of lenses will encourage both those who were severely traumatized in war as well as the rest of you to engage the practices, treatments, and disciplines that can heal your wounding and enrich your lives. I believe that most of you who are reading this have suffered your share of wounding. I believe an exploration of these approaches—some of which are now used with serious trauma—can help heal your wounds and greatly enrich your lives.

Let me ask you a delicate question. Do any of the following apply to you? Did you have a mother who was depressed for a long time after your birth? Did you suffer a traumatic birth? Did your parents divorce before you were seven years old, which suggests that they were miserable for several years prior? Did you have an alcoholic parent or a parent with a serious anger problem? Were you in a serious accident in childhood? Did you have at least one parent who, regardless of how caring he or she might have been, had no clue what it meant to be emotionally present? Did you have a parent who was heavy handed expecting you to adhere to standards well above your age? Did you receive a good deal of empathy and emotional guidance? Did you feel seen and understood by at least one parent? Was discipline meted out firmly with love and respect? I could go on, but I'm sure you get my point.

This is not an indictment of your parents. Most parents are doing their very best. However, you will see that what we need as human beings is just beginning to come to light. And one thing we all need is a good dose of someone being *present* with us, someone who can truly see us and touch our hearts with theirs. When we don't receive what we need, there are consequences—emotional, health, and relationship consequences.

For example, there is one thing that every one of us can learn to do better in this life. That one thing is to let love in. I don't mean this in an abstract sense, but in a real, visceral, in-the-moment sense. When someone is present with you, looking into your eyes with admiration, care, interest, or affection, are you able to feel it, absorb it, and enjoy it? To what degree can you let it in comfortably? Each of us has a limit to our capacity, and the more we are able to take in, the richer we feel. Over years I have seen many clients, and regardless of what they came in complaining of—anxiety, depression, relationship issues, general malaise—all had one thing in common: they were unable to let love really touch their hearts. I know about this. As a young adult, I could not tolerate simple eye contact, and even less so when someone was offering me positive feelings.

This challenge to let love in is not just found among people who suffer from anxiety, depression, or addictions. People who would never consider therapy, who consider themselves healthy and functioning well, have ample room to grow this ability. I use this ability as an example, albeit an important one, because as we examine all the areas of our being that are affected by our wounding, you will see clearly that much more has been affected than you can even imagine. There is growing evidence that love, in the sense that I have been describing, is right up there after air, water, food, and physical safety as an essential human need. Children become wrecks without it. Adults feel starved without it and try to substitute all sorts of things in hopes of feeling it. Many, if not most, human beings walk around with an implicit presumption that love is scarce. In reality, love is the most potentially abundant nutrient in the world, as are air and water. We all need and deserve to experience love, but most of us have to learn how to grow our ability to receive it. What you probably don't know is that one of the fastest growing approaches to psychotherapy focuses powerfully and directly on helping you grow this ability. It is called AEDP[2] and was founded by Dr. Diana Fosha, a New York psychotherapist and professor. From my point of view, you don't need to have a "disorder" to benefit enormously from such an approach.

Chapter 1 begins by clarifying what I believe most of you really want in life. I believe you want to be present in your life, to feel engaged, to have good health, vitality, and genuine love connections with those close to you. I believe you want to feel free in the sense of knowing that your choices are respected and that you have the space to be yourself. Of course, I know you want to age with grace. Often many of us say we don't have the slightest idea what we really want. Sometimes, our conditioning and wounding are such that we never learned how to know ourselves well and know what we truly want and need.

In Chapter 2, I will share the three insights that made a monumental difference in the course of my life. You will come to understand what I mean when I say that *normal* is not nearly good enough. When I look around at what we take to be "normal," it makes me sad. There is so much more to life, and it has little to do with an accumulation of material goods and so much more to do with our evolvement as human beings, capable of living with peace and love in our hearts.

The second insight is that those wounds of life don't just affect your psychology or your emotions. They affect the very cells, tissues, and structure of your body, your brain, your nervous system, your beliefs about who you are, and your relationship capacities. Therefore, to come close to your full potential, you must address all parts of you. I include in this even the quality of the fluids that course through your body. You are 99 percent water in terms of the quantity of molecules in your body, and 70 percent water in terms of total volume. That is a whole lot of water; we are just beginning to understand the implications of this biological fact for our well-being.

The third insight that shook me to my depths was that our physical health, our mental health, and our relationship health are all related. Perhaps this isn't too surprising to you, but twenty five years ago, when it was beginning to dawn on me, it was a big one. It may be for you, too.

In Chapter 3, I describe what it is I believe we should all be striving for. It is a concept that brings together your body, your personality, and your relationships. To state it simply, it is a state or condition in which both individual freedom and global cohesion are maximized. This concept is called coherence. Consider a close relationship, for example. A close coherent relationship would mean one in which you feel free to be and express yourself and at the same time feel very connected to the other. We will return to this concept frequently; for example, it will help you understand the importance of addressing your body to heal and enrich your life.

Chapter 4 will help you understand the importance of having someone who is emotionally present, especially during the first few years of life. You will see why both your nine months in mom's womb and your experience of being born could have long-lasting effects. We will examine the specific emotional nutrients that children require for optimal growth towards becoming coherent human beings. There are consequences to not receiving these nutrients, just as there are consequences to not receiving an adequate supply of each vitamin and mineral.

In Chapter 5 we explore how we bond, and whether your first relationships were secure or not. Our early bonding experiences are of the utmost importance and affect our relationship capacities throughout our lives. Within this context of gestation, birth, and bonding, we formulate our deep, core model of who we are, how good we are, whether people can be trusted, whether our needs will be met, and so forth. These are questions you have answered emotionally by the time you are four or five years old. We go on to address these in Chapter 7.

In Chapter 6, I share my relationship story. In retrospect, I consider myself almost retarded in relationships when in my twenties and early thirties. It's hard to divulge that part of my life; I only do it to show how much change can occur in a lifetime and what is involved in making those changes happen.

Chapter 8 shows you how an important part of your brain—an

area of what is called your prefrontal cortex—requires the emotional nutrients we have been learning about in order to develop well. Not receiving these emotional nutrients sets the stage for stress to become very problematic in your life. And as you will see in Chapter 9, stress is *not* about having too much on your plate. It is so much more about how well certain neurological and psychological structures have developed in your early years. It is about your capacity to meet the demands and challenges of life well.

Good health and vitality are qualities we all want, but we have not known enough about how to achieve them. In recent years, we have accepted that stress is a factor in illness, but not many people understand how that works. You need to know how stress affects you so that you can increase your ability to deal with life's challenges effectively. Chapter 10 continues with stress, explaining how it relates to your health. In language as simple as possible, I have presented what you need to know about stress. As you will see, stress affects your immune system, and therefore, it is implicated in most illnesses. It also affects your brain and your cardiovascular system. Having this understanding and knowing how to "feel and deal" is essential to your health, your well-being, and your relationship happiness.

This leads us naturally to consider stress in its overwhelming form—rapes, muggings, serious accidents, and war. What mechanisms are involved when what is called PTSD develops?

Although there are clear markers of PTSD, I have found that it is essential to understand that many symptoms of PTSD, such as shutting down, hyper-vigilance, and hyper-arousal, are part of the make-up of a large percentage of us who don't have PTSD and who could benefit enormously from working on these issues. To better understand this, we need to know how the autonomic nervous system functions. This is the subject of Chapter 11. Your doctors will tell you to exercise, eat well, and "reduce stress." I hope these chapters will give you—and them—a better understanding of what that means.

In Chapter 12, I give you a new perspective on your heart. It is so much more than an elegant pump. When I speak of the ignorance in our culture, lack of appreciation for the human heart is among my indictments. Fortunately, a growing body of science is shedding new light. When your heart is awakened and cleansed of all the hurts and grievances most of us hold, life has a very different quality. You will learn the importance of cultivating positive feelings, such as appreciation and gratitude. You will learn to see that your heart is a full partner with your brain as an organ of intelligence.

A favorite expression I use in this book is, "It's your whole organism." So, next we consider our very tissues, our flesh and blood. Psychologist, psychiatrists, and social workers are our culture's authorities on well-being, mental health, and relationship satisfaction. Yet, many have very little idea what our bodies—their tissue quality, movement quality, and structural quality—have to do with health, relationships, and well-being. Chapter 13, as well as Chapter 3 and Part Two of the book, will leave you no doubts about their importance. As an illustration of that importance, I include a story of a medical drama I went through in 2001. In medical lingo, I had what is called a myocardial infarct or, in everyday language, a heart attack. I will tell you the story in Chapter 13—and it really is a good one.

Chapter 13 concludes our "landscape." In Part One, you will learn what children—and you, as well—need in order to develop optimally. You will acquire a new set of lenses concerning such ideas as normality, growth, mind, body, relationships, stress, health, and love. You will understand the importance of your gestation, birth, and bonding experiences, and how you form your model of self and the world, and how your brain and relationship capacities are formed during the early phases of our lives. Most important, however, you will learn that it is never, ever too late. At our essence, we are adaptable and resilient. Positive change and growth are of our very nature.

Throughout Part One, I have given you exercises and reflections to help you grow. I consider the set of practices at the end of Chapter 6 to be especially important, because when you come even close to mastering them, your intimate relationships will be awesome. Nevertheless, I believe you will find all the practices and reflections to be quite helpful.

In Part Two, I outline my professional journey and then delve into eight different disciplines, processes, and treatments that I believe everyone should at least know about. They made a huge difference in my life.

The primary source for my research is my own life, followed by the lives of my many clients and students over forty-five years. Sprinkled throughout these chapters is my own story, a story that began under the most challenging of conditions: being unwanted, a near-death experience at birth, and severe physical and emotional abuse from early infancy through adolescence. The deck was well stacked against me. I entered adulthood as somewhat of a wreck.

Now in my seventies and defying the odds, I would say that my life has been an adventure for the past forty years, and I have been thriving for the last twenty or more. This is a story of hope, a story of victory against hellish odds with a clear message of "If I can do it, so can just about anyone else."

You can grow continuously, regardless of your age and regardless of the hand you were dealt. You can increase your capacity to let love in. You can become more coherent human beings.

1. See, for example, the works of Bessel Van Der Kolk, *The Body Keeps Score*; Marion Solomon and Daniel Siegel, ed., *Healing Trauma,* and Peter Levine's, *Waking the Tiger* and *In an Unspoken Voice.*

2. AEDP stands for Accelerated Experiential Dynamic Psychotherapy. Based in the neurosciences and psychodynamic theory, it is a relational approach. We will examine it in Chapter 19.

PART ONE: THE LANDSCAPE

CHAPTER 1

WHAT WE REALLY WANT
(EVEN IF WE DON'T REALIZE IT)

"Connectedness is an organizing principle of the universe."
~ David Bohm

Genuine connection means to be seen and understood. After almost fifty years of working as a psychotherapist, I have formed several convictions about what most human beings want. We want good relationships, at least one in which we are really seen and deeply understood. It is very special when someone knows us, not just superficially, but all of us: our challenges, our victories, our dreams, our hopes, and the different and complex parts of our personality. It is a priceless gift when someone sees who we are beneath our social façade. It is an experience of love to be seen, enjoyed or admired, and related to.

What is really sad, and far too common, is to live your life to the end without ever feeling seen and known. But there is a catch here: in order to be seen and known, deeply, you must be able to soften or release the protective structures that you have built. We all have these structures. They can be soft, light, and simple and easy to open when we wish, or they can be rigid, complex, fragmented, deeply engrained, and seemingly impenetrable. And the more impenetrable the structure, the more difficult it is to feel seen and known. The majority of us are somewhere in the middle of that scale.

Most of us, although certainly not all, want a satisfying, long-term intimate relationship. Human connection provides the nourishment that is nearly as important as food. Impoverishment of human connection has consequences. I like drawing an analogy between the nourishment of connection and the nourishment that comes from what you eat. Both provide quantity and quality. Yes, it is true that some in our culture truly do not have enough to eat, the majority of us ingest more than enough. However, as is obvious, quantity does not guarantee quality. The same holds true for human connection. Yes, there are people who have little or no social connections, but most of us engage in ample social interactions. Once again, though, quantity does not guarantee quality. Further, just as our bodies may be starved for certain nutrients without our knowledge, so too we may be starved for certain types of human nourishment, and we may or may not know it.

Autonomy and Closeness

In our committed relationships, we want to feel autonomous, free to make our own choices and pursue our own interests while, simultaneously, feeling connected and close to our partners. I realize that this may seem like a contradiction or a zero-sum proposition. In other words, it is common to think that the degree to which I am free within myself reduces the degree to which I can be close to you. But it's not a zero-sum situation, at all. I believe most of us want both. More about that later.

Self-worth and Resilience

We all want to feel good about ourselves and to think well of ourselves. We want to feel and believe that we matter, that we contribute to partners, friends, family, work, church, and/or community. We want to be strong enough to formulate an intention and carry it to fulfillment. We want to be resilient, to be able to bounce back from defeats, frustrations, and disappointments and keep moving in the direction we have chosen. We want to be strong enough not to become addicted to what harms us.

Presence

Presence is having all your energy and attention at your disposal and not inaccessible because of worry, distraction, or anxiety. Frequently, people have so much unfinished emotional business or so many chronic conflicts that the amount of their energy and attention available to harness in any given moment is far less than what could be possible for them.

To Live, Move, and Age with Vitality and Grace

It is a wonderful thing to enjoy moving our bodies—dancing, running, swimming, playing golf, or just walking. It really is lovely to be comfortable in our skins, to enjoy our natural sensual nature, and to be relatively free of chronic aches and pains. Yet, we humans struggle with our bodies in many ways. We struggle with the way we look, the way we feel, and how much we weigh. Each year, we spend billions trying to look better and feel better. What is so sad is that most of us don't realize that our personal history and cultural assumptions have conspired to disconnect us from our bodies in significant ways, and *this disconnection is the source of so much of our discomfort.*

> *"Let my love, like sunlight,*
> *Surround you,*
> *Yet give you illumined freedom."*
> ~ Rabindranath Tagore

So, how do you achieve these things? How do you develop a healthy, robust sense of self? How do you strengthen your capacities for relationships? How can you become able to let love in while not compromising your freedom and autonomy? How can you enjoy the movement and sensuality of your body while living and aging with vitality and grace? How can you live from your core self and not from the protective barriers you constructed before you completed adolescence? How do you go beyond feeling that you are a separate entity to knowing that you are part of a greater whole and that there is intelligence in that greater whole? In other words, how can you enrich your life, no matter where you are at this moment?

This is what I want to convey: *all of us can do it!* All the knowledge, tools, resources, and help we need are increasingly available in our culture today. It is true that not all of them are easy to find and that most of us don't know what's really needed, and these factors, of course, make it pretty difficult. And this is why I am writing—to tell you about the resources I have found and give you the understanding and guidance to know what you need to create a more fulfilling, vital, and satisfying life.

You may ask why I am so sure that almost all of us, if we really want to, can dramatically improve the quality of our lives. The answer is simple: If I could do it given my circumstances, and I did, I know it is possible for you to do it.

Let me give you a flavor of what it was like for me growing up. The story of my early life is rather intense. I will tell it in bits and pieces throughout the first part of this book. In Part Two, I will share the healing modalities that became a huge part of the adventure of my adulthood.

My Wretched Beginnings

I can't remember when the beatings became a daily occurrence. No, I don't mean spankings. What I vaguely remember as always having been part of our relationship are my mother's fire-spewing eyes. In an instant, her frustration would turn to rage. Only God knows how early in my life her rage became a daily event. If I attempted to block her blows, she became even angrier, screamed louder, and continued her attack until she knew she had landed some solid hits. She broke so many wooden stirring spoons across my back and shoulders that for a while she bought only the metal ones. When she bent one of those on me, she went back to buying the wooden spoons.

My momma never could stand a mess. She was revolted by

anything dirty. One evening when I was a year old, we were having dinner with my grandparents. I guess I was really getting into sloshing my food around. When a few "stop its" didn't work, she sent her hand flying across my face. Her father picked up his plate of pasta and stopped just short of throwing it at her. My mother told the story many times. With ignorant audacity, she bragged about it: "He was one-year-old when I gave him his first slap across the face." It was the first of a couple of thousands of those slaps, "the beatings," as she called them. The beatings were always accompanied by her favorite epithets. She had several, but her most frequent was, "You and that no good son-of-a-bitch father of yours ruined my life." Other close favorites were, "You no-good-for-nothing son of a bitch," or, "You disgust me," said with a look of revulsion. In the face of such overwhelming fury, I could only go numb.

Here's another incident that was gouged into my memory. When I was around five, I witnessed a fight between one of my many cousins named Rocky and another boy. When it ended, I ran home, excited, to deliver a blow-by-blow account to my mother and grandmother. "And Rocky called him a fucking—" I had no idea what the word *fucking* meant, but it was the last word I spoke in that sentence. Leaping out of her chair, her eyes nearly falling out of her head with rage, she chased me around the table twice before my grandmother was able to block her path. Thankfully, that time, I was able to escape to the bedroom as she continued screaming, "You ever use that word again, and I'll kill you!"

What a wretched child I must have been to merit such treatment. This is how kids think. They assume they deserve what they receive. She was my mommy, and I was sure I must have done something to deserve it. It has taken me a long time to heal such profound shame and feelings of unworthiness.

I know. It's pretty intense. However, I am not sharing my story as a call for pity. I am sharing it so that you might ask, "How can anyone possibly turn around a life with such wretched beginnings?" Perhaps you have heard it expressed that if you want to understand the great middle, you should study the extremes. My childhood was extreme in its violence, abuse, and ignorance. Substantial evidence suggests that anyone reared in my circumstances is not likely to have a healthy, vital, and satisfying life. Yet, I can claim with gratitude and humility that my life has evolved beyond anything I or anyone else ever could have imagined or predicted.

Through my long journey out of the dark trenches of my childhood and into the sweetness and blessedness of my current life, I evolved a comprehension of what happens to us when we are poorly tended or maltreated, and what happens to us when we don't have sufficient understanding of what it means to be alive in these human bodies. Included in the comprehension I have achieved is an understanding of what it takes to restore the full, rich quality of our humanity. I have learned what it takes to live in a body I actually can enjoy and which is capable of deep, loving connections. I have become appreciative of its sensual nature. These days, I live with mostly positive feelings, such as gratitude and appreciation. I have learned what it takes to have a delightful marriage, replete with deep, intimate communication and even a modicum of sizzle as we journey into our seventies.

Sadly, living this fully is not the norm; yet, it is a potential we all can realize. When you finish this book, I hope you will not aspire to "being normal." By then, you will have realized that what is considered "normal" is very far beneath what you will know is possible.

CHAPTER 2

"Normal" Is Not Nearly Good Enough

"There is a candle in your heart, ready to be kindled. There is a void in your soul, ready to be filled. You feel it don't you?"
~ Rumi

"You are not a drop in the ocean, you are the entire ocean in a drop."
~ Rumi

Have you ever worried about whether or not you are "normal?" Somewhere in the recesses of your mind, do you harbor doubts about whether you are like most other people? Do you worry that you don't "fit in" and that you may never? If you have mood swings or if you have an addiction—to alcohol, drugs, sex, or chocolate—do you believe you are part of a small percentage of the population with a disorder and wish somehow to be normal? Please don't. As you will see in this chapter, we are all on the same boat! Sure, some of us may be sitting towards the front and some of us in the back, but it is the same boat. My experience tells me that this is a much more useful, compassionate, and healthy way to think about your personal journey than wondering if you are normal.

Growing up in my generation, I believed that all illness came from germs, bacteria, and viruses, and, of course, bad luck. My mind was just my mind and somehow related to my brain, and my body was my body. My intimate relationships were something else entirely. Mind, body, health, and relationships all lived in their separate compartments. Further, things were either normal or abnormal.

Obviously, when one is engaged in deep personal and transformational work, many insights appear along the way. Three, based on years of observation, have been central to my understanding over the years.

Three Insights that Shook my Intellectual Roots

The following three insights represented a paradigm shift in my life, and I hope they presage a paradigm shift in our culture. The sands are clearly shifting, and I pray these insights represent a few more grains of sand towards that shift.

1. *All of us have suffered—whether we know it or not—and all of us have ample room to grow.*

Not having your essential needs met is a suffering. Having someone who is emotionally *present* is an essential need. As children we quickly develop mechanisms to avoid suffering. So, most people who say they had a normal childhood felt it was normal because they developed mechanisms not to suffer. Psychologists call these defense mechanisms. Essentially, children shut down parts of themselves. They may have shut down their assertiveness, their tenderness, their trust, their sensuality, or their playfulness. Having shut those parts down, they avoided suffering. Why shut those parts down? When aspects of self are not met or acknowledged, or are explicitly or implicitly forbidden, we have to shut them down or else we will feel overwhelmed and not capable of coping.

In your healing journey, it's not about getting fixed and becoming normal. No matter where you begin, you will always have plenty of room to grow. Before this awareness dawned, I assumed that I was one of a low percentage of emotionally disturbed individuals and that everyone else was "normal." Obviously, this idea was discouraging. If you believe you have been damaged, you probably believe that you are not "fixable." Not so. We are all human, and I believe that we can all evolve and flourish.

What I mean by a healing journey is movement towards

wholeness or, more precisely, coherence, which I will elaborate upon throughout this book. I do not mean curing symptoms so as to become what we call normal. Even in the finest homes where children are cared for and well-attended, our high-speed, high-stress, and high-consumption culture is bound to constrict our potential. Also, the ideas we have about living in these bodies and what they need and our human tendency not to claim all of who we are unnecessarily limit our potential. Therefore, whether fortunate or unfortunate in our upbringing, each of us has room to grow towards realizing our potential as a human being. Fortunately, new tools and resources for that growth have become available in recent years.

2.   *Our whole organism is affected by life's wounds.*

Yes, all of you—not just your psychology, your thinking, or your emotions. The impacts and insults you have experienced affect your entire organism. Therefore, all parts of you (your heart, brain, guts, muscles, connective tissues, and cells) must be addressed in healing. I could have remained in talk therapy forever and would not have explored the depths I have managed to reach once I included the somatic therapies in my healing regimen. As important and valuable as good psychotherapy is, it is not enough.

3.   *Physical health, mental health, and relationship quality are entwined.*

The capacity for open-hearted connections, excellent relationships, good health, resilience, graceful aging, and a body relatively free of major tension patterns are all related. I believe this will become clearer as we proceed. Further, as the science comes in to support this assertion, I believe a new model of health, well-being, fitness, and relationship health will emerge.

But I'm getting ahead of my story. First, what do I mean when I say the impacts and insults of our lives affect us as entire organisms?

Wounds and the Whole Organism

The wounds of life—especially in childhood—negatively affect us as entire organisms. So does well intentioned ignorance. For the most part, I will be using the terms wounds or impacts and insults, rather than trauma. It is quite difficult to examine your childhood in terms of whether or not you experienced trauma. The problem is that the conclusions we draw can leave out a great deal of useful information. Many patients over the years told me that they experienced very little "trauma" in childhood. Initially, they usually say they had a normal childhood. Then, within the next fifteen minutes, they tell me their mom was depressed for two years after their birth or their father was an alcoholic who came home enraged once a week. Many tell me their parents never openly expressed affection to them or to each other, that feelings didn't exist in their homes, and on and on. But there was "no trauma." Theirs was a "normal childhood."

Further, the word *trauma* itself is used in so many different ways that non-professionals can be easily confused. For example, the literature on trauma speaks of the following concepts: big-T trauma, little-t trauma, relational trauma, development trauma, shock trauma, and probably others. This yes/no model of trauma keeps us stuck in a way that suggests treatment is only for those individuals who "have the disease." Yet, most of the symptoms of trauma that are present when a diagnosis of PTSD is given are found to an often considerable degree in many of us who would not be classified with PTSD. For example, many human beings are disconnected from their emotions, from their bodies, or from parts of themselves. Many individuals who would not be classified as PTSD are hyper-vigilant, tense, anxious, or hyper-aroused. To suggest that only those with PTSD should receive treatments is to deny perhaps the majority of human beings access to newly evolving techniques that would be of enormous benefit. Further, it would take even more of the stigma off those with PTSD.

So, for these reasons, I am going to refer to the wounds or impacts and insults of life. We have all experienced them to one degree or another. By ignorance, I am mostly referring to the general lack of wisdom around what it means to be alive in these bodies and what we truly need; what our potential really is—for connection, for living in harmony with each other and with nature, for aging in a very different way, for enjoying the very movement of our own bodies, and much more.

When I say that we are affected as whole organisms, I am referring to your core beliefs about yourself, about others, and about the world; to your relationship capacities; to your sense of who you actually are and to your personality, your brain, and your nervous system. Further, my personal and professional journey have shown me that, without a doubt, your neuromuscular system and your connective tissue system, including the fluids (mostly water) of your body must be included. In other words, you cannot separate body from mind from relationships. You need to recognize the whole of you, and how different systems affect each other.

Let's Forget "Normal"

To be "normal" for this age and time is based upon a set of cultural beliefs and assumptions, and these are gradually being challenged in many quarters, including the natural sciences. These beliefs and assumptions are a barrier to realizing even a fraction of your potential. They keep you stuck in a materialistic, mechanistic view of yourself and your life.

For example, do you want your marriage to be just like your parents' marriage? Do you want to age with the degree of vitality and suppleness your parents or grandparents had? Probably not! There is a huge difference between what is normal statistically and what is possible, and between what is normal statistically and what is ideal. If you knew you could have good relationships, genuine connection, autonomy, closeness, good self-worth and resilience, and good health and vitality, and if the means to achieve those were available, all you would need is the desire to have them. Further, if you knew it was not "abnormal" to seek psychotherapy or somatic therapy, it would be so much easier to go for it.

In time, I am certain, a new model of what it means to be healthy both physically and emotionally will prevail. The model I envision, and am describing, will view relationship health, emotional health, and physical health as interrelated.

CHAPTER 3

COHERENCE—HOW IT ALL CAME TOGETHER FOR ME

"When one tugs at a single thing in nature, he finds it is attached to the rest of the world."
~ John Muir

Dr. Mae-Wan Ho and Coherence

After forty years of exploring body, mind, and relationships, I still lacked a unifying concept. All the pieces were there; I knew the importance of fluidity, of good physical structure, of healthy supporting beliefs, and of good relational skills. I knew that although our current model of health and fitness was a grand leap forward over the ideas of the fifties and sixties, those ideas were quite insufficient. Still, I didn't have a single concept that put the whole picture together. I had all the ingredients to make a cake; I just didn't know what the cake was.

Then, I came upon the work of Dr. Mae-Wan Ho. She has written two books. Her first, *The Rainbow and the Worm: The Physics of Organisms*[1] sent shivers coursing down my spine. It provides ample scientific evidence for the premise that consciousness and our experience of life do not reside only in the brain. Rather, they reside throughout our entire organism. Therefore, life's wounds affect the entire organism. Dr. Ho is looking at the biology of an organism through the lenses of quantum physics, and she is arriving at some fascinating conclusions. It is well beyond the scope of this book to attempt an elaborate explanation of her visionary work. I will simply share what I have derived from reading it. The extrapolations of her thoughts to the structure of the body, the personality, and our relationships are mine.

As science grows, our models change. The prevailing medical/psychological paradigm essentially equates the mind and the brain and views the rest of the body as their obedient servant. This fundamental premise informs our culture's model of health, well-being, fitness, and yes, even relationships. Science is in the process of revising this model significantly, and Dr. Mae-Wan Ho is leading the charge. As Dr. Ho's understanding of the implications of quantum physics for cell biology becomes part of the general scientific and medical narrative, I believe we will become much better equipped to take good care of ourselves and to heal the wounds that limit our potential. Specifically, I believe we will come to understand that physical fitness, emotional health, and relational capacities are all part of a whole and must be thought of as a whole. For example, a fit person is not one who can simply run ten miles or has abs of steel. A fit person is one whose tissues are also *responsive, receptive, adaptive, versatile, fluid,* and *vibrant.* This presents a very different picture of fitness. More accurately what we are pursuing in this model is coherence.

The Jazz Band Metaphor

The Rainbow and the Worm describes the living organism as coherent, which Dr. Ho defines *as a state in which both individual freedom and global cohesion are maximized.* She uses a jazz band as a metaphor to illustrate her point. Each musician does his own thing and in perfect harmony with the whole band. The quality of the music is determined by how well each player performs; the vitality, heart, and soul with which he plays his own instrument; and how well he plays in unison with every other member of the band, which shows how sensitive and responsive he is to his fellow musicians. This is a good example of individual or local freedom *and* global cohesion.

Dr. Ho's books give a rigorously scientific definition of coherence in mathematical terms. However, for our purposes, the metaphor of the jazz band is sufficient and indeed apt. All living organisms, from the amoeba to the human being, are ideally coherent. "They are thick with coherent activities on every scale, from the macroscopic down to the molecular and below."[2] This understanding fortified my conviction that the whole organism is affected by life's wounds; impacts and insults decrease coherence; therefore, you must address the whole organism to achieve full healing. This in itself fascinated me. My own experience had clearly demonstrated its accuracy, but to have it grounded in hard science took my conviction to another level.

Her second book, *Living Rainbow H2O*,[3] presents extensive scientific evidence that it is the very fact that we are composed mostly of water that accounts for our capacity to change. As I read, I realized that water itself provides the model to strive for: water is a model for health, well-being, fitness, and relationships.[4] No wonder I had shivers streaming down my back! In *Living Rainbow H2O*, Mae-Wan Ho applies quantum physics and electrodynamics field theory to the biochemistry of water, concluding that quantum coherence is possible because of the large percentage of water that constitutes an organism.

> Quantum jazz is the music of the organism dancing life into being. It is played out by the whole organism, in every nerve and sinew, every muscle, every single cell, molecule, atom, and elementary particle.... Intercommunication is the key to quantum jazz. It is done to such sublime perfection that each molecule is effectively intercommuni-cating with every other, so each is as much in control as it is sensitive and responsive. And intercommunication is predominantly electronic and electromagnetic, thanks to liquid crystalline water.[5]

This was especially exciting to me as a fluid movement teacher, structural integration practitioner, and psychotherapist. Mae-Wan Ho's work can integrate all three of those disciplines around one concept. She is saying that coherence is the nature of life because coherence is the nature of water, and water, as she puts it, is the means, medium, and message of life. She adds that water is even more essential and integral to life than we have previously known.

"The fluid system is the fundamental system of communication."
~ Emilie Conrad

So, this is how her work landed in me. The more vital, energized, and alive the fluids of our bodies are and the more freely they flow, the more coherent we become. Water becomes your cells and tissues. Even your bones, the driest tissues in your body—are 15 to 20 percent water. All your muscle tissues, including those of your organs and heart; all your connective tissues—the fascia or coverings of every muscle fiber, and, essentially, the wrapping of everything within you, big and small; and all your tendons, ligaments, and cartilage come from water and are water-drenched, Your brain is about 70 percent water. All your tissues come originally from water, and water saturates most everything. So the coherence—think of it as vitality—of your fluids affects the quality of your tissues, your physical structure, and your experience. In Chapters 13 and 16, we will investigate this even further.

Coherence at the level of tissues means that the tissues, particularly the connective tissues and muscle tissues, are elastic, supple, receptive, responsive, vibrant, and free to move as they were meant to move. Coherent tissues are fluid, like a well-soaked sponge. Tissues come together to form organs and a whole physical structure. From my perspective as a Hellerwork Structural Integrator, this is how I see coherence—ideally—in the whole physical structure. First, every joint in the body is free to do what it is meant to do, without impediments or constrictions. And each joint is in harmony with every other joint in the body. There is a sense of balance, and the body seems to be supported by gravity rather than engaged in a losing battle with gravity.

Human structures have personalities, and personalities can also be seen in terms of coherence. No matter whose theory of personality we use to understand personality, I think we can apply the concept of coherence. Every aspect of the personality has its place, but it is how it plays its tune in conjunction with every other aspect of the personality that determines the quality of the music.

Human structures and personalities exist in relationships. Once again, life provides a model for the ideal relationship; it maximizes both freedom and cohesion. It is my belief that maximum freedom as well as maximum cohesion is exactly what most of us long for in our relationships. Often, we can feel either smothered or too distant emotionally. How odd and how wonderful that water itself can provide both model and *ideal* for human relationships.

Again it is important to keep in mind that each aspect I described affects and is affected by every other aspect. So, the quality of your fluids, the quality of your tissues (including your brain and nervous systems), the quality of your structure, the quality of your personality, and the quality of your relationships all influence and are influenced by every other aspect. As Dr. Ho said, intercommunication is the key to quantum jazz.

When each molecule, cell, tissue, muscle, organ, joint, structure, aspect of self, and person in relationship is freely doing what it is designed to do, and in harmony with every other molecule, cell, tissue, muscle, organ, joint in the body, aspect of self, and person in relationship then we have a coherent human being. It includes health, well-being, fitness, and relationship. This is coherence. In the realm of fitness, if we strengthen muscles while simultaneously limiting the movement of joints, that does not enhance coherence. If we shorten muscles from their optimal length, that diminishes coherence.

The implications of Mae-Wan Ho's work are staggering. One implication concerns consciousness as one with the whole organism. A fundamental premise of neuroscience research, however, is that consciousness is located in the brain. Obviously, the brain is a critical organ of consciousness; but listen to what Dr. Ho says after she has considered the implications of quantum physics for biological organisms:

Whenever people speak of consciousness, they usually locate it in the brain where ideas and intentions are supposed to flow, and which through the nervous system, is supposed to control the entire body. I have always found that odd, for like all Chinese people, I was brought up on the idea that thoughts emanate from the heart. I have come to the conclusion that a more accurate account is that consciousness is delocalized throughout the liquid crystalline continuum of the body (including the brain), rather than just being localized to our brain or to our heart. By consciousness, I include, at the minimum, the faculties of sentience (responsiveness), intercommunication, as well as memory.[6]

What might it mean to accept that consciousness is located throughout the liquid crystalline continuum of the whole body? What might that mean for physical education and physical fitness? What might it mean for health and self-care? Would not disciplines such as Structural Integration and practices such as Continuum Movement be seen as belonging in the forefront of health care rather than on the fringes? Certainly from the science of Mae Wan-Ho, we can intuitively sense the absolute correctness of considering the organism as a whole.

"Take a drink. Inside you the water whispers: 'And now you are a million years old.'"
~ Mary Oliver

Another phenomenal implication of the fact that we are comprised mostly of water is that we are able to make profound changes and develop strong resilience. Water is famous for its capacity to adapt and change. Neuroscientists now tell us that the human brain has the capacity to change and improve throughout the life span, using words like neuroplasticity, neurogenesis, and synaptogenesis. This is certainly true, but we cannot stop with the brain. The science in Dr. Ho's books is clear—the whole organism is involved because the organism is mostly water, which circulates throughout the body. What has more adaptive capacity than water? It can present as hard (ice) or as soft (air.) You can clean with water and quench your thirst. Rain can sprinkle or fall torrentially. Water can present as a gentle stream or a raging current. It can receive us gracefully or toss us into the sand. Every raindrop takes the shape of an almost perfect sphere whose surface tension makes it tough enough to blast microscopic bits out of any landscape. Water is fluid, and yet, what power it has! And so, too, is our nature—fluid and powerful.

You can bounce back or recover from trauma and abuse, loss and disappointments, defeats and frustrations. You can give and receive love, manifest the courage and strength to direct the course of your life, be gentle and receptive, and connect deeply with others while taking good care of you. Most of all, you can grow the capacity to be deliciously nourished simply by being alive and awake in your body. To become more coherent means to become more present and to be better able to take in love; and to take in love helps you be more coherent and more present. From my perspective, becoming more coherent means recognizing that you are connected to all living things; therefore, any action that harms others renders you less coherent. So what I am pointing to in describing growth is what I believe to be at the heart of all spiritual practices. As you become more coherent, you become more appreciative of the web of life—and of your freedom within it, which is coupled with a deep sense of belonging to and being a part of all life. As you become more coherent, I believe, you recognize the folly of rigid polarities and develop a more compassionate, loving, and peaceful heart. What could be more important? And without a doubt, the journey isn't just for those our medical system diagnoses with a DSM disorder.[7]

Let's all go forward together!

1.   Ho, Mae-Wan, *The Rainbow and the Worm: The Physics of Organisms*, World Scientific Publishing, 1998.

2   Ho, Mae-Wan, *Living Rainbow H2O*, World Scientific Publishing, p. 4, 2012.

3.   Ho, Mae-Wan, *Living Rainbow H2O*, World Scientific Publishing, 2012.

4.   I would add community building and government as well, but I do not have the qualifications to engage such a discussion.

5.   *Living Rainbow H2O*, pp. 4-5.

6.   Ho, Mae-Wan, *The Rainbow and the Worm: The Physics of Organisms*, World Scientific Publishing, p. 185, 1998.

7.   Diagnostic And Statistical Manual of the American Psychiatric Association.

CHAPTER 4

Simple, but Not Easy! What Children Need from Gestation through Childhood

"Too often we underestimate the power of a touch, a smile, a kind word, a listening ear, an honest compliment, or the smallest act of caring, all of which have the potential to turn a life around."
~ Leo Buscaglia

From conception, children require quality tending for optimal development. It begins with gestation and birth. Both events can have profound developmental consequences. Children have an overarching need for a parent—ideally both parents—to be with them, and not just physically there, but present, awake to their own bodies, sensations, and feelings. Parents capable of quality tending are capable of focusing quality attention on their children. It isn't about being a helicopter mom, always hovering, always ready to intervene; it is about being able to meet the child, about being receptive, responsive, empathic, and caring, while simultaneously being present and responsive to your own needs. Not receiving quality tending is insulting to the organism.

The Importance of Gestation

Dr. Frederick Wirth devoted his medical career to prenatal parenting. In his book, *Prenatal Parenting*,[1] he states little-known facts about a fetus.

•A fetus has more nerve cells with many more connections among them than an adult.

•He has a memory of his experiences before birth.

•He develops consciousness and a sense of self separate from his mother before birth.

•He can hear, smell, taste, and see before birth.

•His in-utero experience begins to build the brain architecture that will determine his behavior after birth and probably for the rest of his life.

•He communicates with his mother biochemically, as well as through his senses.

•He shares his mother's emotional experiences.

•His mother cannot hide her most intimate thoughts and feelings from him.

•He is born looking for meaningful relationships and knows how to develop them.

•Each infant is born with a distinct temperament that may require specific parenting techniques for proper nurturing after birth.[2]

These are clinical conclusions of a medical practitioner who devoted his career to improving the quality of gestation, birth, and the infancy of his patients. Some of his statements are arguable, such as the baby having a separate sense of self while in the womb. Nevertheless, what is becoming less and less arguable is just how important a period of life those nine months are.

Given just how much is occurring and how much is developing during gestation, it makes good sense that the quality of this period of life can and probably will significantly influence the whole of a person's life. As any gardener knows, the soil in which a seed is planted and in which it germinates greatly affects the life of the plant. Psychologists and psychiatrists have not yet paid much attention to the influences of the gestation phase of life. Dr. Wirth forgives this neglect, compassionately attributing it to the lack of instrumentation for adequate study of gestation.

Dr. Wirth's lifework started with caring for fragile preemies and progressed to teaching mothers how to care for, love, and nurture their preborns. Mom's state of being throughout her pregnancy affects the quality of the fetal environment. Is she delighted to discover she is pregnant, or is she distraught? Does she have the support of her husband and family, or does she feel alone in her new adventure? Is she confident that her family's finances can handle the new addition, or is she thrown into a state of anxiety? Does she have the knowledge and firmness to avoid alcohol, tobacco, and other toxins, or does she have a "what's-the-difference" attitude? Does she look forward to the enormous commitment of childrearing, or is she feeling mild dread? No, the fetus is not impervious to these factors.

Dr. Wirth recognizes how many different factors besides drugs, tobacco, and alcohol can affect the life of a fetus. He discusses the effects of stress, of negative self-talk, of negative emotions, and of the quality of relational support a woman receives from her family during pregnancy. He tells us how an individual's ability to regulate his emotions can be negatively affected by his experiences in the womb, and he wonders how much psychotherapy in later life is enough to remedy the challenges. As you will see, psychotherapy alone will always be at least somewhat insufficient. As I continue to emphasize, our whole organism is affected and our whole organism must be addressed. And it all begins there in the womb.

From the moment of conception, our genes are interacting with our environment. How our genes are expressed is influenced by the environment in which they are expressed. For example, a child born with a genetic propensity for shyness can, with support, learn to be social enough. This child may never become an extrovert, but with care and support, he can learn to socialize and enjoy people. In an unsupportive or hostile environment, beginning in the womb, that same child may be so painfully shy that any peer engagement is next to impossible. This interaction of genetic expression and environment begins in the womb and continues throughout life. The intrauterine environment is our very first environment. Yet, even though the imprints of this time are profound, the knowledge and tools to work with them when we are adults are still developing.

The Importance of the Birth Process

Birth is a profound transition; it sets an imprint upon which all future experiences may be shaped. Many years ago, Otto Rank, a psychoanalyst and an early student of Sigmund Freud, hypothesized that birth has a strong effect on the personality. Not very many of his colleagues agreed with him, and the concept fell by the wayside for decades. However, in recent years, a great deal more attention is being paid to both the birth experience as well as to factors that influence intrauterine life.

One way we can think about the birth experience is that it creates a template, a structure of expectations, for how the transitions in our lives will proceed. Of course, that structure of expectations will be substantially modified by subsequent experiences, but if those early experiences in some way reinforce our birth experience, then a very firm foundation of expectations is established. A traumatic birth followed by years of warm, loving, and attentive caretaking will produce different results than a traumatic birth followed by years of poor caretaking or maltreatment. Deeply ingrained patterns of expectations can very well have their roots in the quality of our birth. For example, a newborn who is not truly welcomed into the world and who grows up in a somewhat rejecting environment is likely to carry expectations of not being wanted wherever he goes.

During the process of birth, we are exceptionally vulnerable to serious impacts. If you had a breech birth or if forceps or vacuum extraction were used, the effects could be substantial. Interruption of the birthing process can also have consequences. Preplanned Cesarean births have become quite popular, and in some cultures, Brazil for example, they are now routine.[3] According to Kristi Ridd-Young,[4] president of the Midwives College of Utah, currently 34 percent of births in the US are Cesarean. Yet, going through the birth canal and participating in the struggle to arrive is a design of nature. It is important! In my opinion, interfering with this design of nature simply for the sake of convenience smacks of hubris.

Adoption and incubation of the newborn also can have profound impacts. One woman in my practice was adopted at birth and never told that her new family was not her birth family. For twenty-six years, she felt like she never fit in, didn't belong. Finally, the secret slipped out, and at long last, she began to understand the feelings that had so haunted her during her lifetime. Another young woman remembered that she had been incubated for two weeks immediately after birth and was not allowed to be touched except with rubber gloves. For years, she felt that she was relating to people through some impermeable substance (like glass) and had difficulty getting close to people. In short, during the birthing process, as well as during the time immediately following birth itself, patterns can be established that affect an entire life. On occasion, a client with a relatively benign childhood is mystified by the challenges she has faced in life, and deeper inquiry suggests that birth impacts are a plausible explanation.

The importance of gestation and birth as life-influencing events is not universally accepted among scientists and clinicians. However, awareness of their importance is growing. Listen to Beate Ritz, MD, Ph.D., and Michelle Wilhelm, Ph.D:[5]

The time between conception and birth is perhaps one of the most vulnerable life stages, during which the environment may have tremendous immediate and lasting effects on health. The fetus undergoes rapid growth and organ development and the maternal environment helps direct these processes, for better or for worse. Evidence is accumulating that environmental exposures can cause infants to be born premature (before 37 weeks of gestation) or low weight (less than 2500 grams, or 5.5 pounds), or to be born with certain birth defects. These babies are far more likely to die in infancy, and those who survive have high risks of brain, respiratory, and digestive problems in early life. The impact of environmental exposures on fetal development may be far-reaching, as data suggest growth and developmental delays *in utero* influence the risk for heart disease and diabetes in adulthood.

Whether or not psychologists and psychiatrists accept gestation and birth as having significant effects on a person's life, they all agree that the next few years are critical in forming who we become. A great deal has been written on how those years affect our personality, and in recent years, a great deal has been written on how our brains are affected by early childhood experiences.

Before we examine what an infant and child need in those early years—in addition to healthy nutrition and a secure abode—I will share a little of my story. When an organism receives outlandish insults and harsh impacts as early as I did, the wounds are deeply embedded. It takes so much more effort to ever feel whole. This is why, for me, wholeness has been a lifelong journey.

My Gestation and Birth

My mother did not want to be pregnant. With her husband about to be shipped overseas, having a child was the last thing she wanted. In 1942, abortion in a Catholic family was unthinkable, but my mother, I believe, considered it. Even in considering it, the guilt must have been unbearable, so she confessed it to the parish priest. Evidently, he was not gentle with her, because from that day forward, except for weddings and funerals, she almost never entered church again. Not feeling wanted was a theme I worked with for many years; its residuals linger to this day. Then, came my birth.

It was a clear and sunny day in May. According to my mother, I was born blackened from asphyxiation and with the cord wrapped around my neck. She said that what saved my life was the consummate skill of the obstetrician. Immediately, I was incubated. In one moment, I was part of another human being with every need taken care of, and in the next, I was not getting enough air to breathe and struggling for my very life. Terror and a profound sense of isolation were another two of my most deeply ingrained issues throughout my life. Terror and isolation go deep; they affect one's whole being at every level, but they can be successfully worked with over time.

Our pets don't know about life and death, and yet, take away their air supply and they will fight for it with every fiber of their being—as I did. I survived, but then I was alone in a strange, isolated environment called an incubator. It was as if I was sound asleep, deeply and blissfully asleep, and then suddenly I was being strangled. Welcome to the world!

Those first hours on this earth affected the rest of my life. My neck and throat were among the tightest, most constricted areas of my body for most of my life. The area was so tight I could barely feel anything below. Today, it is so different.

WHAT YOU CAN DO: REFLECTION

Is there a story about your gestation and birth? What do you know about how things were for your parents during your gestation? Was your delivery easy? Were there complications? Was your birth Cesarean?

Over the years, I have become convinced that many seemingly intractable patterns that human beings struggle to change have their roots in gestation and birth. Just knowing your story can be very helpful in bringing you more self-compassion.

Presence: An Essential Human Nutrient

We all agree that children need love. No one would deny that love is a fundamental need. But what does that really mean? "Of course, I love my child," people will say, but is that sufficient? There was a time when food, shelter, discipline, and moral guidance were thought sufficient. In fact, the way we have generally thought about love is in terms of commitment, care, guidance, kindness, and so forth. I do not mean to diminish these in any way. They are important and necessary. However, we are realizing that they are not enough.

Human connections—and especially love connections—are as essential for the infant as food or air. We humans cannot survive without it, and we require it in good doses. It provides the ground for the growth of all other positive human qualities. Ideally, out of our very first connections, a sense of basic trust is born. Basic trust is trust in the benevolence of self, others, and the world. A reliable, stable, enduring sense of connection gives us trust that our basic needs will be met, that our food, warmth, care, and contact will be provided reliably. As trust grows, it bodes well for how we navigate closeness to other beings throughout our lives.

Today, we know that it is not enough to simply say that a child needs food when assessing nutritional requirements. Just so, it is insufficient to say that a child needs love. What a child needs is a balanced diet—interpersonally and emotionally as well as nutritionally. What are those interpersonal nutrients that provide brain and heart with the substances they need to thrive? There are several that we all need as children. However, they all flow from presence.

I consider "being present" the overarching requirement for meeting the needs of a child. "Presence" is not a simple concept to define. It refers to the quality and quantity of energy and attention that you can bring to a situation or person. It is being available for a heart-centered engagement in which a person is "touched" by another's being. It is like a light from the heart that shines through your eyes and reaches the other, who feels it. In such a moment, there are no distractions. There is recognition of the other's "Being." A person who is chronically not present may love another inside, but the other will rarely *feel* it. There will be hunger, a longing for a quality connection that is not forthcoming. Here is another way of looking at presence. In a championship ski run, a competitor can be nowhere else in her attention. Every cell in her body must be focused on exactly what she is doing. This level of athletic presence is required for the course of the event. At the other extreme, imagine a ticketing agent looking at his Facebook page, watching the girls go by, and absentmindedly handing out tickets to an occasional customer. Presence exists along a continuum of this nature. Of course, people can be present with nature or in their sport or with things; and, at the same time, not be able to be present in the presence of another. Real intimacy can be very frightening for many, if not most, people. Real intimacy requires two people to be present.

A skier must be able to adjust to the demands of the terrain. A parent must be able to adjust to the demands of the moment. Some moments call for warm empathy, some for consolation, some for fun and play, some for discipline, some for light conversation, some for wisdom, and so forth. So, to be present is the sine qua non of good parenting. *You cannot do something well if you are not there to do it.* In a way, meeting the child's other needs naturally flows out of being present.

I want to offer another image to give you an understanding of presence. Imagine that a human being is an ornate chandelier with a hundred tiny light bulbs. Your degree of presence is the number of bulbs that are lit up at any given moment. My experience has convinced me that almost all of us can turn on far more lights than we suspect. You can learn to replace your burnt-out bulbs with intention, practice, knowledge, guidance, and the resources provided in this book. When the bulbs are mostly lit, and when the glow passes from you to another, that is a moment of love.

Coherence and Presence

Our coherence as human beings is what defines the limits of how present we can be. The more coherent our organism—at all the levels we have described—the more light bulbs we can turn on. Incoherence turns off the light bulbs of our being.

So many things can diminish our capacity to be present: life circumstances such as an alcoholic mate, financial worries and strain, a feeling deep inside that you are inadequate, insecurity, excessive and chronic tension, tightness or compression in the body, feeling overwhelmed or over-committed—any or all of these can diminish the quality of your presence. Most important of all, if you have not received an abundant dose of love transmissions in your lives, it challenges your capacity to show up for others.

The presence I am describing is not just physical presence. If a parent is actually "there" when he is there, and if that parent conveys to his child a sense that he is still with him in heart and mind when he is on the road, for example, this is what counts. Whenever someone is present with you, whether a friend, a lover, or a storekeeper, this evokes a special feeling. The presence of another human being is a gift. This is what I consider the transmission of love.

WHAT YOU CAN DO: PRACTICING PRESENCE

While walking:

First, make an intention to practice presence for the next three or four minutes of your walk. As you begin, notice your mental dialogue. You are probably thinking about something that has occurred or will be occurring. Don't try to forcefully cut off your thoughts; instead, begin to sense the movements of your arms and legs. Soften your eyes and notice what they are seeing without labeling or describing them. Just take in the shapes, colors, objects, the landscape, and people. Do the same with the sounds—just notice them. Notice the movements of your abdomen and ribs as you breathe. Feel the sensations on your skin, especially your face. Allow thoughts to come and go without focusing on them.

While engaging in conversation with another:

Naturally, when conversing, you will be looking at your friend, but for this practice, simply include yourself in your field of attention. The aim is to practice including awareness of your body, sensations, feeling tones, emotions, sense of spaciousness or constriction, and whatever else may be occurring within you, as well. This is a feeling kind of attention, not a mental laundry list of what is occurring in you. The greater the degree to which two people can be with themselves in this way while they are with another, the greater the potential for a nourishing connection.

What can Flow from Presence (It's all love)**

Attention

Both children and adults need quality attention from those close to them. As obvious as this may sound, there is a wide range of quality in how people pay attention. Over the years, I have had many patients who seemed to be starving for attention. Most of them described a mother who was self-absorbed; that is, she had difficulty attending to her child without needing to take center stage in some way.

A mother tiger provides a good example of quality attention. When she is grooming or feeding her cub, she is not also looking in the mirror and brushing her hair, talking on her cell phone, or planning her dinner menu. Mother tiger is right there, all of her engaged in what she is doing. This is what quality attention looks like.

Attunement

Attunement is a refined and mutually engaged form of attention. Mother and infant, two lovers, or therapist and patient are responsive to each other's subtle expressions in tone of voice, facial expression, and breathing. The two are in sync, and they are creating a resonance. Each feels the other. Receiving this level of attuned attention is a beautiful gift, and in infancy, it is a necessary one. The feeling when someone is attuned to your moment-to-moment nuances is sublime. It is an experience of love. Many people stay in therapy for years because it may be the only place where someone really attunes to them.

As an adult, you can learn to attune to those close to you. As a therapist, I get to practice all the time. Over the years, as I have released some of the deep constrictions and fear in my body, it has become so much easier.

In the first years of life, visual experiences, particularly mother's emotionally expressive face, are critical to the child's emotional development. The infant's intense interest in mother's face leads him to track it, especially her eyes. This is called state-to-state communication. Mom and infant are engaged in a dialogue. To do this, mother must tune into the infant's behavioral expressions and to the internal states they reflect. As these interactions increase over the first two years, mother and infant are forming a powerful bond, each contributing to the other's emotional experience. Because the infant's brain and nervous system are maturing, he depends on mother for a variety of life-sustaining functions that eventually become self-regulated. Self-regulation occurs through these powerful nonverbal interactions, as well as the ability to engage in state-to-state communication throughout life.

But what if Mom never had this experience herself? What if she didn't receive it as an infant, as a child, or as an adult? In such a case, it can be very challenging to provide this essential nutrient to her infant. Nevertheless, as mother becomes more aware and can appreciate the value of this state-to-state communication, she can learn how. Learning how to do it with her infant will also improve her ability to give and receive quality attention in her adult relationships. Remember, the brain can change for the better, no matter how old you are. And, as you will see, so can the whole body.

Safety

Safety is a fundamental need of human existence. We all need to feel safe, especially during infancy and childhood. We need to feel physically safe from harm, and we need to feel emotionally safe from judgment and harsh criticism, as well as from neglect or abuse of any kind. When an infant or child is in distress, he needs someone to be there, to let him know he is not alone in his distress. This sense of aloneness when a child is dealing with difficult feelings can come to permeate his inner landscape. Out of this grows a belief: *No one can really be with me, or no one can really understand me. I am essentially alone.*

Empathy

Empathy is another level of attunement. The infant knows Mom is with her; she knows that Mom is feeling, or grokking, what she is feeling, as well. The effect is, *"Somebody really gets me."* This too counteracts a sense of aloneness or isolation.

In infancy, empathy is expressed nonverbally. As the child begins to engage in language, statements that reflect understanding are important: "I understand how you must feel." Empathy helps a child understand what is occurring inside. Mom says, "Your feelings got hurt, and then you got angry because you wanted to play with the toy, too, huh?" This empathic statement helps a child understand his feelings and needs.

Acceptance

Acceptance is another essential need. It provides a sense that who you are, your traits, qualities, choices, and feelings, are respected. Acceptance feeds a child's sense of himself, his sense of self-worth. He feels like a basically good person. When you like someone, you tend to accept them. It doesn't mean you accept everything the person or the child does. It means that you care for and respect who the person is. It means that you do not hold on to moral judgments about the person and then make the egregious error of assuming your judgments are facts. To have the many aspects of self seen and accepted is an enormous gift.

Affection

Affection flows from liking someone. It makes us feel lovable. So many human beings walk through life feeling basically unlovable because they did not receive a sufficient and consistent dose of affection throughout their early lives. A warm smile, a hug, or even a gentle head nod can feel delicious to receive. Speaking of hugs, I want to add that affectionate touch is important to children (as well as to adults). It is important for children to be able to cuddle with their parents, as in front of the TV, or to snuggle in bed. This may seem obvious, but I know there are many adults who are challenged when it comes to physical displays of affection.

Notice that when you feel affection towards someone, you want to touch. It's natural!

Appreciation

Appreciation is essential. When someone really appreciates you, you can see a certain gleam in their eye. It conveys a sense of prizing, delighting in, and recognizing another's potential. We show appreciation with our words, but also with the tone of our voice, the smile on our face, the nodding of our heads. Appreciation inspires confidence. It also is such an important quality to bring into any personal or professional relationship. We all like to feel appreciated. People bloom when they feel appreciated.

What I am describing—affection, acceptance, empathy, attunement, attention, appreciation—are processes of the whole organism. Observe a mother and infant and witness the facial expressions, the many muscles involved in the process, the movements of the head and neck, the changes in the pupils of the eyes.

Allowing

Allowing your children to make their own age and maturity appropriate choices helps develop their sense of autonomy and inner authority. So many adults don't know, *really know*, that they can make their own choices and still be close to someone; getting close to another can threaten your sense that you can still make your own choices. Your autonomy may feel precarious. Sometimes parents hold on too tightly and underestimate a child's capacity for self-direction. This undermines the development of self-confidence as well as the sense of inner authority.

Structure/Discipline

Providing structure is part of allowing. Allowing cannot be without borders. Even in infancy, when the amount of permission is at a maximum, a certain amount of structure is necessary. Bedtime rituals, mealtime consistency, limits, and discipline are part of providing a predictable and safe environment. It is important for children to know there are limits; that we cannot always do what we wish or get what we want. Children are social beings, so learning the value of reciprocity and sharing and accepting frustration is important. Structure includes firm but flexible limits and certainty about who is in charge. But, sometimes parents can be too heavy-handed in the socializing process with expectations that are not age-appropriate. A three-year-old should not be expected to behave like a college grad.

Guidance

Children need social, physical, and moral guidance to grow their comprehension of the world and develop good judgment. There is a lot to learn in every area of life, and children need parents to guide their development and show interest in their progress.

A Positive Environment

A positive environment is important to a child's growing sense of well-being. Recently a client told me that, unlike her partner, she had a good childhood. Except—oh, by the way, her parents divorced when she was three, her mother married her father's best friend and they divorced two years later, and then her mother soon remarried her father. Even if both parents managed to remain aligned and somewhat balanced, this woman, as a child, was breathing in and absorbing through her pores the emotional vibrations of the household. Children feel the emotional tones of their homes.

Even if both of your parents were doing their best to care for you, if they were chronically anxious, angry, or depressed, those feelings seeped into you. Like sponges, we take in the water we are placed in.

What Can Flow From Presence

Attention

Attunement

Safety/Discipline

Empathy

Acceptance

Affection

Appreciation

Allowing

Structure

Guidance

A Positive Environment

Good tending means meeting the essential needs described in the preceding diagram. Most human beings have had some of these needs fulfilled and others not fulfilled. When the scale tips in the direction of a majority of these needs *not* being met, the scale is registering poor tending. Human beings shut down, to some degree or other, when we do not receive what we need. It is not only high-impact traumatic experiences that make us shut down. Shutting down occurs gradually as a result of the neglect of our needs. For example, if our assertiveness is not supported, that part of us will shut down. It is important to understand that it is not just assertive behavior that goes underground; our tissues and our muscles that are involved in assertive expression also lose some capacity. They too are part of our assertiveness.

My scale was off the charts in the wrong direction. My case leaves poor-tending behind and enters the land of serious maltreatment and abuse. Therefore, if I wanted any real satisfaction and fulfillment in this lifetime, it was imperative for me to understand what it takes to move in the direction of greater coherence.

WHAT YOU CAN DO: PRACTICES TO SUPPORT CONNECTIONS

1. Become comfortable with eye contact. In the right circumstances, practice really seeing the other, be it a friend, child, lover, or parent. Stay with their eyes for a second longer than you are comfortable with. The eyes are, as we know, the gateway to the soul; and it is your soul that wants to be seen. Many people are very uncomfortable with eye contact. Notice how it is for you. Practice taking that extra second to expand your comfort level.

2. Be generous with your acknowledgements and appreciation of your partner, children, and friends. Strive to create a positive environment for each relationship. Be generous to yourself. Most people are much more likely to spend time criticizing themselves and very little time appreciating their good qualities or accomplishments. A good time to engage this practice is before bedtime.

** See Richo, David. *How to be An Adult in Relationships*. Boston: Shambhala, 2002 for an expanded presentation of those needs in adult relationships.

1. Wirth, Frederick, *Prenatal Parenting*, Regan Books/Harper Collins, 2001.

2. Ibid., p. 6.

3. This has been reported to me by several friends in Brazil, including a pediatrician and an oncologist.

4. Ridd-Young, Kristi, President, Midwives College of Utah, Personal Communication, 2014.

5. Ritz, Beate, M.D., Ph.D., and Wilhelm, Michelle, Ph.D., "Air Pollutant Impacts on Infants and Children," UCLA Institute of the Environment and Sustainability, Southern California Report Card, Fall 2008.

CHAPTER 5

HOW WE BOND

"The poverty of being unwanted, unloved and uncared for is the greatest poverty. We must start in our homes to remedy this kind of poverty."
~ Mother Theresa

The wounds of childhood profoundly affect our relational capacities. Regardless of the quality of gestation and of birth, the next several years of childhood make a huge difference in how a child's life will unfold. During this time, the child will develop a secure relationship with his parents—or not. His experiences will influence every part of him: his model of the world, his sense of himself, his relational capacities, his brain, his nervous system, and his tissues and fluids. In other words, our coherence as human beings is profoundly influenced by our first bonding experiences with our caretakers. And, of course, these will, in turn, influence his future relationships. Many, if not the majority, of adult intimate relationships are filled with significant distress, and they follow specific patterns that begin in early childhood. You can learn about your relationship patterns as the first step in making positive changes.

It is becoming increasingly clear and obvious that the quality of the relationship between infant and parents is critical to the infant's psychological development. Yet, in the 1960s, that assertion made world-famous psychoanalyst John Bowlby a heretic in his profession. Until Bowlby, the general assumption was that the infant is a package of biological drives that can be tamed and channeled in the process of development; parents mediate and intervene between the cultural prescriptions and the infant's instincts. Further, disturbances arise when internal conflicting drives within the infant are not well negotiated. In other words, in those days the emphasis was intrapsychic, meaning that the conflicts or challenges were considered to be within the psyche of the child and had little to do with the actual relationship between child and parent. Later known as the father of Attachment Theory,[1] Bowlby turned the world of psychoanalysis around with his emphasis on the relationship itself as a primary driving force within which the personality developed.

His work was seminal, generating volumes of research over the years. In recent years, it has provided a theoretical framework for many systems of psychotherapy, both individual and marital therapy. It is a helpful framework within which to understand adult intimate connections, and in particular, it provides a way to make sense of distressed relationships. Bonds are classified as secure or insecure. When a marriage is characterized by lots of distress, almost always, one and often both partners have had an insecure bond with one or both of their parents.

The fundamental question—the answer to which determines whether a relationship is secure or insecure—is, "Can I count on you if I need you? Will you be there for me, emotionally?" If deep in her heart a child can answer yes to this question, if there is sufficient acceptance, presence, and emotional connection, the child will feel safe in the relationship. She will feel secure and have no need to be vigilant. Her parents are providing a secure base from which she can explore her world and a safe place she can return to repeatedly for comfort and nurturance.

Within the context of this bonding process, a great deal is occurring in the development of a child. In the previous chapter, we saw the emotional ingredients that a child needs. Your model of self, other, and the world—which we will examine in Chapter 7—begins in gestation, is influenced by your birth, but is most influenced by the process of bonding. How your needs were met during this time, in particular, contributes mightily to your development. There are profound psychophysiological differences in children who are quite securely bonded with both parents versus children who are insecurely bonded with one or both parents. Our capacity for sustaining satisfactory intimate relationships as adults is momentously influenced during these early years of bonding.

As we look at the different styles of bonding, it is important to keep in mind that there are degrees, nuances, and textures within each category. It is not all or nothing. These are general styles.

Secure Bonding

A *secure* bond provides the foundation for a healthy life, and it is also an antidote for life's wounds. Securely bonded children have a sense that their needs will be met; that they can count on Mom; that she is tuned into their feelings. They feel safe, lovable, and have a mostly positive model of self, other, and the world. Research has shown that infants who feel secure are highly sensitive to mother's presence and may be more or less distressed if left alone, but they are eager to rejoin mom when she returns. They make eye contact and are easily reassured. If threatened, these infants seek closeness. When reassured and comforted, they quickly and confidently return to play and explore. If these children are victimized by an accident or a social event, such as war, they are less likely to suffer PTSD than children who are insecurely bonded to their parents.

Parents of securely bonded children are likely to be well attuned to their child's needs. They tend to be responsive to both positive and negative feelings. In other words, they are much more likely to be attentive, affectionate, accepting, appreciative, and allow their children an appropriate range of freedom while providing a steady structure.

Rupture and Repair

Understanding the process of rupture and repair is important in all significant relationships. It is important for spouses and for friends, and it is important for parents and children. When there is a rupture in the connection or a break in that warm, positive sense of the other, it is time to reestablish it. Here is an example. Mother and infant are gazing lovingly into each other's' eyes when the infant unexpectedly tugs on Mom's hair, causing a sharp pain. With highly evolved video equipment, we can see the split-second look of anguish and fury flash across Mom's face, and fear on the baby's face. It doesn't last more than a fraction of a second, but it is visible on the monitor, and both feel the momentary disconnect. When a smile quickly returns to Mom's face and baby registers it by smiling back, the rupture has been repaired. What is important here is not to allow those moments of hurt or anger to fester or accumulate.

A Secure Base and Safe Haven

Optimally, a secure base and a safe haven are constructed in the relationship between caregiver and baby. It is from this secure base that the toddler begins to venture forth to explore his world. The mother of a securely attached child is available when the child returns from an adventure and can appropriately respond so as to provide modulation and regulation. It is to this safe haven that he returns for nurturance, comfort, and reassurance. For many years, life will be a series of excursions and returns. When the quality of the bonding is secure, that security is internalized as a very fundamental core sense of "I am okay. The world is a safe place." The "I" is rooted in this core sense, and it allows for risk-taking in exploration. It allows for a willingness to be open and reveal oneself. The secure toddler knows that distress will be comforted and hurts will be soothed.

Nevertheless, a good foundation is present! In adult intimate relationships, those who were provided a secure base and safe haven will have the internal structures to provide that for their partners. Also, they will have a much better chance of not contracting a chronic illness, as we will see in Chapter 10. When you have a secure base and a safe haven in your partner, you will feel free to live your life to the fullest, knowing that when you are bruised in the world there is a place of solace.

The Good-Enough Mother

No mother can be attuned all the time. A famous British psychoanalyst by the name of Donald Winnicot coined *the term the good-enough mother*. Research has shown that the good-enough mother is attuned to her infant approximately 30 percent of the time. This fact tells us that it is not possible to remain tuned in to another on an ongoing basis. It is important to know this. I once had a patient who felt so awful whenever a boyfriend mis-attuned that it signaled for her the beginning of the end of the relationship. She was a lovely, bright, and aware woman; no one could figure out why she ended so many relationships with good men. Fortunately, she realized this dynamic and learned to attend to her extreme sensitivity and need for attunement and connection. This was a new beginning for her. She was able to compassionately accept herself and also became able to sustain a quality relationship. No person can be attuned to another 100 percent of the time.

What distinguishes good-enough mothers is their ability to "repair" whenever they notice they are not attuned to their child. Repeatedly, they repair any ruptures in their connection. Repair is vitally important. It shows the infant that it is okay to be out of synch because togetherness will be back soon. The infant and child are learning to be secure and to trust at a very deep level. If that trust isn't established, it can have lifelong consequences, one of which may be a serious challenge whenever an ongoing intimate relationship is attempted.

When Mother engages in interactive repairs after a disruption, she is teaching her baby's whole being. As she mirrors or empathically tunes into her infant, she is providing emotional nourishment and teaching the baby's neurobiology to tolerate more stimulation and disruption. When she mistunes and repairs the transaction, she is teaching recovery. To use a thermostat metaphor, the heat has gotten too high so she turns it down. Or, the temperature is too low so she turns the thermostat up. An infant does not have the neurological structures necessary to take care of the thermostat by himself. He relies on Mom's neurobiology to help him develop these functions. This is an essential aspect of health and well-being.

Securely Attached Children as Adults in Relationship

"Sometimes our light goes out, but is blown into instant flame by an encounter with another human being"
~ Albert Schweitzer

This internal thermostat is the sine quo non of satisfying adult relationships. People whose internal regulator doesn't function well might have difficulty controlling impulses, be moody, and might not handle frustrations and demands well. Further, a good thermostat is necessary to allow real closeness or to permit distance, as well. Closeness can generate intense feelings at times. A good internal regulator allows you to modulate those feelings so that they don't either drag you to the bottom or have you bouncing off the walls.

As adults, those who were securely attached as children have a much better chance in intimate relationships. There are two dimensions in a relationship that each couple negotiates—mostly implicitly—on an ongoing basis. These are closeness and power. Adults who have experienced a secure relationship as children can manage these negotiations with greater ease and less distress. They can enjoy closeness, and they can enjoy solitude. They can accept differences, argue, and work out issues without reacting as if the world is about to end. They can be in charge or be the one who knows or the one who decides in some areas; alternatively, in other areas, they can feel comfortable following their partner's lead or having their partner know more or make decisions. There is fluidity in the power and closeness dimensions, a give and take. Each can feel free internally and simultaneously closely connected to his partner. In other words, the relationship leans towards coherence.

Ruptures occur frequently even in very good adult relationships, The difference between those that are satisfying and secure versus those in which distress permeates is that in secure relationships, the ruptures are quickly repaired. It is important that we are able to identify ruptures and become skillful at repair. This requires paying attention to the quality of the ongoing connection between you, so that you can know when repair is necessary. In the Practice Section at the end of Chapter 6, I will give you more specific instructions in the practice of detecting and repairing ruptures in your relationships.

Insecure Attachment

In contrast to securely connected children, insecurely connected kids live in a different kind of psychosocial world. Three types of insecure attachments have been identified.

Avoidant ("I don't need anyone.")

In the avoidant insecure bond, it is as if the young child has concluded that his needs are not going to be met, so why bother. Expecting to be rejected, he shuts down or withdraws from the relationship. Mothers of avoidant infants are likely to subtly block and reject the infant's bids for comfort. Therefore, to protect themselves from the pain of not having their needs for comfort or emotional contact met, these children are likely to express minimal feeling and to be withdrawn or hesitant in their interactions. They tend to avoid physical contact.

As adults in intimate relationships, they are the ones without apparent needs. They act as if they don't need anything from their partners except to be given freedom from the other's emotional demands. They have learned to push away experiences and feelings they don't like. They can appear independent or autonomous, but in attachment terms, they are compulsively self-reliant, meaning they are afraid to be dependent on anyone. Underneath, they often feel

55

inadequate; they are afraid they don't really measure up, and find it hard to believe that they can be truly loved. Deeper still, they long for acceptance.

Insecure-Preoccupied ("I know you're going to leave me.")

In another style of insecurity, the child seems preoccupied with Mom's presence and shows little interest in exploration and play. This style is called insecure preoccupied or insecure-resistant. During research studies, these kids became highly distressed when Mom leaves, but they are not easily comforted when she returns. They want to be close, but then resist comforting. Their yearning for closeness is mixed with ambivalence and anger. The caregiver of the preoccupied infant is likely to be highly inconsistent in response to the infant's needs. At one time, the caregiver may continue to provide stimulation when the infant is signaling a need for diminished intensity. At another time, when the infant is signaling a need for activity, the parent may regard the infant as a nuisance and provide insufficient stimulation, contact, or comfort. The infant is left not knowing what to expect. It is as if these infants are trying to attract the attention of the unresponsive or withdrawn caregiver but do not expect to succeed. At the same time, they are angry and don't easily allow soothing.

As adults, these children may desperately cling to relationships, thinking their security lies out there somewhere. "Are you there for me? Are you going to leave me? My world revolves around you. What can I do to make you happy?" They can appear loving, close, and intimate, but in attachment terms, they lack healthy individuation or healthy boundaries and may be compulsive caregivers. They are inclined to undervalue themselves, not knowing their own self-worth, their own natural goodness, or what they genuinely have to offer others. Of course, underneath, they are lonely and quite sure that no one will really be there for them. Deeper, they are longing for someone to really be there for them.

As ways of being in relationship, both the avoidant and the

insecure-preoccupied styles can vary in intensity, ranging from slight tendencies to deep entrenchment. In my years of counseling couples, one of the most common patterns I have seen is one in which one partner—frequently the woman—displays what we have called the insecure-preoccupied pattern. She will be the one who insists on counseling, is frequently angry at her partner, and complains about his emotional unavailability and lack of commitment to the relationship. Her husband, exhibiting the avoidant insecure pattern, will lament that if only she weren't so emotional, so easy to upset, then everything would be just fine. He will present as having his emotional life together, stable and calm. However, as counseling proceeds, it doesn't take long to uncover that he is afraid and feels inadequate. His façade covers those feelings with an I-don't-need-anything attitude; yet underneath, he is scared. Even deeper, he longs for her acceptance and approval.

She, on the other hand, is covering deep loneliness with her rants as well as fear that no one will really be there for her—that she will not able to depend on him. She feels unlovable and longs for her mate to show up and provide that reassurance, presence, and love. If he begins to come forward, however, she will be pushed up against her fear of being unlovable.

When the couple can come to recognize their deeper feelings and needs and communicate them to each other, they can create a secure bond. As long as they continue the conversation at the level of their self-protection—their complaints against each other—they will simply reinforce their sense of insecurity in the relationship. From the perspective of coherence, as they become more authentic, they can begin to feel both cohesive as a couple and free as individuals.

Disorganized Attachment ("Please come close; I dare you.")

There is one more style, and it is the most severe. Generally, it is associated with abuse or serious neglect. Clearly, it is my story. The trajectory of my life, established in gestation, birth, and the early years of bonding, was an unswerving path towards, at best, a very difficult life.

What happens when the very one who, biologically, is supposed to be a haven of protection, comfort, and nurturance is instead a source of danger and threat? The internal conflict becomes intolerable!

Behaviorally, the infant will show a variety of contradictory patterns. In research studies identifying this pattern, the infant nestles up to Mother but averts his eyes and looks dazed. He approaches Mom and then has an outburst of aggression. He sometimes demonstrates vacillation between the two insecure styles described above. He becomes frightened, but makes no effort to seek Mom. More than likely, this child will have a great deal of freeze[2] in his system. There is a longing for closeness and at the same time a strong desire to get away. In benign moments, such a child may be coping with an impossible situation by imagining he is far away on an adventure. In more threatening or abusive situations, he might drop into a void of helplessness and terror, paralyzed to take effective action or cope in a skillful way. Seen in adult relationships, this type of bonding presents the most dramatic difficulties.

My personal story is a vivid and poignant example of a disorganized attachment. We can see that the bond is very strong. My mother and I were undeniably bonded, but the nature of the bond was disorganized. I will share my relationship story in the next chapter to give a picture of what disorganized attachment looks like, but mostly to inspire hope that no matter where you are now in your relationships, you can make them better.

WHAT YOU CAN DO: REFLECTIONS AND PRACTICES

What is important in order for you to feel safe in a relationship?
Here are some questions to pose to yourself based on characteristics I would be looking for if I were looking for a relationship, now.
Does the other keep his word?

Does he honor his commitments, promises, and agreements?

Does he let me see who he really is? That is, do I get a sense that he is sincere and genuine?

Does he speak from his heart or is there usually some kind of a wall or façade or pretense there?

Does he tend to hang in there when the going gets a bit tough, or is he searching for the nearest exit?

Of course, it would be good to answer these questions about yourself. If you want someone to depend upon you and trust you with an important part of his life—to be a father or mother to the children you will have together, for example—then you, too, have to be trustworthy and dependable.

Practice repairing ruptures in your connection.

This is an exceptionally important practice if you want to maintain good relationships. Close relationships are characterized by a flow of good feelings between two people. But, as you saw above, even the flow of good feeling between mother and infant is frequently ruptured. Learn to detect those breaks when your heart closes— maybe even just a little bit. To repair a rupture often doesn't take much—a smile, a kind gesture or word—but it restores the positive feeling. If you ignore these little breaches, they grow and accumulate.

Reflect on the following: What do you do when your feelings are hurt by your partner or closest friend?

Can you let him see you are hurt?

Does it turn into anger?

Do you blame him or yourself?

See how fast you can let go of the anger. I have not yet reached a point where I can simply not get angry when my feelings are hurt. However, I challenge myself to see how quickly I can let go of it, focus on the deeper feelings underneath, and then determine what it is I need to communicate.

1. For in-depth treatment of Bowlby's Attachment Theory, research, and application, see the following texts: Ainsworth, M., Blehar, M.C., Waters, E., and Wall, S. (1978), *Patterns of Attachment: A Psychological Study of the Strange Situation*, Hillsdale, NJ: Erlbaum Books. Cassiday, J., and Shaver, P., ed. *The Handbook of Attachment: Theory, Research and Clinical Application*, Guilford Press, 2010.Johnson, Susan, *Emotionally Focused Couple's Therapy*, New York: Guilford Press, (2002).Fonagy, Peter, *Attachment Theory and Psychoanalysis*, Other Press, LLC, 2001

2. Freeze/collapse is a psychobiological phenomenon covered in more detail in Chapter 11.

CHAPTER 6

MY RELATIONSHIP STORY

"Real isn't how you are made," said the Skin Horse. "It's a thing that
happens to you. When a child loves you for a long,
long time, not just to play with, but REALLY loves you,
then you become Real."
Marjorie Williams, *The Velveteen Rabbit.*

Momma

If only I could have hated her, it would have been easier. But to make matters complicated, I really loved the woman. Momma and I were intensely bonded. In the rare moments when she was tranquil, I could feel her care. Her love came through her eyes, and I felt it deeply. Plus, she was always there. I was never neglected or ignored. I was controlled, beaten, humiliated, and terrified, but she was always close by. So there I was, terrified of the person to whom I was so drawn and whom I so much wanted to please. I longed to be close, yet I was petrified. I did what most children do under similar circumstances: *I froze*, unable to move towards her and be close, and at the same time, unable to move away from her and become truly independent.

Living in that environment was frightening. I felt my parents' constant frustration and anger and never knew when the next beating would come. Terror is not an emotion that a child—or anyone for that matter—can handle. Handling an emotion means you can feel it, tolerate it, name it, and tell someone what you are feeling. In other words, you can experience, reflect, and communicate. Terror twists and distorts the mind and soul. It prevents us from being present and plays havoc with our physiology. When there is no escape, you can only freeze. You can't run, and you can't fight.

I recall an incident that occurred when I was not quite four years old. One Sunday morning, I wanted to jump in bed with my mother. She pushed me away, saying I was too old. One of my uncles was living with us at the time, and I ran to his room and asked him to go beat up my mother. My hurt and the rage had nowhere to go. She told me later, and often, that she did not believe in physical affection for a boy beyond the age of three—of course, she didn't give much affection before I was three, either. That's how, according to her wisdom, boys became gay. By the time I was six, I couldn't tolerate physical affection when it was offered. If my grandmother, whom I adored, tried to put her arms around me, I would kick her shins. Ouch! A pattern was established. I longed for affection and at the same time would somehow punish anyone who tried to get too close.

I could neither move towards my mother, nor could I move away. Expressing affection to her was not possible, and neither was expressing anger. Moreover, as much as I wanted to, I could not please her. No matter what I did, it was never good enough. When a child is frozen like this, there is also a feeling of helplessness. There was nothing I could do about it. It was the way my life was; it was how the world was; it was who I was. That was the most painful part of all, the sense that, at my core, in my very essence, I was rotten. What can you do when you feel that your very core is bad? Authentic self-expression or communication is not something that even makes sense. Unconsciously, we have to protect ourselves against the dreadfulness of feeling worthless. I protected myself by living in fantasies. One day, I would be a great prize fighter. Interesting choice, eh? Or one day I would play center field for the Yankees.

As just one more example of my mother's intensity, I want to tell you how an Italian, whose father was from Italy, as were his maternal grandparents, came to be named St John. My parents planned to name me John after my paternal grandfather. However, during her pregnancy, my mother got into a fight with him, and out of spite, she named me Don, after no one in particular, which is highly unusual in an Italian family. For some reason, the Catholic priest refused Don as a Catholic name when he baptized me, so they put John on the baptism certificate and then forgot about it. For five years, I was always Don. Until I went to Catholic school, that is, and they were not interested in my birth certificate. My baptism certificate said John, so John it was to everyone who knew me at school. Facetiously, I tell my friends that I took Don and John and made myself a saint for putting up with all the bullshit.

Pop

In contrast to the strong bond between my mother and me, there was almost always an uneasy distance with my father. I was two years old when I saw him for the first time. This memory would be humorous if it were not emblematic of how my relationship with him turned out. It occurred on the day he returned home from the war. My father was a barber, and in his absence, a barber friend of his would come to our house and cut my hair. I had long, brown, curly hair, and I despised haircuts. I refused to sit still, frustrating the poor man to no end. So, on this morning in August of 1945, my grandmother held me in her arms while my mother waited at the top of the stairs as my father opened the door at the bottom. As he began climbing, my grandmother said, "Here comes the barber!" Immediately, I vomited. I really disliked haircuts.

Unfortunately, my relationship with my father did not get much better until many years after I left home. I cannot recall ever experiencing an iota of affection, either for him or from him, throughout my childhood. When I was eighteen, two days after my high school graduation, I left to join the US Air Force. At the train station, my father took my hand and said, "Goodbye, my boy."

I was stunned! "Good bye, my boy." It was the most affection I remember receiving from him during the first eighteen years of my life. When he died, I did not shed a single tear. Whatever bond we had was weak and negative. An internalized good father is such an important structure in the development of a child. For a boy, it relates to sexual identity, a sense of competency, a strong male structure, and the ability to love a woman. In my early life, there was a big empty hole where dad should have been.

Nonna (Grandma)

My grandmother was the primary solace in my family. In all the years I knew her, she never spoke an unkind word against anyone. Many times she stopped my mother when the beatings occurred, and always she spoke to me with kindness and care. She meant the world to me, but as I said I couldn't let her get close. It was too painful.

Nonno (Grandpa)

Grandpa was the strong, silent type. But he always greeted me with a smile and usually with a quarter in his hand. Even though I don't recall ever having a long conversation with him, his presence always provided comfort.

First love

Who can forget their first love? At the time, mine seemed so unique in its certainty, depth, and its sense of tragedy as it came to an unexpected end. However, my clinical practice showed me it was a phenomenon played out in many lives. A boy or girl grows up in horrible circumstances, enduring a painful and lonely childhood. Then, in adolescence, the girl or boy of your dreams appears, and for a brief moment in time, both are transported. Heaven could not feel better. Soon, the bottom falls out, and the effects are shattering. I have seen that so many times.

So it went with me. I was seventeen and working in an amusement park, making pizzas. Fran, nicknamed Candy, was a very mature looking fifteen-year-old. Curvaceous in tight denims and voluptuously endowed, she looked well beyond her fifteen years. It was the spring 1959, and I was completing my junior year of high school. A friend told me Fran would be *easy*. I never questioned the source of his knowledge; it just piqued my interest. I had seen Fran a couple of times around town and was trying to get up my courage to ask for a date. I was beyond surprised when she not only said yes, but did so with enthusiasm.

Losing your virginity was a very high adolescent priority, and what could be more appealing than a striking girl who was easy? An hour into our first date, I found out that my friend was dead wrong. I tried to score, of course, but got my face slapped. We immediately liked each other, and three weeks later, I asked her to go steady. It was another world.

It was a blissful year. We were together whenever I wasn't working throughout that summer, and when school started, I picked her up in the morning, drove her home at night, stayed until about five pm, went home, ate dinner, and returned to her for a couple more hours. Whenever we were alone, we made out.

Someone really cared about me! What an exhilarating experience it was. Of course, my insecurities were always ready to leap to the fore, and in our first few months, I broke up with her several times. But we settled into a routine that could be called "fifty shades for adolescents who want to remain technical virgins."

In the evening, I hung out with her family. I loved being with them because they treated me like a human being. I was "Johnny," and they all, including her parents, aunt, uncle, and cousins, were accepting and affectionate. I was especially moved by how Fran's three young cousins treated me like a favorite uncle. They showered me with attention whenever we visited their home. With Fran's family, I was a person, not my mother's son. In my family, regardless of how affectionate a relative might be, they knew I belonged to my mother, and her fierceness was legend. It was deliciously novel to be treated as if I were an independent human being for the first time in my life.

Fran and I had a strong compatibility. The chemistry was vibrant, but neither of us had any interpersonal or emotional skills. There was never any emotional conversation between us. We called it love. I always thought of it as love, and we fantasized that it could last forever. Of course, it could not and it did not. We were biologically adults, but emotionally and socially, we were children.

As graduation approached, so did reality. I had no idea what I wanted to do or what I *could* do; I felt a dire lack of skills, aptitude, and interests. So, I did what so many kids from blue-collar families do when they wander aimlessly out of high school. I enlisted in the military. Hoping to find something to do in life, I signed up for four years with the US Air Force. They offered technical training and there were no signs of war in 1961; thus, it seemed an intelligent thing to do. So, I began my four years of military duty. I was eighteen and Fran was sixteen, beginning her junior year of high school. It seemed so reasonable: I would learn a career as some type of technician; Fran would graduate from high school; and then we would marry.

I imagine that in the age of digital communication, the letter from home doesn't have the same cherished significance as it did then. Ask any old veteran; he or she will tell you that mail call is the most anticipated moment of the day. Almost every day, I received a romantic letter from Fran; I read each one a dozen times.

To my surprise and consternation, Fran began to insist that we get married when I returned home. I knew her father would never allow his sixteen-year-old to marry before finishing school. Attempts to reason with her were futile, and besides, I didn't dislike the idea. Somehow, I had come to trust her; given my history that was no small accomplishment. But was it really trust, or was it naiveté?

I yielded and agreed that on my first leave we would elope. I did the necessary research and developed a plan. Approximately two months before completing tech school and my first leave, I received my next assignment. I would be spending two years in Bermuda. The excitement was mounting. Just one more month, and I would be home marrying the girl of my dreams. So, initially, when her daily letters dwindled to one every three days, I just assumed she was busy making wedding plans. When I received only one in the last two weeks before my leave, I started feeling a vague anxiety.

It is still a blur. I was home for four weeks before heading to Bermuda, and what happened in those wretched weeks was mostly drowned in alcohol. Her father had found out and raised holy hell. Fran was getting shaky at the knees, and another guy had showed up on the scene. All this happened in a four- or five-week period. It was over. Bathing in self-pity and reeling with miserable loneliness, I took off for Bermuda to begin my next tour of duty. It was 1962. Ray Charles had a double hit: "Born to Lose" and "I Can't Stop Loving You." Conveniently, Seagram's Seven and excellent scotch cost just $2.90 for an imperial quart on the Air Force base; predictably, my locker was never without a bottle. Over and over, I listened to Ray wail what I deeply felt. Indeed, I was born to lose; and for sure, I would never stop loving her. Now I know that it was my inability to really feel the pain, process the grief, and move on that kept me stuck in suffering. The situation was a recapitulation and intensification of the aloneness I had felt for so long after the fantasies of baseball and boxing greatness had collapsed.

Those next three years had a hellish quality. I didn't become an alcoholic, probably because I would awaken from my stupors with intense migraine-type headaches that kept me away from the bottle for two or three days at a time. Or maybe I just don't have the gene. Anyway, I sure drank a lot, and I got into a great deal of trouble as a result. In one barroom fight, I almost lost a finger. Another time, I held a broomstick against a roommate's throat and might have seriously injured him if several buddies had not slammed into my room and taken me to the floor. On another occasion, one month after I was selected division Airmen of the Month at MacDill Air Force Base in Tampa, I was thrown in jail in Daytona Beach for disturbing the peace.

It wasn't always awful. After several months of attempting to make a mechanic out of me with dismal results, an opportunity arose for me to try my hand as an office administrator. It worked! I was good at it. My boss, Chief Master Sergeant Robert Sanders, was one of the most decent leaders I have ever met. He cared about his troops and was genuinely kind. He was one of the first of several very good men in my life who filled the empty place in my heart where my father should have been. Some of my young fellow airmen called him Dad. I didn't; it was not a word I used with anyone. In return for his good treatment of us, we all worked hard and the shop was a place of palpable camaraderie.

Day times were fine. It was at night that the demons came, and they just kept coming. I felt broken and unfixable. I was drawn to Hemingway's *The Sun Also Rises*, and James Baldwin's *Go Tell It on the Mountain* and *The Fire Next Time*. I spent my off-time drinking, reading, prowling after women, and listening to Ray Charles.

One day, a buddy and I were in an "it's-time-to-get-good-and-drunk" mood. We purchased a bottle or two of whiskey and twelve cans of beer. Sometime during the evening, a third friend joined. When we had consumed most of the liquor we had, we decided it was time to drive to Clearwater, which was perhaps thirty minutes from Tampa, so we could go clubbing. Of course, I can't remember a single frame from that evening except that I was howling and hollering so much that when I awoke in the back seat of my car, I was bleeding from my throat. That was when I knew I needed help. In the Yellow Pages, I found a psychiatrist who worked on Saturdays.

So began the journey that continues through this day.

Marriages

Tina and I met at the University of South Florida, where I was completing an undergraduate degree with a major in psychology. By this time, I had been in traditional psychotherapy for about three years. The one thing that changed in my life as a result was that I decided to get an advanced degree in clinical psychology. This was no small decision. With a very poor high school education—because I had emotionally and intellectually given up at the beginning of my sophomore year—and having had no realistic ambitions ever, making that choice and going for it was truly a momentous occasion in my life.

After a grand Greek wedding, Tina and I drove to Lawrence, Kansas, where she began her career as a school teacher and I began mine as a clinical psychology graduate student. How ironic that I did so well in a clinical graduate program and did so poorly as a husband. I could not tolerate any kind of genuine closeness. When you are filled with shame and guilt, as I was, how can you self-disclose? What do you share about yourself? I simply didn't. I was clueless; I had no sense of what my emotions really were.

I also avoided intimacy by finding something to fight about when it appeared that Tina was interested in getting close to me. I began to suspect that I was doing something strange, but I could not admit it, even to myself. I simply did not know what a human connection was. I was becoming a star in the clinical psychology program, and I had yet to feel a genuine human I/Thou connection, a heart-to-heart connection. My anguish begged to be drowned in booze. I had a constant longing for I knew not what. Ironically, when it was offered, I ran in fear. I longed for closeness and was simultaneously terrified of it. As it was in the beginning, so it was as an adult.

One very effective way to insure against closeness is by attempting to completely dominate your mate. And that is just what I did. I masked my deep sense of weakness with a false bravado. The game that Tina and I played together was to act as if I was the capable, decisive one and she was the needy, helpless one. Thus, she deferred all decisions to me, and in any crisis she expected me to take charge. This was a wonderful charade because it convinced me of my strength and capability. After all, she needed me for almost everything.

When I say that we played a game together, I do not mean that we consciously said, "Hey, you act like this because that way I won't feel threatened by your power and femininity, and I will act this way so you don't have to take responsibility for your strength. You can continue to believe that men are powerful daddies who will always take care of their little girls." If we could have verbalized these strategies, perhaps we would have found our way out of that rigid bind. We could not and did not. As you may have guessed, the type of bond I had with Tina is called *disorganized-insecure*. I longed for closeness but closeness was a threat. If she attempted to come close, I fought.

It is ironic and amusing that the very moment we separated, I fell into a helpless depression. Fortunately, it only lasted a couple of weeks. As soon as we separated, I felt almost incapable of putting my socks on in the morning. Tina, on the other hand, learned to tune up her car and overcame a phobia of flying in planes. Surely, God was laughing. I, always so strong and in charge, and poor, helpless Tina had reversed our roles on the stage of life.

This is what I mean by playing charades. We each played pretend-not-to-rock-the-boat, and we each suffered. Tina was terrified of being left, and I was terrified, period. I pretended to be strong and in charge, while she pretended to be weak and helpless. We were emotionally much too young to embrace and contain those disparate fragments. When we separated, the deeper truth surfaced.

Three marriages came and went as I doggedly pursued growth and improvement. I was determined to get it right. When my wife Diane and I first dated, it was touch and go for a while. However, by then, each of us had acquired more skills and capacities than we had ever had. With the grace of God and the courage to hang in there, we just kept learning and growing together. Today, thirty years later, we are constantly grateful and appreciative for the relationship we have built. It seems to continuously get better.

When we examined the skills and capacities that have so enriched our relationship, we came up with twelve that I want to offer here. Some I have mentioned already, and some I will mention again in different contexts. Your entire organism affects your ability to engage these skills: the fluids in your body, your brain and nervous systems, your tissues and physical structure, your beliefs—everything. Yet, if you engage the skills directly and do your best to learn them, I guarantee you will bring more loving connections into your life.

"My humanity is bound up in yours, for we can only be human together"
~ Desmond Tutu

WHAT YOU CAN DO: PRACTICES THAT ENRICH RELATIONSHIPS

1. Speak from your heart. This is also called transparent self-disclosure. It can be helpful to ask yourself: What is the simple truth? Learn to identify when you are simply saying it like it is without adding an element of attack, blame, or criticism. You want to be known. We all long for someone to know us deeply. Practice letting yourself be seen and known. Here is an example: "I like you, and I am afraid to get closer because I don't know if you have really separated from your last boyfriend."

2. Listen to your partner. Listening to your partner means paying attention. Try to understand what your partner is saying. This may seem obvious, even trivial, but consider how often you are formulating your response or thinking about something else while someone is speaking to you. Intend to become a better listener. To become a better listener, you have to be willing to be changed by the other person.

3. Attune. Attunement is a type of listening that involves your heart and requires an ability to demonstrate through your facial expressions that you really are getting what your partner is saying. It is a mutually engaged form of attention, and it creates resonance. It is often experienced as love. Let yourself be affected by those close to you while in conversation. Notice if your facial muscles feel engaged or if you are trying to hold a particular expression. Genuine interest is not feigned interest; let yourself feel what is being communicated.

4. *Learn to detect ruptures in your relationship and repair them skillfully.* Sometimes, we describe the intimate connection as a filament between two hearts. From time to time, the filament gets very thin or tears and needs to be restored. In most relationships, there are frequent moments of little annoyances, exasperations, or forgetfulness that can create tiny—and sometimes not so tiny—ruptures in your connections. The flow of good feeling begins to diminish. Pay attention to these ruptures so that you can catch them and repair them quickly. If they persist too long, and especially if they accumulate, it does not bode well for your relationship.

5. *Release frustration, irritation, disappointment, and resentment gracefully.* It is characteristic of a good relationship that the vibes between the couple are mostly positive. If disappointment, resentment, or frustration tend to linger, and especially if they characterize the tone of the relationship, the odds of a long-term and satisfying relationship drop. Make it your priority not to dwell in negativity. This is not easy but very much worth cultivating given the effects of negativity on your health and well-being. The first thing required is your sincere desire not to dwell in negativity. Then, the moment frustration, for example, occurs do not allow yourself to go into a mental story justifying it; rather, feel the sensations in your body, feel its effects; then take several deep breaths and imagine or sense those effects dissolving with every exhalation. Then decide what action, if any, you want to take to improve the situation.

6. *Self-soothe*. Self-soothing and the ability to let go of negative experiences are important aspects of self-regulation. Talk to yourself gently and clearly. Guard against self-talk that induces self-pity, feelings of victimization, or defensive anger. Listen to how you speak to yourself. In what tone does your inner voice speak? Is it harsh, demanding, or critical? Is it self-indulgent or excusing? How would you speak to yourself if you really liked yourself? Sometimes, it is important to be firm and clear. Sometimes, it's important to be comforting. Sometimes, it's important not to speak at all, just to feel and be.

7. ***Choose your response; don't just react***. This may be the most challenging of all our practices. It is also the most powerful in terms of promoting self-development. The story of Dr. Victor Frankl is among the most inspiring stories of courage and wisdom that I have ever come across. Victor Frankl was a Jewish psychiatrist and author in Austria during the reign of Hitler, when he and his family were captured and placed in a concentration camp. His entire family was killed and his papers and books burned. What else can be done to a human being? As horrendous and painful as these experiences undoubtedly were, they did not crush Victor Frankl's spirit. We might say that he became enlightened as a result. Here is a quote from his marvelous book, *Man's Search for Meaning*. "Between stimulus and response there is a space. In that space is our power to choose our response. In our response lies our growth and our freedom." Practice choosing your response. If your mate, child, or employee disappoint you and you are just at the edge of a verbal barrage of berating and belittling, pause. Count to ten. Speak from your heart after you have calmed down. Ask yourself how you want to be in your relationships. Do you want to be the one who blows up, criticizes, and puts down? Or do you want to be able to speak clearly and firmly, with care and consideration?

8. *Remain centered while engaged in difficult conversations.* For many couples, distance may develop gradually over time, and the relationship begins to lose its appeal. Often, a contributing factor is avoidance of difficult conversations. You see, if you go with the easy way out (avoidance), you will pay a price. You must be willing to be uncomfortable and/or to allow your partner to be uncomfortable. If you can stay centered and remain open, available, and receptive, your partner will probably be able to stay engaged in the conversation. How, then, can you stay centered? If you keep part of your attention in your lower body—your abdomen, pelvis, and legs—it will help keep you centered. Feel the support of your lower body; feel the strength of your back, right there behind you. Feel your heart, too, and your intention to strengthen the relationship.

9. *Make room for new aspects of yourself to emerge.* Who you are carries a tapestry of possibilities. If you are unaware of aspects of yourself, especially those you deem unacceptable, they tend to unexpectedly emerge in others around you. Alternatively, you may constrict yourself in an effort to cut that part of yourself away. If you can recognize those parts and embrace them, your sense of yourself expands, and conflicts can resolve more organically. In your essence, you have the possibility of moving fluidly among different "selves" as called for by the situation. A good way to approach this practice is with judicious use of the word *and*. For example, I can be tender when called for *and* assertive when called for. I can be silly and playful when appropriate *and* quite serious when necessary. If you find you can't move out of a particular way of being, for example, if you are always serious, regardless of the circumstances, then this is an area for you to develop.

10. ***Embrace and support your vulnerability.*** When the conditions of your first years, from minus nine months to, say, four or five years, are optimal, there is a bright glow to that soft, tender part of you. It has been held in a way that is conducive to feeling safe and secure. But if the wounds have been significant, your vulnerability gets tucked away behind a wall of protection. Embracing vulnerability involves taking risks. If you are scared, unsure, or tender, it is easier to keep it under wraps, protected. Practice allowing your partner to see and be with you when you are feeling vulnerable. Sometimes, it doesn't even require words. However, in order to be okay with your vulnerability, you must be able to support it. In fact, it is essential. If you don't believe you can support your vulnerability with strength, you are not likely to expose it in the first place.

How do you support it? If, for example, you tell your partner you're afraid and he laughs at you, it is important to let him know, clearly, that you do not allow anyone to make light of your vulnerability. When choosing a partner, it is important to observe how he responds when you are vulnerable and can he display his vulnerability? Deep intimacy and vulnerability go hand-in-hand. You can't have one without the other.

11. ***Cultivate an attitude of gratitude and appreciation.*** If you want to live in an environment that feels good, that contains humor and care and delight and affection, it is up to you to create that environment. Lots of people respond to that suggestion with, "It takes two to tango." I suggest a more useful attitude is, "It takes one to tango." If you can keep the focus on what is positive, if you can be generous in expressing appreciation and gratitude, if you can feel free to acknowledge what your partner means to you, your chances for reciprocity along the same lines are so much higher.

12. ***Engage in mindful self-care***. It is your responsibility to take care of yourself, to listen to your heart, to care for your body, and to honor your nutritional and spiritual needs. It is your responsibility to handle what needs to be handled.

From my perspective, the above capacities are so much of what life is all about. If you can take good care of yourself, live with gratitude and appreciation, embrace and support your vulnerability, welcome new aspects of yourself to emerge as life conditions change, remain centered in difficult conversations, not allow your reactions to take over but pause and respond according to your values, self-soothe, let go of negative experiences gracefully, become skillful at repairing ruptures in your connections, attune to and empathize with your partner, be a skillful listener who can hear the music between the words, and speak from your heart, unguarded and without vigilant censorship, that would be quite a group of skills.

It would be hubris of me to claim mastery of them; however, I can assert without hesitation or doubt that in my late twenties I would have been classified as retarded in most of them, if such a classification existed. Today, however, that is clearly not true. It is possible to change and grow substantially!

I want to emphasize these are capacities that involve the whole organism. Recently, as you will see later, neuroscientists have begun to understand how certain areas of the brain must develop so that these capacities can flower. I am adding to that. I am saying that it is the brain, the nervous system, the heart, the whole structure, the tissues, and, yes, the fluids themselves. All are involved.

Next, we will visit our model of self, those core beliefs and assumptions we unconsciously hold about ourselves, others, and the world.

CHAPTER 7

What "Creating Your Reality" Really Means: Core Limiting Beliefs and Your Sense of Self

"Home is knowing—Knowing your mind, knowing your heart, knowing
your courage. If we know ourselves, we are always home anywhere."
~ Glinda, *The Wizard of Oz*

The wounds of childhood profoundly influence what you believe to be true about yourself, others, and the world. You may be amazed to discover how much of your quality of life and your relationships are influenced by what you deeply believe to be true. Limiting beliefs may be at the roots of many of your challenges. Further, you probably formulated these beliefs in early childhood, at birth, and perhaps even in the womb. These beliefs will function as a perceptual filter, allowing in what is consistent with them and keeping out what isn't. Discovering what they are can change your life in a big way.

Model of Self, Others, and the World

Long before a child utters his first words, he has begun to formulate beliefs about himself, others, and the world. These are implicit, emotional beliefs; they are pre-rational; and they profoundly influence your sense of who you are. By the time you have reached the age of three or four, you have internally answered the questions, "Are others dependable? Can I count on people? Is the world safe or dangerous? Will I reliably get the nourishment and nurturance I need? How consistent are others? Can I trust? What happens when I express myself strongly? Is anger allowed? Is my distress tolerable to others?

Will I get help when I'm distressed? Is it okay to need? Will I be much better off if I focus exclusively on things outside myself and ignore my own feelings and needs? Is it okay to enjoy my body?" Obviously, these are important questions.

When a parent is able to notice that her infant is signaling a need, discern what that need is, and respond to it in a timely manner, she is positively affecting many developmental processes in the child. The infant is learning, "The world is a safe place. My needs can be met," or "I am capable of making a positive change in my world" or "Other people are dependable and responsive; I can rely on people." These foundational beliefs influence and form the very core of how you view yourself and the world.

These are not rational considerations. As a two-year-old, you were not thinking about these questions. Nevertheless, you were drawing conclusions about them—emotionally—based on the kinds of interactions you were having with your parents, your experiences, and the quality of your environment. So, in the first three or four years of life, you began to form an internal model of reality consisting of your basic operating principles or core beliefs, and these substantially influenced the course of your life. These are foundational and will continue to influence your perceptions, your behavior, and your organism as a whole.

For example, if you have a core belief that people are not to be trusted, you will interpret a situation—say, being short-changed by a merchant—differently than you would if you believe that people are basically trustworthy. In the first case, you might assume that the merchant was out to make a quick buck; in the second, you might assume it was accidental and give the merchant the benefit of the doubt. In the first case, you are more likely to be tense in the situation. Over time, that belief can cause more chronic tension or a certain level of vigilance to insure that you are not being mistreated. You can see how your core beliefs play an enormous role in the evolution of your close relationships.

Two Kinds of Dysfunctional Beliefs

There are two kinds of dysfunctional beliefs we human beings hold: beliefs that offer a positive outcome if you conform to expectations, and beliefs that offer no hope.[1] The less severe are the beliefs that offer a positive outcome; however, they are dysfunctional because they are conditional. An example is a belief that the only way to be loved is to always be nice. Another is that if you ever show anger, you will be abandoned. So to be loved, you can never show your anger. Even though there are limitations and restrictions, there is also hope. "Yes, I can be loved. I can be accepted—as long as I pay the price."

The more severe are the beliefs that offer no hope. No matter what you do, you are doomed. An example is a belief that no matter what you do, you will never really be loved. Another is that nothing you do is worthwhile. Or, you may believe that if you open up and get close to someone, you will be hurt, or if you let your guard down, you will be annihilated. These offer no hope of love, acceptance, or a positive sense of yourself. They are distress-producing and detrimental to your well-being. Much of our human suffering is related to these pain-producing and limiting beliefs. Ferreting them out is a worthwhile endeavor, although it's not necessarily easy. I will suggest some ways to do just that.

I recall reading a book by Jane Roberts, *The Nature of Personal Reality*, which argues that our beliefs create our reality. At the time, I was working in a children's clinic where we had a playroom with a dartboard. For an entire year, I had been playing with those darts, and I had never put more than two or three of the six darts in the bull's eye. As I was reading Roberts' book one day during lunch, I had a jolting realization: At my core, I believed that *nothing I ever did or could do was worthwhile.* My whole body felt the jolt. I stood up and threw all six darts into the bull's eye! A core belief had come to light, and as we will see below, bringing a core belief to light is the first step in changing it.

These beliefs are emotional constructions generated out of feelings of distress. When an infant or toddler's predominant experience is distress, when there are chronic insults or serious impacts, then "I feel bad" is how he comes to know himself. The "feeling-bad" state gets embedded as, "I feel bad; therefore I am bad." Again, this is not a cognitive process. It is a feeling of deep shame, and its effects can show up in many different ways. For example, clients will reveal that they always felt they were somehow a disappointment to their parents, or an inconvenience, or that somehow they are flawed or defective. Sadly and tragically, this lies at the core of many, many human beings. It is a feeling/belief that keeps us from disclosing ourselves openly and honestly and makes the expression "love yourself" seem like a foreign language. How can you love yourself when at the deepest layers of your constructed "self" is this sense of "I am bad, flawed, or defective?" You "know" you are inferior, unlovable, unwanted, or defective. You are likely to be hypersensitive to criticism, rejection, or blame because you agree that you are essentially bad. You must then always keep some part of you hidden, and true intimacy becomes impossible. This is a situation in which love cannot get in.

Again, these deep emotional wounds affect all of us, not just mind and emotions or even the brain. They affect how we breathe, how we hold ourselves, how we move and engage in the world.

The Child's Solution: Construction of an Image

The child constructs a solution: he creates an image of self that he attempts to project outward so that nobody can ever see how bad he really feels about himself on the inside. He may become tough, rebellious, with a "nobody-is-going-to-hurt-me" attitude. Or he may become super-helpful: "I'll-always be here for you, but I will never need anything." He may become rational and intellectual, always happy to share his thoughts and opinions, but "Feelings? What feelings?"

These constructed images are not just the result of a mental or even an emotional process. They are constructed with your whole somatic being and are intended to *protect* the very vulnerable, tender places inside that you don't feel good about or want to be seen. Real love, real, genuine connection from being to being does not occur when you are relating image to image. Image-to-image relationships are hardly rare. An example is a couple I worked with in Seattle who came in for therapy after she discovered he had been having an affair. As therapy progressed, she discovered she didn't know him below the surface. She was in love with the image. He was handsome, professional, athletic, and could take care of whatever needed handling. He had never learned to open up and reveal his deep feelings. It was only when he slowly became able to reveal himself that she began to know him (and he her), and a real, intimate relationship began to form.

Your Beliefs Create Your Reality—but they ain't necessarily true

It is obvious that such core beliefs will result in interpersonal distress or avoidance. They also produce a heightened sensitivity to anything that confirms the negative perspective, which is another way of saying that your beliefs create your reality. If you are certain you will be rejected or abandoned or invaded or criticized, then you will notice and respond to every cue that could support that belief. The cues are evident and in clear view. Conversely, you will overlook, not see, or minimize those environmental cues or events that contradict your deep beliefs. In your reality, they will tend not to exist.

The model you generate of self, of other, and of your world is vital to how you function in life, vital to your relationships, vital to your successes and failures, and vital to your health. When important developmental needs have been chronically unmet or in cases of serious impacts or maltreatment, your core beliefs, which are the organizing structures of your personality, will generate pain and distress. They become rigid, unconscious, and therefore resistant to change. They are a chronic form of stress that compromises your vitality and whole-heartedness. The areas in which you formulate these beliefs include your body, your lovability, your competence, your attractiveness, your sexuality, and your food and money. In short, the whole of your life is influenced by what you deeply believe to be true. Remember, however, these core limiting beliefs are just that: beliefs. They are not the truth about who you are.

WHAT YOU CAN DO: PRACTICES

Ideally, at the center of self, are beliefs that you are lovable, capable, and basically good; beliefs that the world is relatively safe and others are fundamentally trustworthy; and that, perhaps with some effort, your needs will be met, you will be nourished, and you will get the love and attention you need. Of course, we all have some limiting beliefs. Preferably, they are the ones that provide hope and are not so rigidly adhered to.

At this point, you might be wondering how to discover what you deeply believe to be true, when, as I said, our deepest beliefs are often outside of our awareness. You also might wonder what is the value of bringing your beliefs to consciousness.

Honestly reflect on the state of your life.

Honestly reflecting about the state of your life is one of the surest ways to ferret out what you believe to be true. If, for example, you have had a series of failed relationships, it would be valuable to examine what you believe to be true about yourself in relationship.

The first step is to sincerely want to become aware of what is running the show of your life. The next is to ask yourself to allow this to be revealed. Do not examine your challenges and conflicts from the point of view of "my bad luck" or "it's always these other people's fault." Examine them constructively. Ask yourself whether you have some belief that is contributing to how these challenges and conflicts play out in your life.

By seeing them in the light of day, you have taken the first step towards challenging their reality and coming to see yourself in a better, more expanded way. For example, if you realize that you believe you will be hurt if you let yourself get close to someone, you can test that belief. More than likely, the belief originated very early on in your life.

You are not that child. You can bring new tools, comprehension, and skills into your current relationships. Once you uncover this core limiting belief, examine it closely. How does it manifest in your body? Imagine getting close and open with someone; sense what happens inside of you.

When you have a good sense of how this belief manifests in your life, ask yourself, "Is this really true?" Take your time with this and see what comes up. Then ask, "What if the opposite were true?" With support from friends, you can test your beliefs in current time: Will I always get hurt if I let myself get close? Do I do something that increases the probability of my getting hurt? What if I didn't do that next time; might it go down differently? Do I choose people who bring a high probability that I will be hurt? In this case what if you would be deeply nourished if you got close to someone? Remember, what was true in your infancy, does not have to be true today.

Sometimes a good course of psychotherapy is the best way to reach these deep structures. Whatever orientation of psychotherapy it may be, it is likely to uncover beliefs you didn't know were there that were significantly influencing your life.

Obviously, if your sense of self is grounded in positive beliefs and you experience life as an abundance of flow, love, joy, peace, and good health, there is no need to begin a quest to uncover what programs are running the system. But, if your life has distress, pain, dissatisfaction, and ill-health, such an examination can bear good fruit.

Who are You? Your Sense of Self

Who am I? It is a question that theologians, philosophers, and psychologists have pondered since time immemorial. A definitive answer to this question is above my pay grade, since I am neither philosopher nor theologian. However, this much I do know—we are so much more than we think we are! If you ask an astrophysicist, he will tell you that every atom in your body originated in ancient stardust. We know from science that our bodies are mostly fluid. At birth, we have the potential to learn any language on the planet. Also—and this is one of the main messages of the book—no matter how egregious our beginnings, we have the ability to continue to change in a positive way.

What does it mean that, as organisms, we are made mostly of water? It tells me that, like water, we are adaptable and filled with potential. However, as a result of the wounds of our lives, along with an insufficient comprehension of what it means to be alive in these human bodies and what we need, typically our sense of self gets truncated, rigid and even fragmented. So much human suffering results from people identifying with only a small aspect of themselves—their tribe, for example—-and hating what they consider *other.*

If your beliefs are supportive and realistic, if you feel lovable, capable, and filled with potential, if you can hold apparent opposites, it means your sense of self is more coherent. For example, do sexuality and spirituality live together within you in harmony? Can you integrate these two aspects into your sense of who you are? A blatant example of *lack of* coherence and a sense of self that is *not* integrated is the fire-and-brimstone preacher who gets caught at the local brothel.

Can you be serious and playful, rational and intuitive, strong and vulnerable, dutiful and carefree, productive and relaxed? As you can see, "self" has many aspects. How well they coexist and support you are key. Another question to consider is whether you are open to discovering new aspects of yourself. Whenever I hear someone say, "I'm the kind of person who…" or "That's just the way I am," I cringe.

Why do I cringe? Your "self" as fluid potential has far more possibilities than that, as you will learn when we explore the Psychology of Selves in Part Two. Whenever we rigidly identify with one aspect of self and exclude other related possibilities, we are cutting off some of our wholeness.

Here is an example of how a sense of self is developed that does not necessarily bear a strong relationship to reality. As a little girl, my wife was always told she was a delicate child. Therefore, she was not allowed to engage in many physical activities, such as riding a two-wheel bike, until she was an adolescent. She was well into her adulthood before realizing that, at five-foot-nine and having a rather solid bony structure and musculature, she was anything but delicate. Yet, she had a strong sense of herself as delicate, which was inculcated by parental propaganda and strongly influenced her relationship to physical activity. After all, she was a "delicate child."

Coherent Beliefs: Embracing "And"

How do the jazz-band metaphor and "maximum individual freedom and maximum global cohesion" apply to your sense of self?

Let's begin at the cognitive level. In a coherent personality, beliefs are self-supportive and not self-negating, self-destructive, self-minimizing, or self-aggrandizing. A person with a coherent personality is able to make a realistic appraisal of his strengths *And* weaknesses, with no need to diminish *or* inflate. Coherent beliefs are consistent with the fundamental reality of our nature and include self-acceptance *And* self-love.

A person with a coherent sense of self would have a fair amount of tolerance for ambiguity and what I call "*And*" consciousness, by which I mean an ever-growing awareness that she is multi-faceted and multi-dimensional.

Here are some examples. A friend of mine has been in a relationship for about a year. A part of him is eager to commit and set the date, but another part isn't. Something "doesn't feel quite right." In a situation like this, my counsel is to make room for both parts. A part of him wants to be in this relationship *And* a part of him does not want to be in this relationship. It would be helpful for him to listen to what each part has to say and to assess how each part feels. The more fully he can embrace each aspect of self that is involved, the greater the possibility that the situation will flow organically and clarity will come.

A majority of our human suffering comes from our inability to embrace a bigger sense of ourselves. For example, if I make a commitment of monogamy without embracing all of who I am and then have sexual feelings for another, I am racked with guilt. But if I can acknowledge that a part of me has no interest at all in monogamy, then I can make a choice freely. Personally, I choose monogamy, And I acknowledge that, of course, it would be fun not to be monogamous!

WHAT YOU CAN DO: PRACTICES

1. Look for opportunities to insert an *And* after a position you hold or a view of yourself. Explore what happens. Notice sensations in your body. Notice any "voices" that emerge from your mind. All of this is useful information! See if you can locate within yourself some dimension of what you take to be *other*. An obvious example is, "I am a man, *And* I have feminine aspects of myself that help me to empathize with and understand the females in my life." Or, "I am a strong, competent, and efficient woman, *And* I have a luscious, juicy part of me." If you are a conservative, I am not trying to make you into a liberal; but practice making space for opposites, even though one side may be much stronger than the other (and vice versa, of course. Intense polarization, whether at the level of politics or personality, does not reflect coherency).

2. As you discover limiting beliefs that are interfering with the fullness of your life, make a two-column list. On one side, write down a limiting belief you have discovered. Opposite it, in the second column, write down the belief you want to be true for you. Here's an example. In the left column, let's say the discovered limiting belief is, "If I really open up with a man, he'll run away." In the second column, you might write something like, "Even though a couple of men have left after I shared my vulnerability, many men would welcome an honest, deep relationship."

You know, there really are many men who would. But if the first belief is operating, then you are likely to see and respond to the very first sign of a man shutting down and miss all the signals to the contrary.

1. Young, J., *Cognitive Therapy for Personality Disorders: A Schema-Focused Approach*, Sarasota, FL: Professional Resource Press, 1999.

CHAPTER 8

GROWING A BRAIN THAT DIGS RELATIONSHIPS

"What flows through your mind sculpts your brain. Thus, you can use your mind to change your brain for the better—which will benefit your whole being, and every other person whose life you touch."
~ Rick Hanson, *Buddha's Brain*

The wounds of childhood affect our brain, and the consequences are serious. My purpose here is simply to show how interpersonal experiences provide nutrition for the brain—specifically for the prefrontal cortex—and how certain psychobiological and relational capacities require the development of the prefrontal cortex, which in turn requires positive emotional experiences for its development.

It is difficult to fathom a three-pound structure that feels like Jell-O and is capable of solving the most complex calculus equations or writing a symphony or mastering several languages. Yet, our brains are capable of that and so much more. These three pounds of tissue contain over 1 trillion cells, including 100 billion neurons, or nerve cells.[1] The brain works as a whole, so any attribution of function to a single substructure is generally an over simplification. For the reader interested in a deeper exploration of neuroscience and psychological health, many good texts are available.[2]

Even if you did not receive the good tending in childhood needed for optimal brain development, you can change your brain now, as an adult, through learning to have good relationships and engaging mindfulness practices.

A Thumbnail Sketch of Your Brain

To create a simple visual impression of the location of the

structures within the brain, fold your thumb into your palm and fold the fingers over the thumb. Now, turn the palm so you can see your fingernails. Imagine that your wrist, hand, and fingers symbolize the brain. The fingers folded over the thumb represents the *cortex*, the most evolved and human part of this marvelous brain. The area from your knuckles closest to the fingernails, down to the fingernails, represents the *prefrontal cortex*. In the center of the prefrontal cortex, behind the orbits of the eyes, is an area called the *orbitofrontal cortex*, which sends and receives signals from all the other major areas of the brain. It also controls the autonomic nervous system via the *limbic system.*

Now, lift your fingers and expose your thumb, which symbolizes the limbic system. The evolution of the limbic system corresponds to the evolution of mammals. Mammals give birth to their babies, while reptiles hatch eggs. Mammals and reptiles also have very different orientations towards their offspring. Reptiles are detached and disinterested in their progeny, while mammals are capable of engaging in subtle and elaborate interactions. The limbic system is one of the prime mediators of those interactions. It is the neurological center of emotion and motivational states.

The area of your wrist represents the *brain stem* or *reptilian brain*. This is the oldest part of our triune brain. In essence, it is a bulbous elaboration of the spinal cord, located just as the cord enters the *foramen magnum*, that large hole at the base of the skull. Physiologically, this is the area that governs survival. Vital centers such as those that control respiration, heartbeat, and the startle reflex are located here. The reptilian brain receives information from perceptions, from our bodies, and from the outside world.

Human Capacities that Require a Well-Developed PFC**

Human beings are designed to learn and grow throughout the life span, not just in the first eighteen years of life. This means we have the capacity to change throughout our life span. There were times in my twenties and early thirties when life looked hopeless. My habits were self-destructive and my relationships were chaotic and seemingly futile. Millions and millions of individuals are in such straits. It is possible for them, for all of us, to change. Change is possible because of the plasticity, resiliency, and growth potential of our brains *and*, as we have already discussed, of our entire bodies, which are over 70 percent fluid. We can become healthy—in body, mind, and relationships.

In Chapter 4, I discussed the emotional nutrients we need for optimal psychological growth, such as attention, affection, acceptance, and so forth. We saw how they contributed to our model of our self and to our experience of security with our primary caretakers. Now, we will understand that experiences in which someone else is truly present with us influence the development of our prefrontal cortex. It has been known for a long time that brain development is experience-dependent. As children learn to distinguish shapes, sizes, distance, numbers, words, and concepts, their brains are fed and grow. However, only recently have we discovered that the qualities that make us most human, such as self-regulation, attuned communication, empathy, control of fear, self-soothing, response flexibility, self-reflection, a good moral compass, and the ability to trust your heart and gut feelings depend, in part, on the development of a certain area of the brain. Further, in order for that area of the brain to develop optimally, the emotional nutrients discussed earlier need to be provided.

According to Dr. Dan Siegel from UCLA, who is one of the founders of a field called interpersonal neurobiology, the development of an area of the prefrontal cortex (PFC) is necessary for the following human capacities to flourish.[3] This area of the brain is deeply connected into both the limbic system and the autonomic nervous system. As we will see in Chapter 9, the limbic-autonomic connections are major components of the stress response, and their optimal functioning empowers the organism to deal effectively with challenges from both within and without.

Self-Regulation

At birth, an infant lacks the ability to regulate his own feelings. Distress, delight, surprise, and anger are some of the basic, biologically-based emotions that we express as infants. There are ups and downs. The infant is dependent on Mother for regulation because he does not yet have the biological equipment to do so. As Mother provides it to the best of her ability, the infant develops the neurological and the psychological capacity to take on the job himself. The ability to regulate affect (excitement, energy, and feelings) is among the most important biopsychosocial skills a child must learn for adequate functioning.

To understand this idea better, let's return to our thermostat. Whatever temperature it is set for, there is a small allowable range above and below. For example, if it is set for 68 degrees, when the room temperature drops below 66 degrees, more or less, the thermostat kicks in and turns the heat on. When the temperature in the room rises above 70 degrees, more or less, it does the opposite. Now, imagine what would happen if the temperature kept rising and the thermostat did not kick the heat off. Or what if the temperature continued to fall and the heat did not come on? It would be a problem. We rely upon the thermostat to regulate temperature for us.

Good regulation is the ability to regulate or modulate emotion or our response to psychosocial challenges, and it is the foundation of a good life. When well-developed, self-regulation becomes the foundation for the growth of psychosocial competencies throughout the life span. When poorly developed, it leaves deep marks and renders us susceptible to a variety of stress-related difficulties, as we will see further in Chapter 9. In fact, bi-polar disorder is an extreme case of poor self-regulation.

Examples of poor self-regulation

• Inability to control your temper, which can be set off by the slightest provocation

• Getting frustrated in a traffic jam and being upset for hours

• Having a hard time restoring your spirits after a slight disappointment or defeat

• Being upset for days after a difficult conversation or a confrontation

These are just a few examples. Some people's lives are so chaotic that they have a constant frenetic quality and can't calm down and relax. Others' lives are so constricted that they rarely venture beyond very narrow borders. They may be afraid to try anything new, afraid of change, afraid to venture into unfamiliar territory, and even afraid to travel. Not knowing what they might encounter, they don't want to risk having any feeling they can't manage or any situation that might derail them.

Of course, people don't admit or even know what is really motivating their preferences. No one comes out and says they are afraid to go on a trip because they don't believe they can manage the emotions that may arise. They put forth a more personally acceptable rationale.

Self-Regulation and Shame

Shame is a difficult emotion to deal with because it is accompanied by a desire to hide. Frequently, we don't even know that what we are feeling is shame. Your guts and the tissues of your face may feel tight. You may feel flushed and hot. Your perspiration may have a different odor. You may think you are feeling frustration or anger—or almost anything else but shame. Shame can be insidious, and because it is so dreadful to simply acknowledge and face shame, it is a difficult emotion to regulate. If you could simply feel it, name it, and express it to another, it would not be the insidious emotion that it is. When ashamed, we don't want to be seen. It's too painful. We feel defective or deficient. To address shame requires courage and a relationship in which there is great safety. It is the hardest emotion to deal with. Whereas guilt is associated with something I either did or did not do, shame says "I am bad, deficient, defective and unlovable."

Biologically, as an innate affect, shame serves a purpose. It lowers your happiness or excitement level when it is not safe for it to be up, and it returns you to yourself when you are attempting to connect with someone who is unable to be present with you.[4]

Here is an example. A toddler is excited and about to knock Aunt Sadie's favorite vase off her coffee table when mother emphatically says, "No." Not only is toddler very excited, but he had been resonating positively with Mother and was expecting more of the same. That is, he was expecting Mother to match his increasing excitement as he reached for the novel and stimulating object in his path. Mother's "mistuned" response deflated the child's high sense of excitement. This deflation is called shame. As Mother is able to attune to his experience, his energy returns, and that rupture has been repaired.

A few years ago, our friends were with us for dinner along with their then two-year-old son, Vinay. As we were finishing dessert, Vinay, who was playing by our living room window, reached for the blinds, which, had he pulled, would easily have come down. In a moderately loud voice, I said, "Vinay, no!" His deflation was immediate. I had interrupted his excitement and interest. Fortunately, his mother's repair was just as immediate. She spoke to him with soothing words and made certain that he knew that it was the action that was wrong, not him. As she did, I watched his energy quickly fill back up.

This is regulation. As we saw above, the infant is dependent on Mother's more mature structures to provide that regulation. Two important events now occur. One is that the child internalizes these breaks in his excitement as stored images. Soon, he will be able to call upon these images in the absence of Mother and provide his own regulation. Second, regulation of these deflation and repair experiences literally helps important parts of the child's brain and nervous system to grow.

Although these repair transactions often have a verbal component, essentially they are vibrational. The whole sequence can occur without words. It is critical that a child learn how to rebound from such a state. Recovering from moments of shame is a crucial aspect of effective self-regulation. With Mother's attuned participation in these transactions, the child begins to develop an internal sense of himself as effective and to view his interactions as positive and reparable and his caregiver as reliable. The child is learning that he can come up when he is down, and come down when he is up. He is also developing the neurological structures that will enable him to control the process himself.

Often, an individual who is deficient in this capacity will avoid close, intimate relationships. Relationships that involve removing your clothing, sleeping with another, revealing your deepest fears and hopes, and being seen in your raw, more primitive moments—all require us to regulate our affect. Certainly, there will be moments of shame or embarrassment, and if you can't quickly recover from their impact, you will tend to avoid situations that potentially could evoke those unwanted feelings. This is why self-regulation is a foundational capacity for a healthy life.

Attuned Communication

The next capacity that requires the participation of the pre-frontal cortex is the ability to *engage in attuned communication*. It is the wonderful feeling that someone is really with you. It is a feeling that the other is tuned in, connected, and is being affected by you. You can feel that he or she is there.

People are starving for attuned communication and, sadly, few know it is what they are starving for. Having those moments when someone is so with you that their facial muscles are reflecting the movement in your facial muscles and their eyes reflecting the feelings in your heart is something we humans long for. You can call it the experience of love. It is soul food for the brain, the heart, and the nervous system. Indeed, we pay a price when it is not provided. The capacity to provide this level of exquisite attention requires a well-developed pre-frontal cortex. It requires facial muscles that are free enough to express nuances of feeling.[5] If you did not receive attuned communication it is difficult to offer it. However, once again, it is never too late to improve and refine our capacity to be with someone in this way.

Empathy

Very much related to attuned communication is the next capacity that requires participation of the pre-frontal cortex. It is the *ability to express empathy:* "I know, feel, and sense what you are experiencing, and I can let you know that I know." When you have an abundance of attuned communication and empathy in your life, you feel rich no matter what your circumstances. If you don't have these nutrients, if they are not coming from somewhere, you feel hungry, no matter how materially rich you may be. Like attuned communication, empathy is an essential nutrient, and it is my impression that the majority of human beings are living with a nutritional deficit. In a very real sense, even if you have others who care for you, provide for you, and have sex with you, if you are not receiving the nourishment these capacities provide, you have a deficit.

Control of Fear

Fear is a fact of life. We humans are burdened and blessed with the knowledge of our mortality. A three-year-old is learning to master her fears when she play-acts that a really scary monster is in her room and then Daddy appears and saves the day. Adults are vulnerable, too. As much as we would like to think we're in control, deep down we know that life can turn on a dime. We may deny our fears. Many people do.

So, then, if you don't want to repress or deny your fear and if you don't want to let it run out of control, what options are left? You can recognize and embrace your vulnerability as an intrinsic part of being human. You can feel the sweetness and poignancy of life and get to know it and appreciate it. You can protect yourself without erecting impenetrable walls of defense. You can form a realistic sense of what you can control and what you cannot. These options require a well-developed pre-frontal cortex.

Self-soothing

When my then three-and-a-half-year-old granddaughter was demonstrating her jumping twists from the sofa to the ottoman and back, she missed her landing and bumped her head hard on the edge of the ottoman. Of course, she wailed; but only for less than a minute as I held her and kissed her "boo-boo" to help the hurt go away. Earlier in our visit, she told me that she had hurt her finger in gym class but didn't cry. She didn't say it explicitly, but she was telling me that she self-soothed. She was learning how to do it, and she is learning to self-soothe because an adult has always been there to teach her how.

Countless situations require us to soothe ourselves. If your relationship breaks up, or your lover or partner gets angry at you, or a promotion you were expecting doesn't materialize, or you just had a bad day and are either criticizing yourself or feeling criticized by someone else, these situations call for self-soothing. If you do it well, you are likely to tell yourself something positive or optimistic, or you may simply attend to the part of yourself that feels hurt and sad. You are able to let go of the frustration or agitation relatively quickly and return to a positive state. Without this ability, you are likely to indulge in too much food, alcohol, or drugs; watch too much TV; or play too many video games. All of these behaviors are efforts to soothe yourself and feel better. Again, it is a well-developed Pre-Frontal Cortex that makes self-soothing likely.

Response Flexibility

Response flexibility is the ability to respond instead of react. Development of the PFC is the capacity to create some space between a stimulus and your response. It is a type of flexibility, and it means that, between a provocation and your reaction, you can take a moment, count to ten, breathe, have a cup of tea, or take a walk. Taking that time means you can choose to respond differently than you would if you had just reacted in the moment. Developing this capacity also allows you to see different options instead of always doing something the same way.

It takes a great deal of maturity to not react to provocations with blame and counterattack, especially when those provocations touch a vulnerable spot.

Self-reflection

The next capacity is the *ability to self-reflect*, to examine your own behavior and see how you may have contributed to an interaction. So many people walk around feeling that they are life's victims. They blame others; they blame their circumstances; they blame God for their challenges and failures. What they rarely do is calmly ask themselves how they might be contributing to the situation and look for other options may be available. Over years of working with people, I see over and over again the sense of empowerment that comes when someone realizes he has a choice in his situation and can develop the skills to engage those choices effectively.

A Good Moral Compass

If the opportunity presented itself to cheat on your spouse with a very attractive person, would you do it and do your best to cover your tracks? Would you do it if you were guaranteed you would not be caught? Would you refrain from doing it because you're afraid you'd be caught and the consequences would be brutal? Would you refrain from doing it because you could not imagine hurting your mate? Would you refrain from doing it because it just isn't right and you made a vow not to?

Clearly, the last two reasons suggest a more evolved moral compass. And once again, at the level of our neurobiology, a well-developed PFC is necessary to keep this compass in place.

Ability to Trust Your Heart and Gut Feelings

A few years ago, my wife and I moved to Salt Lake City to be near our family, especially our grandchildren. It was a major uprooting, and the transplant shock took several months to wear off. Before we left, a client asked how we knew it was the right decision. Immediately, I understood her question. I could easily imagine how difficult such a choice could be. In Seattle, my wife and I had so much: private practices, friends, church, community, and a beautiful home. It was a great question.

Of one thing I can assure you: it was not a decision arrived at through a rational process. It was one of those instant moments of just knowing. It was a heart feeling and an inner knowing.

We all receive intuitive information, whether we receive it as a heart feeling, a gut feeling, a sudden but clear image, or a sense of just knowing, it is information that we can learn to trust and value. Of course, we should then submit the "feeling" to a rational review, but we have the opportunity to cultivate those non-rational sources of information. Yes, a developed PFC is important here, again.

Obviously a well-functioning PFC is at the heart of our humanity. When it is chronically compromised, we have a situation where self-regulation, control of fear, attuned communication, empathy, self-reflection, self-soothing, a good moral compass, and trust in our gut feelings are low. When we move along the continuum from poor tending toward maltreatment, we see situations in which the child frequently is left in distress. *The brain of an infant who experiences frequent neglect or maltreatment is exposed to intense states of biochemical imbalance. Evidence exists that when an infant is continually left in states of distress, without interactive repair, the result could be cellular death of areas of the brain that are involved in feelings and emotions. There is evidence that adverse social experiences can result in permanent changes in the brain's receptors for important neurochemicals. Changes in these receptors may be the mechanism by which intense stress leaves permanent marks on the growing brain.*[6]

My upbringing was clearly at the awful end of the continuum, and my life appeared destined to proceed along the trajectory in which it began. But thanks to God and some wise choices on my part, my life changed course and continues in a positive direction as I age. I now know in my bones and in my heart that, regardless of the hand you were dealt, it is eminently possible to take charge of your life and make it better. I can say unequivocally that life offers so much more than most of us ever imagined; the spiral of your life *can* turn, and it can *continue* in a positive direction.

Presence in relationship provides the nutrients for the growth of the brain's pre-frontal cortex. And even if you did not receive it in childhood, you still can receive it as an adult.

WHAT YOU CAN DO: REFLECTIONS AND PRACTICES

Consider the nine capacities described in this chapter. Make note of where you want to see improvements in yourself. The practices listed in Chapter 6 cover most of these. In fact, the practices throughout this book, as well as the somatic therapies and psychotherapies that I describe later, will all contribute to growing these dimensions in you.

Here is an oldie but goodie: When you feel the rising heat of anger or rage, do not speak. Instead, focus your attention on taking a deep breath and begin counting to ten. Doing this takes will power, but realize that letting the words fly in such moments only makes your life messier. Bring a quality of firmness and commitment to this practice. As you learn to stay inside your body as you engage in difficult conversations, without anger or blame, you will feel your sense of power grow. And as your sense of power grows, you will get enraged less and less. The hot rage reflects a sense of powerlessness, a sense that you have no control in the situation. As you practice engaging in difficult conversations as described in Chapter 6, your confidence in yourself will grow. As your confidence grows, explosive anger will recede as an issue.

** I owe much of the material in this chapter to a course I took with Daniel Siegel, whom I cite below.

1. See Koob, Andrew, *The Root of Thought*, Pearson Education, Inc., 2009.

   The remainder are glial cells, which were once considered to be merely supporting cells for the neurons, but scientists are now taking a new look at glial cells, especially one type called astrocytes. Researchers think it is possible that these cells may be information storage sites in the brain.

2. See, for example, the works of Daniel Siegel and Rick Hanson.

3. Some authors talk about the medial pre-frontal cortex, some about the ventrolateral pre-frontal cortex, when discussing which part of the prefrontal cortex is involved in the capacities I will be describing. For simplicity, I will simply refer to the pre-frontal cortex. See Dan Siegel's, *The Developing Mind*.

4. For a thorough analysis of the origins and effects of shame, see: Nathanson, Donald, *Shame and Pride: Affect, Sex and the Birth of the Self*, 1992. Also, Kaufman, Gershen, *The Psychology of*

Shame: Theory and Treatment of Shame-Based Syndromes, 1996.

5. This notion that the muscles need to be free to fully express one's feelings will become clear in later chapters.

6. For an extremely thorough and in-depth examination of this, see Schore, Allan, *Affect Regulation and the Repair of the Self,* 2003.

CHAPTER 9

STRESS: IT'S NOT ABOUT HAVING TOO MUCH ON YOUR PLATE

This is where you will begin to see how everything we've covered so far ties together. Good tending is important for good relationships, positive beliefs, and a well-developed brain. As the quality of tending decreases or impacts increase, you are more vulnerable to stress and its consequences, including health issues.

On August 13, 2012, *The New York Times* reported the death of Dr. William C. Reeves. He was sixty-nine years old. From 1992 to 2010, he directed research at the Center for Disease Control and Prevention in Atlanta in one of the most contentious subjects in contemporary medicine: chronic fatigue syndrome. The article went on to say that at least one million Americans suffer from the syndrome, which includes severe fatigue, muscle soreness, difficulty concentrating, and sleep problems—*and* it has no known cause. For years, Dr. Reeves searched for the cause, for a virus or bacteria responsible for this affliction. According to Dr. Thomas Folks, a colleague, "He tried desperately hard to find the etiology, whether it was physiological or an infectious disease or whatever." When Dr. Reeves began to suspect that stress and a history of physical, sexual, or emotional abuse were contributing factors, he incurred the anger of many patients.

Why would people get angry when told that their problem might have stress or abuse as a contributing factor? The answer is not necessarily simple.

First, patients know that they are genuinely suffering, and that the suffering is in their bodies. Second, if stress and abuse are contributing factors, that might mean that the problem is "in their heads," which is not an acceptable diagnosis when the pain is clearly something they feel in their bodies. Third, if stress and childhood abuse are factors, and the problem is systemic, there is no easy, tangible cure. No single medication or surgery is going to solve the problem.

Okay! So, what gives?

What gives is recognizing that the complaining patients are absolutely correct. The problem is in their bodies; the difficulty is with the medical model. For years, the medical model has ignored the possibility that mind and relationship factors can cause physical symptoms. And even the words *body* and *mind* are misleading.

Quality of Tending in Childhood

We have already seen how good tending in early childhood results in a strong and positive internal model of self. We have seen how a secure bond is essential to the development of both psychological and neurological structures, and that these structures provide the foundation for resiliency, adaptability, good health, and good relationships. With a good, strong foundation, an individual has the capacity to meet life's challenges—socially, interpersonally, and professionally. This does not mean that such fortunate individuals are immune to the disorganizing and painful effects of excessive impacts and insults that can occur later in life. It does mean, however, that they have a stronger base, a foundation to which they can return.

Children who are poorly tended, especially children who are maltreated, are more likely to deal with serious illness, both as children and as adults. Good tending is the beginning of a healthy lifestyle. Children who are poorly cared for are much more likely to develop poor habits of self-care. They are more likely to smoke, eat poorly, not exercise, drink excessively or use recreational drugs. And, as we learned in the previous chapter, they are likely to have a less developed pre-frontal cortex with all its accompanying challenges.

Many factors influence the quality of tending that parents provide.

- The parent's emotional, spiritual, and social maturity, which inform their ability to be present with their children.

- Ability to discern their children's' needs and respond to them in a timely manner.

- Their everyday level of stress and anxiety

- Their comfort with touch, play, and sexuality

- Their love for each other

- Ability to handle conflicts well

- Ability to set firm limits and discipline with love

- Ability to see other's uniqueness and honor other's individuality while maintaining a cohesive family unit

- Willingness to be available to engage, to guide, to teach, and to inspire.

Obviously, this is an ideal worthy of aspiration. What wonderful parents are those who even come close to this ideal! Looking at the continuum of tending, as we move away from the ideal, we find a large percentage of truly "good-enough" parents, who raise wonderful, bright, and healthy kids. Still further away from the ideal, we find another large percentage of parents, who, because of their own history and challenges, are emotionally unavailable and generally provide less than adequate care for their children. At the furthest end of the continuum is where we see maltreatment, neglect, and emotional, physical, and/or sexual abuse.

The Executive Function of the PFC

In Chapter 8, I presented a thumbnail sketch of the brain, emphasizing the pre-frontal cortex (PFC) and its links to the limbic system and the autonomic nervous system. To recap, when the PFC was not optimally developed or was chronically compromised, a situation exists in which self-regulation, attuned communication, empathy, self-reflection, self-soothing, a good moral compass, control of fear, and trust of gut feelings are likely to be low. This information sheds light on many of our social ills, including how we become *more susceptible to chronic illness and disease.*

For decades, physicians dismissed any relationship between stress and disease because the physiological links could not be satisfactorily elucidated. Now, as the research grows, we can begin to comprehend the vital importance of human connection for the development of those physiological structures that support our health and well-being. Because, as you are about to see, chronic stress contributes greatly to chronic disease. Furthermore, whether or not life's events enter our perception as challenges that we are ready and eager to tackle or as stressors with negative effects depends on the foundation that has been established in the early years of life.

The pre-frontal cortex is involved in self-regulation and serves a kind of executive function relative to our limbic system. Two structures of the limbic system I want to mention here are the *hippocampus* and the *amygdala*. The hippocampus is a small, layered, and folded structure. It is necessary to the formation of explicit, factual, or autobiographical memory. It is concerned with the context and sequence of events. The second structure, the amygdala, is tiny, almond-shaped, and lies deep under the cortex, close to the hippocampus. It assigns emotional significance to experiences and is important for processing highly charged events. It is our 24/7 alarm center, always on the alert for threat or danger. It sets off the fight/flight response and carries emotional memory.

Here is an example of the relationship between the PFC and the amygdala from the world of business that will give you a sense of how all this comes together. Let's say a middle manager, in charge of a sales and marketing project, realizes that the plan he is implementing is not working. In fact, his data reveals that his company's competitors are getting an edge because his project did not do what he expected. Panicked, he tries even harder to make it work. However, his CEO has a much better perspective on the organization, its competition, and the sector they are in. The CEO, who represents our PFC, counsels the manager, who represents our limbic system, to remain calm. Without operating from panic, he points out what needs to be done.

If the PFC is not well developed, the amygdala, which sets off the fight/flight response, operates without executive supervision, meaning it is much more likely to kick you into fight or flight. So, in addition to the compromised development of the qualities and capacities mentioned in Chapter 8 (self-regulation, attuned communication, empathy, etc.), you are also subject to more frequent fight/flight responses with less provocation than an individual with a strong foundation. More situations or events feel "stressful."

Here is an example of an individual with a poorly developed PFC who responded with fight/flight in a situation most folks would see as innocuous. Several years ago, my wife and I took in a young man, a member of our church, who was having serious challenges in his life, including a brush with the law. After eighteen months and some rather intense psychosocial education from both of us, and having completed his GED, he was ready to go off on his own and begin community college. He found an apartment with some other students. On the day of his move, we drove him to his new home. A rather attractive young lady answered the door and welcomed him. I found it fascinating to observe that he turned scarlet and the tension level in his face and neck skyrocketed as he struggled to find simple words like, "Hello, my name is...."

In this case, the saber-toothed tiger was a young lady saying welcome, but his physiology didn't know the difference. Fight/flight had kicked in. In Chapter 11, we will look at this mechanism in depth. For now, it is important to note that the stronger the foundation established in the first few years of life, beginning in gestation, the more difficult it will be later in life to unbalance an individual with a "traumatic" event.

How the Mechanisms of Stress Relate to Health

You will better understand how stress translates into poor health by knowing more about how the mechanisms of stress relate to health. In the human organism, these mechanisms represent an elegant and complex interweaving of the PFC, the limbic system, the autonomic nervous system, the cardiovascular system, the endocrine system, the immune system, and the neuromuscular and connective tissue systems.

Think of an orchestra. Different instruments do their own thing, yet they do it in complete harmony with every other instrument. It is a beautiful arrangement. However, as in an orchestra, if one or more of the pieces are out-of-tune, the whole is affected, and the physiological soil is set for the growth of emotional *and* physical difficulties.

There is mounting evidence that stress is an influential factor in a wide variety of physical and emotional disorders. It has been estimated that the cost of stress-related disease is $200 billion per year. [1] This astronomical figure includes the cost of a variety of physical illnesses, such as heart disease, hypertension, asthma, diabetes, allergies, and other immune disorders. It includes syndromes such as migraine headaches, fibromyalgia, chronic fatigue syndrome, and numerous digestive disorders. There is a growing movement of medical educators who want to shift focus from treatment to prevention. To be effective, this movement towards prevention must understand and fully embrace all the factors included in quality of life and health. Let's examine the stress response. What is it?

Definitions of Stress

The word *stress* may rank among the most commonly used words in the English language, yet from the very beginning of its usage, its definition suffered from vagueness and ambiguity. What exactly do we mean when we say we had a stressful day at the office? It could mean many different things.

Stress as a stimulus

In its original sense as physics' term, stress refers to strain exerted on an object that can alter the shape of that object. In this definition, stress is a stimulus, an external force that affects an object or organism.

Stress as a response

Stress also can be defined as a response, that is, as what occurs inside an organism as a result of perceiving a stimulus. More specifically, stress is what occurs physiologically when a situation or event is perceived as stressful, including its ensuing effects on internal or "target" organs. Target organs include the heart, brain, lungs, kidneys, adrenals, and pancreas. The mind can be a target organ, too. That is, stress can affect our perceptions, judgments, cognitive functioning, and even our personalities. In other words, your perception of an event affects your physiology and psychology.

Understanding of how stress relates to health and illness has been evolving over many years. The grandfather of that understanding was Hans Selye, a Hungarian researcher who was responsible for putting the word *stress* on the map. He was attempting to determine the effects of a particular hormone on the body. Lore has it that he was particularly clumsy in handling and injecting the hormone into his experimental rats, and periodically he dropped the little critters and had to chase them around to capture them again. When he conducted his examinations, he discovered that his experimental rats had peptic ulcers, shrunken immune tissues, and enlarged adrenal cortexes. Being a good scientist, he of course gave a neutral stimulus to a control group, so that he would not erroneously conclude the results he observed were a function of the hormone he had injected. To his chagrin, he found that the control group, the one where the rats had been injected with a benign solution, displayed the same responses as the group he had injected with the hormone. They, too, had ulcers, shrunken immune tissues, and enlarged adrenal glands. What was common to both groups of rats? Selye was handling both groups the same way. The effects were not from the hormone he was injecting, but from the handling process itself!

Daunted but not defeated, Selye wrestled with the problem. Finally, he arrived at the conclusion that there exists a nonspecific response to external demands, in this case, his handling of the rats. In other words, in response to any demand, the body has a *general stress response*. This is *normal, natural*, and *adaptive*. The organism's resources mobilize to meet demand, any demand. However, when the situation is prolonged, physical problems can occur. Selye termed this the *general adaptation syndrome*: The first response to threat is an *alarm reaction*; it is followed by a mobilization of resources, which he called the *resistance phase*. If the mobilization continues, resources are depleted. Selye termed this the *exhaustion phase*. In his theory, it was this exhaustion phase that resulted in illness.[2]

The stress response itself is a normal, adaptive, and healthy response to demand; human beings require challenges in order to grow and develop optimally. In this sense, stress is good. We need challenges, and we have the psychophysiological mechanisms to handle them. However, when the demand or impact is overwhelming and is too much for our resources, or when it continues for too long, difficulties will occur.

Keep in mind that, to an infant or small child, receiving inadequate nurturing or having a parent who is not emotionally present much of the time is a very disturbing situation. For example, if the mother is depressed for a long time or if a parent is chronically anxious, worried, and not very nurturing, the child will feel a chronic level of distress. Just being mishandled by a clumsy scientist was too much for Selye's rats. The wounds of childhood are often a source of chronic distress.

Acceptance of Stress's Role in Health and Disease

Stress plays a crucial role in health and disease, but there have been impediments to the general acceptance of that notion. As the medical community begins to accept stress as a serious factor in health and disease, then we may begin to take self-care more seriously than we have to date.

Impediments to general acceptance

The major impediment has been a hundred and fifty years of medical success based on the "one cause for one disease" theory. Another has been uncertainty about how stress translates into disease. In order for science to accept that A causes B, it is necessary to show exactly how that occurs. Until recently, how exactly stress caused disease was not well explained.

Although it may be intuitively obvious that stress translates into disease, the mechanisms involved have been anything but obvious. Hans Selye's general adaptation syndrome described an "exhaustion" phase, in which structures have been worn down. This was a beginning, but hardly a sufficient explanation, even if it makes sense intuitively. Science requires far more than intuition. Selye's theory just did not stand up to scrutiny, especially in the face of a hundred and fifty years of one cause/one effect being "just how it is."

Several different theories have attempted to explain how stress translates into disease. For example, one theory—developed by a psychoanalyst named Alexander French—states that specific psychic conflicts result in specific conditions, such as repressed hostility resulting in migraine headaches. Again, although there are certain conditions under which this theory might seem to have intuitive validity, it simply does not meet scientific standards.

Another theory states that individuals are genetically predisposed to respond to stressful stimuli with a particular pattern of psychophysical reactivity. If, for example, an individual is born with a "weak" stomach, under stress, it will be his stomach that is most affected by stress. In other words, when a specific organ has a genetic weakness, and there is frequent stress activation, that organ will be the one to suffer first. Once again, this particular theory of translation makes much intuitive sense but fails to account for all the data.

Yet another theory proposes that disease is not the result of direct stress, but of insufficient motor expression.[3] This view suggests that our sedentary lifestyle is to blame for how stress translates to disease. These scientists point to the fact that the role of our musculature goes far beyond locomotion. It is well known that our striated muscles have a role in circulation, metabolism, and endocrine balance; they also serve as outlets for our emotions and nervous responses. Thus, it is conceivable that the great loss of mobility that has occurred over the last hundred years could be responsible for stress resulting in disease.

All of the above theories probably contain a degree of truth. Some cases of stress are due to the wear-and-tear effect; others show the effect of a predisposition for certain organs; and in yet other cases, the culprit is the great spread of a sedentary lifestyle. However, none of these explanations alone is sufficient to explain the phenomena to scientists' satisfaction.

Limbic Hypersensitivity Phenomena—a Common Denominator

Synthesizing decades of theory and research, a couple of Harvard psychophysiologists[4] arrived at a model that elegantly explains the pathogenic mechanisms in diseases that are considered to be related to stress and emotional challenges. The basis for the model was a consistent observation that certain technologies resulted in a greater capacity for relaxation and ameliorated or at least lessened the severity of a wide variety of diseases. These were technologies such as meditation, biofeedback, and yoga. Since learning to relax can improve a wide variety of psychosomatic conditions, it seemed to follow that those conditions have a common denominator. Reviewing the experimental and theoretical literature, researchers concluded that the common-denominator condition was something they called *limbic hypersensitivity phenomena, a state in which the limbic system is either chronically "aroused" or has such a low threshold that it is easily aroused.*

This condition gives rise to a wide variety of physiological and emotional disorders. Discovery of a latent condition that can manifest clinically in a plethora of physical and psychological disorders has obvious and profound implications for prevention and treatment.

This limbic hypersensitivity theory accepts what is common to all previous attempts to explain the linkage from stress to illness: organs that are overstimulated for long enough eventually manifest disease. The dysfunction may be a result of wear and tear, biochemically-induced trauma or toxicity, predisposed organs, or visceromotor fatigue or exhaustion. All of those explanations have some validity. However, *this model places its emphasis on the limbic system itself.*

It states that a wide variety of etiological or causative factors—including emotional, cognitive, environmental, social, and biochemical—can result in limbic-system-based neurological hypersensitivity. In turn, this state activates a variety of stress axes, such as the neurological, neuroendocrine, and endocrine axes, which can, through their effects on target organs, manifest as disease.

Limbic hypersensitivity phenomenon is a common denominator factor of a wide range of conditions that can be called arousal disorders.

Included in this classification would be all anxiety-related and stress-related conditions, both physical and psychological. Physical illnesses can include gastrointestinal disorders, such as peptic ulcers, ulcerative colitis, irritable bowel syndrome and esophageal reflux; they can include cardiovascular disorders, such as essential hypertension and coronary artery disease; they can include respiratory disorders, such as asthma and allergies; and they can include many other disorders, such as migraine headaches, fibromyalgia, chronic fatigue, and chronic pain. Anxiety-related disorders include panic syndromes, generalized anxiety, and post traumatic stress. It is also likely that many forms of depression involve limbic hypersensitivity phenomenon. The implications of understanding limbic-hypersensitivity cannot be overstated.

Recall that the pre-frontal cortex is a regulator of the amygdala, which sets off the fight/flight mechanism. We have examined the consequences of not having essential needs met—and especially of severe wounds and impacts—for the development of the pre-frontal cortex. *This is one route to limbic hypersensitivity.* In Chapter 11, we will look at other routes to this same phenomenon. In Chapter 13, we will take an in-depth look at what I mean by the quality of tissues. Here, I will simply say that the skeletal muscles play a critical role in sustaining an aroused limbic system. The Harvard scientists I mentioned before reviewed research showing that individuals suffering from any one of these stress-related disorders had higher levels of chronic muscle tension in their bodies. They concluded that *chronically contracted muscles bombard the limbic system and perpetuate its functioning in a high state of arousal.*[5] It is a circular process. Stress and anxiety lead to chronic muscle contraction. The biochemistry involved in chronic muscle contraction bombards the brainstem, limbic system, and cortex, thus sustaining limbic sensitivity.

I believe that the effects of stress in our culture are revealed in medical statistics, in the high prevalence of anxiety and depression, in the general malaise that many endure, in the divorce statistics, and in the relationship challenges many of us face. *The chronic stress of being unsupported, harshly criticized, not emotionally well-nourished, or just not well-tended are sufficient to produce this picture.*

Positive Change is Possible

Neurogenesis refers to the brain's ability to grow new cells throughout its lifetime. Scientists did not accept that this was possible until the end of the twentieth century, when a scientist by the name of Elizabeth Gould[6] demonstrated that the adult rat continues to produce new cells in an area of the brain called the *dentate gyrus*, which is part of the hippocampus. She also found that increased levels of cortisol and stress could suppress the production of these new cells, putting the process on hold.

Neuroplasticity refers to the brain's malleable, responsive, and resilient nature. In the process of learning, the brain actually remodels and reconfigures its very structure. Both neurogenesis and neuroplasticity are central to learning and memory processes, and both are put on hold in times of stress. This is a protective feature and another example of the adaptive nature of those stress mechanisms. If the stress is terminated, then both neurogenesis and plasticity resume, and there is no permanent damage to the brain. However, when the stress situation is chronic, protection becomes damage; a temporary restructuring becomes diminished connection or shrunken tissue. Just these facts should be enough for us to take stress seriously. Fortunately, research and my personal experience have shown that positive changes are possible even when the effects of stress have been severe.

My Health as a Child

As I have been saying, you must understand and deal with your organism as a whole when seeking healing and realization of your full potential. You already know a little of my history, so it should come as no surprise that I was not a healthy youngster. At age three, I started getting migraine-type headaches, nausea and all. By the time I was in my late 20s, I was getting severe headaches of this type three or four times per month. They were the awful ones during which I sometimes tried to vomit just to get a respite from the throbbing pain. In addition to these, I also got another three or four a month that were not severe enough to put me to bed. It was a lot of headaches!

Looking back, it is hard to believe how low my energy usually was. Fatigue accompanied me everywhere, even as a child. And why wouldn't it? My self-care sucked! Beginning when I was a young child, I preferred cream pies and coffee for breakfast, followed by numerous candy bars and caffeinated soft drinks throughout the day. When I was a child, I loved to play, but by the time I was sixteen, exercise meant standing on the curb and sticking my thumb out for a hitchhiking adventure. I smoked over a pack of unfiltered camels every day, beginning at age sixteen. Of course, all of these factors don't include the chronic, insidious stress of an organism so incoherent and so unfulfilled in basic emotional needs and so forth. In my 30s, I began to change, but not soon enough to prevent serious damage.

WHAT YOU CAN DO: PRACTICES

Prioritize peace. If you made it your priority to cultivate peace in your heart, what would it mean in terms of what you do, what you say, and how you respond to situations? Setting this intention consciously is a strong, positive step. This is a resource book, providing you with the understanding, practices, and disciplines you can engage to live more peacefully and harmoniously. I do know it can be done.

1. For readers wishing a more in-depth treatment of stress, I highly recommend the work of Bruce McEwan, *The End of Stress as We Know It*, or George Everly and Jeffrey Lating, *A Clinical Guide to the Treatment of the Human Stress Response.*

2. For an in-depth treatment of Hans Selye's work, see McEwan's *The End of Stress as We Know It.*

3. Everly, George and Lating, Jeffrey. *A Clinical Guide to the Treatment of the Human Stress Response.* (note: pp. 50 to 60 describe the attempts to relate stress to disease).

4. Ibid.

5. Everly, George and Lating, Jeffrey. *A Clinical Guide to the Treatment of the Human Stress Response.* New York: Kluwer Academic/Plenum Publishers, 2002, 182.

6. Gould, Elizabeth, et al., (1998), Proliferation of granule cells precursors in the dentate gyrus of adult monkeys is diminished by stress. *Proc. Natl. Acad. Sci. USA, 95,* 3168-3171.

CHAPTER 10

STRESS AND HEALTH: A NEW WAY OF THINKING

"If I told patients to raise their blood levels of immune globulins, no one would know how. But, if I can teach them to love themselves and others fully, the same change happens automatically. The truth is: love heals."
~ Bernie Siegel, M.D.

I hope you are forming a more sophisticated understanding of stress. Stress is not just about too much on your plate. It's more about your deep sense of self and how well your various psychological, neurological, and relational capacities have developed.

From a physiological perspective, a general, nonspecific response to a wide variety of stimuli did not seem to make sense. Scientists had believed that a specific response always has a specific stimulus, and certainly they had believed that specific illnesses had specific causes. The nineteenth-century German physician Robert Koch, in fact, won a Nobel Prize for the discovery of a specific agent (the tubercle bacillus) as the cause of a specific illness (tuberculosis), greatly advancing medical research based on the theory of disease specificity. Hans Selye's groundbreaking theories were the major take-off point for years of research on stress, leading to the radical concept of a common denominator cause for a variety of illnesses: limbic hypersensitivity. This was a new way of thinking.

You will see how you can address limbic hypersensitivity. Again, no matter what hand you were dealt or how poor your early foundation was, you can continue to improve your capacity to meet life's challenges effectively. This is especially true when you understand all that is affected by wounds of life.

Now, let's take another look at the stress response and how stress affects different organs and systems of the body. Stress can be a factor in most diseases. Armed with this knowledge and an understanding of the root causes of stress, you will be better prepared to engage the practices and disciplines described in this book.

The Stress Response

When the stress response is initiated, the organism's attention shifts from long term-needs to short-term needs. For example, reproductive or digestive activity is placed on hold—it's not important in the moment; the neuromuscular systems, however, require an increase of energy. The body is preparing itself to meet a demand, challenge, or threat.

The stress response can be examined along the three different axes: the neurological, the neuroendocrine, and the endocrine. If you are interested in the physiological details of these responses, I refer you to Everly and Laiting's book, cited in the previous chapter.

The neurological axis

The neurological axis is the response of the autonomic nervous system (ANS). It responds immediately when a threat is perceived. This system is so important to our understanding of stress, health, trauma, relationships, and body tissues that we will devote the entire next chapter to it.

The neuroendocrine axis

The neuroendocrine axis begins in the limbic system area of the brain. French surgeon and neuroanatomist Paul Broca first identified a group of organs in the brain that he referred to as the limbic brain. The word comes from the Latin *limbus*, which means *edge, margin, or border*, and it refers to an area above the reptilian brain that is common to all mammals. This area of the brain is at the center of activities dealing with stress, emotion, love, and trauma. The amygdala initiates the neuroendocrine axis.

I recall a client who had a tendency to flare up intensely whenever anyone got upset with her or challenged her. A quality of rage would appear seemingly out of nowhere. This was her sensitized amygdala in action. That is its job—to warn when danger appears and set into to motion your readiness to fight to the death or run like hell. Simply understanding that it was her over sensitized amygdala was helpful in her ability to either not flare up or to have the rage dissipate in seconds. Later, as her prefrontal cortex became more engaged, her ability not to flare, i.e., to regulate her amygdala, grew.

The amygdala signals the adrenal glands, which outpour adrenaline. Adrenaline is one of the two major stress hormones; cortisol is the other. Adrenaline steps up the heart rate and sends more oxygen to the lungs, brain, and muscles. It stimulates secretion of a substance called fibrinogen, which aids in the clotting of blood. If you are preparing to fight or run, you may get wounded. How brilliant is the body to begin clotting your blood—just in case! It also mobilizes the release of glucose and fatty acids from their storage as glycogen and fats, respectively.

Adrenaline increases blood pressure, heart rate, and cardiac output; it decreases blood flow to the kidneys, skin, and gastrointestinal system. Action requires energy, so these physiological activities mobilize energy in preparation for action. The whole body is made ready to engage the situation. This is not a condition to wish for except in the very short term to meet an emergency, which is exactly the design. However, when some of these effects become chronic, then the very systems designed to empower us suffer unwanted consequences.

The endocrine axes

Neural stimulation of the adrenals occurs rapidly. Slower, more prolonged effects occur along what are called endocrine axes. For a more detailed look at these I refer you to books by McEwan and Everly and Lating, cited at the end of the previous chapter. For our purposes, it suffices to say that cortisol is released via a sequence of hormone secretions and also comes from the adrenal glands.

As with adrenaline, the effects of cortisol are both complex and double-edged. One of cortisol's first functions is to replenish the energy supply depleted by the effects of adrenaline. It does this by converting a variety of food sources into glycogen and fat storage. Too much or too little of either cortisol or adrenaline can tip the system out-of-balance, creating problems.

Stress and the Immune System

For almost forty years, scientists have posed questions concerning the relationship of brain, behavior, and the immune system. This field came to be known as psychoneuroimmunology, and it has generated a vast amount of research. The basic question we are concerned with here is this: Does stress affect the immune system? If it does, it must be considered in relationship to a host of infectious, degenerative, as well as so-called psychosomatic diseases. In addition, if severe early wounding in childhood seriously compromises the healthy stress response, and if that, in turn, suppresses the immune system, then the link from early wounding to infectious, degenerative, and psychosomatic disease is established.

In fact, the immune system is an active participant in the stress response. Immune cells are generated in the bone marrow and are carried in the blood; they destroy whatever does not "belong" to the body. When the fight/flight mechanism is engaged, the chance of injury resulting from fighting or running away increases. Therefore, the immune system must prepare to deal with infection in case there is a wound. Initially, cortisol boosts the immune system by sending white blood cells to their battle stations, and then turning off the immune response once an appropriate level is reached. Cortisol also shuts off its own production to keep the stress response from getting out-of-hand. So, when a threat is perceived, cortisol sends out the troops, and if they don't find infections, they return home. When the threat is over, when the stressful stimulus goes away or is satisfactorily dealt with, cortisol sends an all-clear signal to the immune system. This is the sequence of events when the system is functioning effectively and in harmony.

If the protective functions of cortisol are not effective, such as when the perceived threat does not get resolved, the immune system can go into overdrive. Inflammatory and autoimmune disorders are conditions that arise when the immune system gets out of hand. In inflammatory disorders, the immune system goes on the attack in response to stimuli that do not bother most people, such as pollen or dust. Allergies are an example of the immune system on overdrive. In autoimmune disorders, immune cells fail to distinguish self from non-self, similar to what happens in inflammatory disorders, but they carry it one step further and begin attacking healthy tissues. Rheumatoid arthritis and type I diabetes are examples. In type I, or juvenile, diabetes, the immune system destroys insulin-producing cells in the pancreas, which results in dependency on insulin injections.

I think you can begin to see how early impacts and insults play havoc with your immune system, setting the stage for a wide range of physical and/or emotional problems. When your immune system is depressed, you are more likely to get ill.

Numerous studies have demonstrated that the emotions affect the immune system. In one study,[1] a group of medical students demonstrated that loneliness can suppress the immune system. They also found that people caring for spouses with Alzheimer's disease without much social support fared worse in tests of immune system activity than did those with stronger social support.[2] Confirming an experience common to most of us, one scientist found that people were more likely to catch colds during periods of prolonged stress.[3]

In the early 1950s, 126 healthy men randomly chosen from their Harvard graduating class were asked to describe the closeness and warmth of their relationship with their mother and father. They were asked to choose among four answers: very close, warm and friendly, tolerant, strained and cold. Thirty-five years later, 100 percent of the men who had rated both parents low in warmth and closeness had been diagnosed with diseases, compared with only 47 percent of those who had rated both parents as high in warmth and closeness. The researchers concluded that the perception of love might turn out to be a core biopsychosocial-spiritual buffer, reducing the negative impact of stressors and pathogens and promoting immune function and healing.[4] More and more studies are revealing that the emotional dimension contributes to chronic illness.

Stress and the Brain

Previously, I mentioned the hippocampus, a small structure in the limbic area that is involved with memory. It is rich in cortisol receptors, and cortisol is a major stress hormone. The hippocampus is involved in the formation, organization, and storage of memories. Cortisol participates in that process. Stress hormones assist in engraving experiences into our memory. This is why we tend to remember those situations in which we are emotionally involved. This is another example of the adaptive utility of the stress response. However, when stress levels are severe or exceptionally prolonged, the hippocampus itself and its role in memory formation are at risk; excessive or chronically elevated levels of these same hormones can damage the structure of the brain that is responsible for memory formation.

I can't help but wonder how much stress is involved in the development of dementia and Alzheimer's. Remember, in response to stress, the brain puts *neurogenesis* and *neuroplasticity* on hold. This is absolutely fine for a very short time; it is nature's design. However, these mechanisms, which are designed to protect us, turn against us when stress is excessive or prolonged. As I have been saying, it begins in gestation, the birth experience, and the early years of bonding. Our relational capacities, our model of self, and the quality of our PFC and limbic system are all entwined.

Stress and Cardiovascular Disease

The statistics on cardiovascular disease in America are daunting. According to the American Heart Association, it is the number-one cause of death in the United States, claiming the lives of 40.6 percent of the more than 2.3 million people who die each year. Almost 61 million Americans have some form of cardiovascular disease, ranging from congenital heart defects to high blood pressure and hardening of the arteries. According to the Center for Disease Control,[5] about 600,000 people die of heart disease in the United States every year—that means one in every four deaths. Heart disease is the leading cause of death for both men and women. Every year, about 715,000 people have heart attacks. Of these, 610,000 are first heart attacks, and 325,000 happen to people who have already had a heart attack. As with so many contemporary diseases, modern medicine has been brilliant in developing pharmaceuticals and surgical procedures to deal with the symptoms of cardiovascular disease, but it is not so great at recognizing and preventing its root causes. Nevertheless, stress has now been accepted as a risk factor for cardiovascular disease.

Stress and our DNA

It is ironic that a mere forty years ago, medical science rarely considered stress a factor in disease. Now, its role is indisputable, and there is substantial evidence to support the relationship between the two. Now, we know that stress can be harmful even to our DNA. Your immune system, your brain, your cardiovascular system, and even your DNA are affected by stress. Again, however, what is stressful is determined only in part by external circumstances. In a company of soldiers on the same battlefield, some will get PTSD and some won't. It is the strength of their systems, which is so heavily determined by the quality of tending they received from gestation through childhood, that determines how they can handle the impacts they receive. Knowing this, how important it becomes to make healing the wounds of childhood a top priority!

Dr. Elizabeth Blackburn, a Nobel-Prize winning scientist, opened a body of research involving telomeres. Telomeres are repetitive DNA sequences that protect the ends of chromosomes from fraying over time. In general, the older the individual, the shorter are the telomeres. Shorter telomeres are associated with a raft of diseases in adults from diabetes to dementia.

In a fascinating study done in Romania, it was found that children who were raised in orphanages had shorter telomeres than children who were raised in foster homes. This study demonstrates that deprivation, an insidious form of stress, affects children right down to the molecular level.[5] As we saw in Chapter 4, children need someone to be present with them and to attend to their emotional needs as well as their physical needs. Being in an orphanage is an extreme form of deprivation; however, not receiving attention, attunement, empathy, and other emotional nutrients is also deprivation, albeit in a milder form. It is one many adults have suffered. Future research will tell us how our telomeres are affected by lesser forms of deprivation.

Chronic Sympathetic Hyperactivity and Heart Disease

Our hearts are extremely sensitive to any need to increase our responsiveness. Whenever we are aroused, whether that arousal is pleasurable or stressful, the heart beats faster to provide the body with more oxygen and fuel, such as glucose. Elevations in blood pressure help us deal with environmental challenges, even if those challenges are not emergencies. When properly balanced, the stress hormones adrenalin and cortisol provide and restore energy, but they are problematic when out of balance. However, the autonomic nervous system just may be the key to heart disease. Listen to the words of two cardiologists from the Mayo Clinic:

> The status of the autonomic nervous system, although often ignored by clinicians, is a major determinant of cardio-vascular health and prognosis. Excessive sympathetic stimulation and diminished vagal tone not only are markers of an unhealthy cardiovascular system, but also in part *cause* the adverse events. Chronic Sympathetic Hyperactivity increases the cardiovascular workload and hemodynamic stresses and predisposes to endothelial dysfunction, coronary spasm, left ventricular hypertrophy, and serious dysrhythmias. [6]

In the next chapter, you will come to understand even more about sympathetic hyperactivity, but let me say now that it begins with a PFC that isn't well developed. This allows the limbic system to operate without adequate supervision, so the individual's ability to self-regulate is compromised. His amygdala is more apt to kick into fight/flight at a lower threshold. Minor thwarting turns into a major frustrating event. He may be chronically irritated or annoyed or frequently anxious or worried. And remember, I am not describing just a small percentage of the population, but probably at least half.

Stress and Love

Earlier, I talked about love as an attuned connection between two people, which is different from the way it is normally described. Love is an experience that occurs when two people are in sync, connected, generally maintaining eye contact, and feel the delight in their connection, however brief. High levels of stress make attunement almost impossible. To enter into a connection like this requires slowing down enough to feel, to be present. The high-speed, high-stress lifestyle of our times is not conducive to love. There is a Catch-22 here. You need attuned love to develop resilience and the capacity to receive love. The less you receive, the more you need it, and the harder it is to receive it. The comprehension, practices, and disciplines I present in this book are aimed at reversing this cycle and helping us slow down and become more available for love. Love is a delicious antidote to stress.

1. Kiecolt-Glaser, J., Garner, W., Speicher, C., Penn, G. and Glaser, R. (1984), Psychosocial modifiers of immunocompetence in medical students. *Psychosomatic Medicine*, 46, 7.

2. Dura, J.R., Speicher, C. E., Trask, O.J. and Glaser, R., (1994) Spousal caregivers of dementia victims: Longitudinal changes in immunity and health, *Psychosomatic Medicine,* 53, 345-362.

3. Cohen, S., Frank, E., Doyle, W.J., Skoner, D.P., Rabin, B.S., and Gwaltney, J.M., (1993), Types of stressors that increase susceptibility to the common cold in healthy adults. *Health Psych.* 17, 214-223.

4. Russek, L.G. and Schwartz, G.E., (1996), Narrative descriptions of parental love and caring predict health status in midlife: A 35-year follow-up of the Harvard Mastery Stress Study. Alternative Therapies in Health and Medicine, 2, 55-62.

5. Nature: The International Weekly Journal of Science, Published on-line, http://www.nature.com/news/2011/110517/full/news.2011.298.html.

6.   Curtis, B., and O'Keefe, J., (2002), Autonomic tone as a cardiovascular risk factor: The danger of flight-flight. *Mayo Clinic Proc.* 77, 45-54.

CHAPTER 11

A New Model of Your Autonomic Nervous System

"We are hard wired to connect"
~ Stephen Porges

To understand and appreciate the role of stress in health and the effects of early childhood impacts and insults, it is essential to have a rudimentary understanding of the newest model of the autonomic nervous system (ANS). Understanding this system will be enormously helpful in your journey towards wholeness. Healing arts practitioners will find it invaluable for their work with others. In the subsequent two chapters, we will round out our understanding by considering the heart, and the tissues and structure of the body.

I began with what children need and stated that not receiving it insults the organism. Frequently, the insults and impacts are far more serious than simply not receiving enough of what we need. We have seen how these wounds affect our model of who we are, our relational capacities, our brain, our nervous system, and our stress mechanisms. In this and the next two chapters I will finish presenting all the areas that are affected so that we can learn to provide for ourselves what we have been missing. This is about our journey to become more coherent organisms.

The nervous system, as a whole, is composed of the *central* and *peripheral nervous* systems. The central system consists of the brain and the spinal cord. The peripheral system consists of the *somatic* and *autonomic* systems. The somatic system refers to the nerves that direct movements of the head, trunk, and extremities and also direct sensory information from the environment back to the spinal cord and motor command centers of the brain. It is sometimes referred to as the voluntary nervous system because it controls the movements of skeletal muscles.

The Autonomic Nervous System

The autonomic nervous system (ANS) is responsible for maintaining internal stability and responding to urgency. It mediates involuntary movements (although some can be brought under voluntary control with meditation or biofeedback). It is a key to communication among organs within the body, and it coordinates efforts to maintain stability within cells, tissues, and organs. The two main divisions of the ANS are the *sympathetic* and *parasympathetic*. Both are controlled by a structure in the brain called the *hypothalamus*. The hypothalamus plays a key function in both the ANS and the endocrine system. Although it is only about the size of a peanut, it plays a major role in human functioning.

The sympathetic nervous system

The sympathetic fibers leave the hypothalamus and run primarily along either side of the spine. From there, they travel out to the many organs and muscles of the body. Some of the functions of the sympathetic nerves are to:

- Dilate the pupils of the eyes

- Thicken saliva

- Dilate the bronchial tubes of the lungs

- Stimulate the secretion of adrenaline and noradrenaline at the adrenal glands

- Increase heart rate

- Decrease output of urine

• Decrease digestive function

The sympathetic system is associated with the fight/flight response, because it prepares us to defend ourselves by either running or fighting. It is also responsible—along with adrenaline—for many of the feelings we associate with stress, such as pounding of the heart, sweating, and tightening of our muscles. When this emergency measure is evoked repeatedly throughout the day, or when it is never fully turned off, we have a situation of chronic anxiety in any of its many manifestations.

The parasympathetic nervous system

The parasympathetic system's function is to insure that the body's priorities shift back to internal needs after external demands have been met. At the end of a scary roller coaster ride, for example, the parasympathetic returns the organism to a state of equipoise. We can laugh, remember the thrill, and go about our day. The parasympathetic has done its job.

The fibers of the parasympathetic are found mainly among the cranial nerves, a set of twelve nerves that send fibers to all the facial structures, the throat structures, and to the heart and digestive organs. The *vagus nerve* is the principal nerve complex of the parasympathetic system. This system:

• Constricts the pupils

• Stimulates saliva

• Increases digestion and peristalsis

• Decreases heart rate

Until recently, it was thought that the two divisions, sympathetic and parasympathetic, were designed to work in what is known as a coupled-reciprocal relationship. Picture two individuals of about equal weight on a seesaw: that is what is meant by a coupled-reciprocal relationship—as one goes up the other goes down. As we are about to see, the relationship between the two branches of the autonomic nervous system is a bit more complex than that, and a lot more interesting.

The Polyvagal Theory: a New Understanding of the ANS[1]

Most texts describe the sympathetic system as the first to activate in response to an external demand. Remember, when activated, the organism is preparing to mobilize for an emergency. For example, energy leaves the digestive area and heads for the extremities. Our musculature tightens. Adrenaline starts to pump. We are revved and ready for action! Ideally this is not a response we want to kick in frequently throughout the day; nor is it a response to be maintained for long periods. Why, then, would it be the first response to environmental demand, as we have thought it to be for so long?

As it turns out, it's not. Scientists are developing a new model of the ANS. In this model, the first responder to demand is mobilization in the parasympathetic side of the system. This model, developed by developmental neuropsychologist Dr. Stephen Porges,[2] has powerful implications for healing the wounds of childhood. Because of this, I present it in some detail.

Although what follows may seem somewhat complex to those without a background in anatomy, I ask you to hang in there. First, it is as simple and clear an explanation of this model as I have come across. Second, it is an important piece in our understanding that the whole human organism is involved in our wounding, not just our minds or our emotions. Further, I will add to how this is generally presented by emphasizing the quality of the tissues themselves. The literature speaks of the nerves controlling the tissues. However, if the tissues are not capable of all the movements for which they were designed—because tissues compress, harden, and constrict—that diminishes the effectiveness of the mechanisms.

The Vagus Nerve

The primary nerve of the parasympathetic division of the ANS is called the *vagus nerve*. It is Cranial Nerve Number X, and it exits from the medulla, a structure that is considered part of the brain stem. The brain stem is the lowest area of the brain. It is where the spinal cord transitions to the brain. In mammals, the vagus nerve has two distinct parts that exit from different places in the medulla.

One part is *myelinated*, which means the nerves are covered with a kind of tissue that acts as insulation and allows for much faster transmission of an impulse along its fibers. This part is referred to as the *ventral vagal*. It exits from the front part of the medulla and travels to the facial area, the larynx, the esophagus, the lungs, and the heart.

The other part of the vagus nerve is *unmyelinated*, and thus its transmission of impulses is slower. It is called the *dorsal vagal* and exits from the rear part of the medulla. It travels primarily to the area below the diaphragm, the visceral region. It also sends some fibers to the heart, but it does not exert a major influence on the heart.

Three Stages of ANS Development

This understanding views the ANS in an evolutionary context, with three stages of development.

The dorsal vagal

The oldest or most primitive part of the ANS is the *dorsal vagal*. Its primary function is to foster digestion and, to some degree, to slow the heart. Behaviorally, the dorsal vagal is associated with immobilization behaviors. Reptiles, for example, have only a dorsal vagal, so when a reptile is confronted with a novel stimulus or threat, its first response is to freeze. The action of freezing is mediated by the dorsal vagal. This is the first phylogenetic stage of the ANS. In other words, in the context of evolution, the dorsal vagal came first. If the dorsal vagal is overregulated, which is one consequence of high-impact traumatic events, it will immobilize the system. It will "freeze" the organism. This compromises the functions of the ANS. In describing the conditions of my childhood, I stated that my only option was to freeze. I couldn't fight, nor could I run—except in my mind.

The sympathetic division

The second phylogenetic stage is the development of the *sympathetic division* of the ANS, a system which first appears in some bony fishes and amphibians and exists in all mammals. As it prepares the organism to mobilize its resources in response to a strong environmental demand or threat, it *inhibits* the activity of the dorsal vagal's effect on the digestion process. Energy moves away from digestion and sex (which are not important in an emergency) and to the arms and legs. So, besides this transfer of energy, the sympathetic system keeps the dorsal vagal in check. It keeps us from being immobilized by an experience as it prepares us to fight or run, as described in the previous chapter.

If we were to place ourselves in an absolute ready position to fight or run, we would immediately feel all the muscles involved in those two activities. Most of the big outer-layer musculature is involved, including the large muscles of the back, shoulders, arms, pelvis, and legs. The ability to sense and therefore to fully contract and fully relax those muscles is an absolute part of the fight-flight mechanism. To the degree that we have full access to those tissues and the ability to engage them, we have the subjective sense that we are capable of running or fighting. It does not mean we are athletic or super-strong; it simply means that our consciousness must be connected to those tissues so that the mechanisms can function optimally.

Chronic tension, compression, constriction, and disconnection from those tissues reduce our sense of being able to fully engage the mechanism associated with the sympathetic nervous system, i.e., fight-flight. This is not an all-or-nothing situation. It is a gradated situation. Nevertheless, the feedback that we can engage those muscles and movements informs us that we are biologically capable of surviving, of running or fighting, if and when necessary. This is a biological imperative.

The ventral vagal

The third and most recent system to develop is the *ventral vagal*. It makes its appearance among the higher mammals. Its myelinated fibers allow for a rapid regulation of your heart's output, which in turn allows for engagement and disengagement with the environment, *without the activation of your sympathetic system*. In other words, as it disengages, as it lessens its regulation, the output of your heart increases to provide more oxygen to the body. Its activation also inhibits the activity of the sympathetic system and modulates sympathetic activity to allow for a return to equipoise after sympathetic—think fight/flight—arousal.

The ventral vagal functions as a brake: when released, it allows for increased cardiac output without the necessity of engaging the more intense sympathetic system. *The slow release of this vagal brake permits modulated responses to psychosocial demands.* When it is not functioning well, the fight/flight response is evoked in response to situations that may bewilder an onlooker; it may be hard to see the threat to which the individual is responding.

For example, a young lady approaches a young man at a social event, a very innocuous situation. In this case, the young man starts sweating, his heart rate increases, and he starts looking for an easy exit. His vagal brake is not functioning well, so he finds it difficult to respond to a mild social demand. Instead, his sympathetic system is activated, and he has entered the domain of fight/flight. Had he gone into fight, he might have assumed an aggressive or sarcastic posture. Had he gone into flight, he might have withdrawn or become inappropriately intellectual, avoiding any contact. If his vagal break was adequately functioning, he would engage the attractive lady in pleasant conversation.

When high-intensity impact experiences, or shock traumas, occur, the organism freezes to some extent or other. The degree to which you are frozen compromises your capacity to protect yourself, to fight or flee, to feel and deal, to adapt, and to engage in intimate relationships. The function of the sympathetic division is to mobilize the organism for emergencies. When a situation really calls for a rush of adrenaline and a readiness to fight or run, it is vital to your survival that the system is capable of doing that. However, to the degree, that you are in freeze, you will experience some helplessness. This is one way to understand the many people who do not seem aggressive but are prone to eruptions of rage, especially towards those closest to them. They do not have the sense that they are capable of engaging forcefully when necessary. The rage is often an eruption of a feeling of helplessness.

The Social Engagement System

Social engagement is the first line of defense against stress and an antidote to its deleterious effects. Because the ventral vagal complex[3] innervates throat, neck, and facial structures, which are organs of interpersonal communication, we can say that the ventral vagal mediates interpersonal communication as well as self-soothing and calming behaviors. It is impossible to overestimate the importance of this to understanding stress, impacts, and insults.

If that brake is functioning poorly, you will feel at the mercy of internal and external forces that others seem to negotiate with ease. Why? Because, in such instances, the sympathetic is the first level of response to engagement. Again, the vagal brake is meant to be the first level of response. If the mechanism, including the tissues involved, is doing its job, many social situations would not be perceived as threats. In the example above, the young man would be able to respond appropriately to the presence of the female, and his fight/flight response would not be called into action. When it is not functioning properly, you are left with many fewer options for response. Further, you will be interpersonally less available and responsive.

Here is one example of how that vagal brake can be damaged.

Perinatal hypoxia is known to prevent the myelination of nerve tissue. That is, if a baby suffers any type of temporary suffocation in the birthing process, it is possible that the tissues would not myelinate or would myelinate poorly, which means he would live without the benefits of a vagal brake. He would respond to minor psychosocial demands as if they were threats. His sympathetic system, with its adrenalin and cortisol, would over-engage and trigger the behaviors associated with the sympathetic, which are fight or flight.

As we will see, many other conditions, impacts, and insults result in diminished functioning of the autonomic nervous system and its elegant way of providing what we need biologically to feel and deal in the world.

ANS - POLYVAGAL MODEL

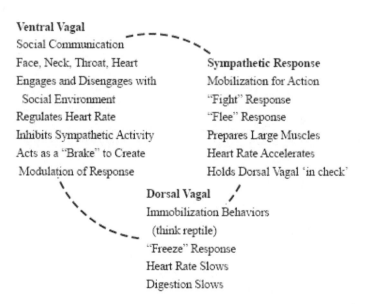

Ventral Vagal
Social Communication
Face, Neck, Throat, Heart
Engages and Disengages with
  Social Environment
Regulates Heart Rate
Inhibits Sympathetic Activity
Acts as a "Brake" to Create
Modulation of Response

Sympathetic Response
Mobilization for Action
"Fight" Response
"Flee" Response
Prepares Large Muscles
Heart Rate Accelerates
Holds Dorsal Vagal 'in check'

Dorsal Vagal
Immobilization Behaviors
  (think reptile)
"Freeze" Response
Heart Rate Slows
Digestion Slows

In recent years, many studies have documented that the experience of being loved and socially connected are primary antidotes to stress. As we saw earlier, individuals who perceive their parents as loving and their relationship with them as close showed significantly fewer chronic illnesses in adulthood than individuals who did not feel close to their parents or perceive them as loving. Repeatedly, the research is showing that people who are socially engaged and have close relationships tend to be healthier than those who aren't and don't. A compromised ventral vagal system may be just one of the physiological substrates that impede the experience of being loved and connected. Why?

Non-verbal Communication and the Inhibitions of Childhood

Much human communication is transmitted nonverbally. Your tone of voice, facial expressions, body posture, and movements of your head and neck all provide information that accompany the words you speak. The ventral vagal complex mediates these expressions. The nerves don't live in isolation, but rather as part of a whole system with the tissues they mediate. When you have suffered serious impacts in life, the functioning of the ventral vagal complex, *along with all the structures they mediate*, are affected. The many muscles and connective tissues of your face and neck will not have their full expressive capacity. They will be restricted. Your range of expression, and therefore of communication, will be diminished. The capacity to connect will be abridged. Life will lose some of its sweetness. Further, many of us have been reared in an environment that allows only a very limited range of human expression. As children, the way we obey the injunctions against expression is to begin tightening our facial muscles. Over time, we lose the ability to engage those expressions. Our muscles simply don't know how to move in those ways. Non-expression becomes automatic and the mechanisms of which the expressions are a part—in this case social engagement—are rendered less effective.

Let's summarize this. There is a phylogenetic—meaning in the development of species—hierarchical structure of responses to stress, impacts, and trauma. The latest response to arrive—found only in human beings—is a deregulation of the *ventral vagal system*, a sophisticated and minute biological adjustment that allows the organism to respond to low-level psychosocial demands in a modulated and stress-free fashion. We can say that this is a physiological substrate of your ability to feel and deal. Also, its activation inhibits the sympathetic system so that tranquility is restored when a threat has been removed, which also facilitates your ability to feel and deal. However, if, for whatever reason, the ventral vagal system is compromised, the next system "up" is the sympathetic. Then, it takes less time for the sympathetic to engage and longer for it to shut down. An individual may exhibit symptoms of poor impulse control or become easily aroused, displaying flares of anger and reactivity. Other examples of fight behaviors in humans include hostility, resentment, anger, sarcasm, irritation, and aggression. Flight behaviors include withdrawal, passivity, not engaging, and avoiding. The implications of how this affects your ability to self-regulate are probably becoming increasingly obvious.

Shock and the Ascendance of the Dorsal Vagal

What happens if the sympathetic division of the autonomic nervous system is overwhelmed? It would mean that the individual is not capable of either fighting or avoiding the danger successfully, as in a sudden car accident, a mugging, or a rape. The fight/flight mechanism doesn't get a chance to do its job.

The story of my childhood is another example. The system in my body that was designed to protect me was frequently assaulted by the very people whose job it was to protect me until my own capacities developed. In this type of situation, as well as in other shock trauma situations, the dorsal vagal ascends. This means it becomes overregulated, and the result is shutdown, freeze, immobilization, and collapse. The inability to fight turns to rage; the inability to flee turns to terror. Neither can be successfully expressed. There is profound helplessness.

This is an example of the sympathetic division being overwhelmed. It remains highly charged, but it is overshadowed by the dorsal vagal. This occurs in cases of extreme trauma—a life-threatening accident, war experiences, a severe assault, or a history of childhood abuse. There is no escape, so you cannot employ the emergency mechanisms of fighting or running. My story is an example of a situation where an organism was frozen at a very deep level. Fight/flight was occurring, but it was dominated by a general freeze response. It is analogous to trying to drive a car with one foot fully on the gas pedal and one foot slammed onto the brake.

This is a description of an organism in shock; and yet, it is possible that, on the surface, the individual appears relatively normal. Under the radar, though, the cells and tissues throughout the body contract and compress. The body feels less spacious or feels numb. These responses may be subtle, or they may be very intense. In my case, there was nothing subtle about it. The shock was intense. People walk around in a state of shock, and even when it is not subtle, they often don't know they are in shock. I didn't; it was normal for me.

Symptoms of Shock

A major symptom of shock is an emotional life that is extremely shallow, with no feeling of vitality and aliveness. There may be bursts of impulsive rage or anger or a chronic sense of dread or anxiety. And some things are just not present—warmth, love, a deep sense of connection to others or nature, and the ability to be transparent and self-disclosing. Additional consequences include not being able to feel your body; sensations are dulled and beg for intoxicants so they can come to life. There may be a chronic state of vigilance and arousal in terms of physiological markers, such as heart rate and blood pressure. There are various ways in which this condition manifests but these are very common.

In summary, in Chapter 9, I mentioned Dr. William C. Reeves and his quest to find the cause of chronic fatigue syndrome. After years of research, he began to suspect that abuse and stress were contributors. It may be clearer now just how chronic stress—and living with the result of unresolved, unhealed wounds—can be at the root of such a disease. Do you recall from Chapter 8 how self-regulation becomes a challenge when the pre-frontal cortex is not optimally developed, and how? Now you can understand, in addition, how, when the social engagement system is not optimally functioning, self-regulation becomes a huge challenge.

Let's look at this from the picture of an individual with a weak or rigid vagal brake. Since a healthy ventral vagal facilitates satisfying, contactful, engaging, warm, loving interpersonal relationships, it is highly likely that an individual with a weak ventral vagal would have interpersonal challenges. The main symptom you might observe is great difficulty in successfully navigating an intimate relationship. Of course, this individual is also likely to show higher levels of anxiety, hostility, and aggressiveness on one hand; or passivity, withdrawn behavior, or depression on the other. All these symptoms are forms of chronic stress. People who are relationship-challenged, people who are easily frustrated and slow to recover, people who are always mildly depressed or anxious, people who struggle with deep feelings of shame, guilt or inadequacy—all are stressed.

We have moved from the pre-frontal cortex to the limbic system, particularly the amygdala, to the autonomic nervous system and to the muscles and tissues of the face, neck, and vicinity. We are filling out a picture that begins with the importance of essential needs to our model of self and other and to our relational capacities. We are seeing how our psychology and physiology, including the quality of our tissues, are all related.

The Straw that Broke the Camel's Back

In spite of the fact that my childhood had been a series of extreme impacts and insults, there was still one area in which I could function decently—my intellect. Reading, writing, and arithmetic was where I could escape into relative safety. So, as I approached high school, I could feel the pull of two worlds. Each was clearly marked. One said *Good* and was the path of education, possibly even a college education. It meant attending Archbishop Stepinac High School, an all-boys' Catholic high school well known for its academic rigor and discipline. The other path was probably best labeled *Aw, fuck it* and was represented by Port Chester High School, where you could, in 1957, if you wished, easily spend four years and not acquire anything remotely resembling an education. This path included other possibilities, such as an entry-level position into the mob as a numbers runner. Runners were well known in my neighborhood, and some of my older friends had already climbed aboard, so it was a very real possibility. A young man could begin as a "runner," and if he had the necessary talents, he could work his way up the mob ladder. The lures were power, rebellion, pocket money, and confirmation of my conviction that "life sucked."

I chose to give life one more chance. I enrolled in Archbishop Stepinac High School. It was a remarkably clear moment of choice; perhaps, I thought, I could do something worthwhile with my life. Based on my entrance aptitude tests, I was placed in a science and engineering track. My four years were completely structured and included math, science, German, and religion classes. Freshman year passed uneventfully. I was accustomed to wearing a sport jacket and tie to school and having a fair amount of homework. Receiving As and Bs, I felt satisfied with my performance, even though my report cards always evoked smirks of disgust from my mother, who had the misfortune of having a son who didn't get straight As, as did one or two of his classmates.

In recent years, the dark underbelly of the Catholic Church has been exposed in countless headlines of sexual abuse and seven-figure payments to victims. Back in the 1950s, sexual abuse was not the only type of abuse inflicted by the priests, brothers, and sisters who had presumably dedicated their lives to the saving of souls. Sadism, or perhaps more accurately in most cases, excessive corporal punishment, came in a close second.

A Day in High School I'll Never Forget

In September of 1958, I began my sophomore year of high school. It was to be a year I would never forget. My biology teacher was a short, round, heavy-set man with a baby face by the name of Brother Bernadine. He would walk up and down the aisles with the thick biology book in his hands. If something about a student's posture displeased him, or if he did not like an answer that was given, he banged the book on our heads. If someone's foot was in the aisle, he really seemed to enjoy kicking his shins. He was a piece of work, Brother Bernadine.

But compared to Brother Kerry, our geometry teacher, Brother Bernadine's viciousness was in the minor leagues. On the first day of class, his face as expressionless as cold stone, Kerry warned that when the bell rang, everyone would be in his seat—no exceptions, no deviations whatsoever from strict obedience to his rules would be tolerated. There was a chilling quality to his tone, a cold look in his eye, and a sardonic sneer that evoked hair-raising fear. On the second day, those fears were confirmed.

As the beginning class bell was ringing, Michael Lelane, a rosy-faced, small, bright Irish kid, was approaching his seat. Unfortunately for Michael, the bell stopped ringing, at least for a full second, before his butt had reached his seat. And no, I didn't intend to write *minute*, I meant a *second*. Without saying a word, Kerry walked over to him, lifted him out of his chair, and pulled him to the front corner of the room. With his left hand, he held Michael against the wall, and with his right, he started swinging. He slapped Michael hard, with a forehand and then a backhand, again and again. It would have been outrageous enough if these were simple slaps, but the bastard was taking full, hard swings. After a while of this, he dragged the now dazed boy back to his chair, dropped him into it, and returned to the front of the room. (I can only imagine the shocked expressions on our faces!) He said, "When the bell rings, you will be *in* your chairs." He opened his text and began teaching, not another word said.

On that day, I intellectually and emotionally dropped out of high school. It was the end of my career in science or engineering. I quit participating. I spent a lot of time fantasizing how I would kill the son-of-a-bitch if he ever put his hand on me. Yes, I did my homework in his class and managed to pass most of my classes, but that was the final straw. The battle for my soul had come to an end. The enemy had dropped a bomb. My will to succeed was overwhelmed. I gave up. Clearly, my social engagement and fight/flight systems were overwhelmed repeatedly. My geometry teacher's assault on a fellow student was context-specific. I gave up in the classroom as well as at home.

I share these stories because they demonstrate how much positive change is available in one lifetime, regardless of the hand we were dealt. The type of psychotherapy I now do requires me to be contactful, relational, open, and empathic. The kind of movement I teach requires me to be extraordinarily fluid. The wounds and the scars have become part of my strength.

WHAT YOU CAN DO: PRACTICES

Most of the practices in this book, as they are mastered, will improve the functioning of the autonomic nervous system. Of course, for many of us, disciplines, such as I describe in Part Two, will be needed. Peter Levine's Somatic Experiencing is designed specifically to improve ANS functioning. Here are a couple of exercises that quickly call one side of the system—the sympathetic or parasympathetic—and then call forth the other side. The idea is to improve the system's fluidity.

To "work" the autonomic nervous system:

Take a hot shower—hot, cozy relaxing, and parasympathetic—followed immediately by a cold shower—shivers, freezing, and sympathetic. Alternate several times. It may sound impossible, but I have found that, except for during the cold of winter, once I do it, I really start to enjoy it.

Build bursts and rests into exercise. For example, instead of walking fast for thirty minutes, walk very fast for five minutes, and then resume at a more leisurely pace for five minutes. Then, walk very fast—or run—for five minutes. (Note: For a fascinating look at how to exercise, rest, and approach work in a way that supports fluidity of the ANS, see Jim Loehr and Tony Schwartz, *The Power of Full Engagement*, 2003, Free Press.

1.   Porges, Stephen, *The Polyvagal Theory: Neurophysiological Foundations of Emotions, Attachments, Communication and Self-Regulation*, W.W. Norton, 2011.

2.   Ibid.

3.   By ventral vagus complex, I am referring to Cranial Nerves III, the oculomotor; VII, the facial; IX, the glossopharyngeal; and X, the vagus. (Nolte, *The Human Brain*, 1993). These nerves function as a subsystem.

CHAPTER 12

REFLECTIONS ON THE HEART

"The best and most beautiful things in the world cannot be seen or even touched... They must be felt with the heart."
~ Helen Keller

It is time for us to return our hearts to their rightful place—to the center of human intelligence. We have taken one organ, the brain, and equated it with human intelligence. Perhaps the single most illustrative and unfortunate consequence of that equation is that the guiding question of science and technology is "What *can* we do?" and never "What *should* we do?" For example, what should we do for the well-being of self, body, and the world? I believe that only the heart in partnership with the brain will even seek to ask the question. We have gone to the moon, we have put gigabytes of memory in the tiniest of spaces; yet, we haven't come close to learning to live in peace and harmony. We have built altars to our rational, logical, and analytic capacities and have, to our great peril, *ignored the wisdom of our entire organism, and particularly of the heart.*

A Heart Brain

There is a field of medical science called Neurocardiology, which is the study of the nervous system of the heart and its relationship to the brain and the autonomic nervous system (ANS). Two physicians Armour and Ardelli, wrote a text in which they asserted that the complexity of the heart's own nervous system qualified the heart for consideration as a "heart brain."[1] The heart has more links to the brain than any other organ and has over 40,000 sensory neurons. These neurons sense pressure changes as well as heart rate and detect circulating hormones and neurochemicals. They send this information to the brain. These incoming signals have a regulatory role over many of the ANS signals that flow from the brain to the organs of the body, including the heart. Again, the heart processes information independently of the brain and the nervous system, and then it interacts with them as well as with other processing centers throughout the body.

We can think of the heart as the center of the primary fluid system. The vascular network, going from the heart to everywhere in the body, and returning back to the heart, travels thousands of miles.[2] The only other organ whose tentacles reach to everywhere in the body is the brain. As I see it, their partnership is a key feature of human wholeness. When the activity of the brain is considered to be the mind, as well as the source of intelligence, while the heart is relegated to the function of an elegant pump, we have the kind of culture where wisdom has little hope of flourishing.

In his book, *The Heart's Code*, Paul Pearsall tells a poignant, heart-wrenching story to illustrate the heart's capacity to "think and remember." He was speaking at a conference to a group of psychologists and psychiatrists when a psychiatrist rose and shared the following story. An eight-year-old patient of hers had received the heart of another little girl who had been murdered. She was brought to the psychiatrist by her mother because she had begun screaming at night in dreams, dreams in which she saw a killer. After a few sessions, the psychiatrist felt she could not deny the reality of this little girl's experience, and with her mother's consent, called the police. Using the description provided by the girl, the killer was identified as the donor's murderer, captured, and convicted. In that room, Pearsall says, there were few dry eyes. What this suggests to me is that mind is not to be equated exclusively with the brain.

To bring clarity, let me repeat Dr. Mae-Wan Ho's statement:

Whenever people speak of "consciousness" they usually locate it in the brain, where ideas and intentions are supposed to flow, and which through the nervous system, is supposed to control the entire body. I have always found that odd, for like all Chinese people, I was brought up on the idea that thoughts emanate from the heart. I have come to the conclusion that a more accurate account is that consciousness is delocalized throughout the liquid crystalline continuum of the body (including the brain), rather than just being localized to our brain or to our heart. By consciousness, I include, at the minimum, the faculties of sentience (responsiveness), intercommunication, as well as memory. [3]

Communication Between the Heart and Brain

The heart is a sensing, feeling, communicating organ. It is a self-organizing, highly complex information center, which continually sends messages to the brain. There are four channels of communication between the heart and the brain. The first three are neurological, biochemical by way of hormonal exchanges, and biomechanical by way of pressure waves. The fourth is electromagnetic. These four channels of communication and the complexity of the heart's nervous system attest to the intimate relationship between heart and brain.

What does it mean that the heart is linked to the brain and has so many sensory neurons? What does it mean that neurocardiologists refer to the heart as a "heart brain?" What does it mean that the recipient of a heart transplant begins to dream and see the man who murdered her donor? The intelligence of the heart is a way of knowing. The heart has a spiritual intelligence with the capacity to understand sacred and profound truths that simply defy rational understanding. It brings clarity and recognition of what is important and what is not.

For example, most religions have their origin stories. Our culture places these stories in *contrast* to the findings of science and evaluates them from a rational perspective. These stories are not meant to be memorized and understood as historical events. *They are meant to elevate the vibration of our consciousness.* Examined from a rational, empirical perspective, they can seem foolish. However, the heart can recognize the fundamental spiritual truths within them, which serve to illumine our consciousness, our hearts, and our minds and allows us to apprehend our essential unity as human beings. These stories can illumine the forces that we must recognize and contend with in our lives. They are spiritual forces, and the open heart, the awakened heart, can hear and see what the eyes cannot. As Helen Keller said, "It must be felt by the heart."

Let me emphasize that when I say something can be understood by the heart, I am not suggesting sentimentality or emotionality. I am speaking about a level of understanding that is transcendent and elusive. It has a felt-sense quality of knowing, and tends to occur in meditative states. I will elaborate on this as I describe my personal healing journey in Part Two. For now, suffice it to say that awakening the heart means another way of living. It is not just about your personal happiness and comfort. It is not about feeling great when things are going your way and bemoaning your fate when they don't. It's about knowing that, no matter the circumstances, no matter what the winds of life deposit on your shores, you can engage, participate, reflect, derive meaning, and become a better person. It's about wanting your life to make a difference, to contribute, whether it's to your family, your community, your country, or the planet. It's about knowing we are all in this together.

"The goal of life is to make your heart beat match the beat of the universe, to match your nature with Nature."
~ Joseph Campbell

The Heart's Responsiveness

The human heart is the most responsive organ in the body. The quality of the rhythm of its beat changes in response to each moment-to-moment interaction with your environment. It is like a cellular conductor, broadcasting its message to your every cell, and that broadcast affects your perception, feeling, cognition, and health. Beating approximately one hundred thousand times per day and forty million times per year, it changes its rate and quality of beat in response to ever-changing environmental circumstances. Within one conversation, the heart shifts countless times to reflect the feeling tone and quality of the conversation. Not only does it change its beat, but it also broadcasts that change to every organ and cell in the body, especially the brain. If this is not intriguing enough, consider that this broadcast also reaches those in close proximity to you. I am saying that your own "vibes" affect you and others. How is this possible?

Let's discuss heart-rate variability. When you take your pulse and record 70 beats per minute, it's natural to assume that the time interval between each beat is constant throughout that minute. This is not so! There is a natural variability in the time interval between beats. I am not speaking here of pathological arrhythmias, but of natural, beat-to-beat fluctuations. Not only does the interval change, but there is a qualitative variability in the time interval between heartbeats. Musicians listening to the beat of a drum hear the quality and pattern of the rhythm. The rhythms of our heartbeat and the patterns of time interval variability have qualities that we can analyze to determine the degree of their coherence.

Research done by an organization called HeartMath[4] has demonstrated that the heart's ever-present rhythmic field has a powerful influence on processes throughout the body, including human feelings. Brain rhythms naturally synchronize to the heart's rhythmic activity. For example, during sustained feelings of love or appreciation, blood pressure and respiratory rhythms, among other oscillatory systems, entrain to the heart's rhythm. Their rhythms are in synch.

On an objective level, the coherence of your heart rhythms refers to the quality of interplay between the two divisions of your autonomic nervous system—the sympathetic and parasympathetic, which we examined in detail in Chapter 11. The quality of that interplay is what manifests as the quality of coherence in the variability of the heart rate. In this sense, coherence means a certain global order in the system, a certain connectedness among parts, a uniform, synchronized pattern. Each part is doing its thing in relation to the whole. This is another aspect of coherence within the human organism. We have previously discussed coherence in terms of supportive beliefs, good relational capacities, and a well-functioning pre-frontal cortex and nervous system. We will in the next chapter see coherence in terms of the structure of the body, its tissues and movement. Here, we are talking about coherence in the rhythms of the heart.

It is really important here to appreciate that high levels of coherence are accompanied by good, positive feelings in the heart. So often, people say that everything is fine when, in fact, they are feeling rushed, pressured, worried, anxious, cynical, resentful, bored, constricted, unappreciated, disconnected, unhappy, unloved, tense, or any other of many negative states. If such challenging states are on the mild side, we assume normality. However, even if these states are only mildly negative, they are reflecting a certain degree of incoherence in the patterns of heart rate variability, and thus in the interplay between divisions of the autonomic nervous system.

When we experience sincere, genuine peace in our hearts—or appreciation, warmth, care, compassion, love, or any version of true positive feeling—those feelings are reflecting a high degree of coherence that has profound and positive implications for your health and well-being. You experience flow, efficiency, and ease.

Of all the body's organs, the heart is the most powerful generator of electromagnetic energy in the human body, producing the largest rhythmic electromagnetic field. As measured by an electrocardiogram, this field can be detected anywhere on the surface of the body. The heart's electrical field is about 60 times greater in amplitude than the electrical activity generated in the brain. The magnetic field produced by the heart is more than 5000 times greater in strength than the field generated by the brain and can be detected from several feet away from the body.[5]

Signals generated by the heart have the capacity to affect people around you. One person's heart signal, as measured by an electrocardiogram, can affect another's brain waves, as measured by an electroencephalogram. When people touch or are in proximity, one person's heart signal is registered in another's brain waves. Thus, the heart is both an organ of perception and feeling and an organ of transmission. Much communication between human beings is generated from heart to heart. The quality of being, the quality of feeling that we experience in the presence of another is driven by heart-to-heart, electromagnetic communication. If the heart is hardened or walled off from our awareness as a result of impacts, insults, or maltreatment, we lose the capacity to feel each other's presence. It is no small loss.

There is abundant literature describing how much communication takes place non-verbally between mother and infant. According to the literature, this communication is mediated mostly via the right brain of the mother to the right brain of the infant. This right-brain-to-right-brain communication provides the biochemical nourishment needed for the synaptic growth of the brain, particularly in the prefrontal cortex areas. Yet, when you understand the electromagnetic strength of the heart and how connected to the brain it is, it is compelling to wonder if the heart is a primary organ of transmission and reception between mother and infant. At the very least, it is a key partner with the right brain in this essential, formative communication.

Pearsall describes an experiment conducted by Russek and Schwartzvi that illustrates the energetic connection between hearts and between hearts and brains. Two people sat opposite one another in the same room with their eyes closed and not communicating in any way. Using a complex measurement process that included ECGs and EEGs for both people, they recorded the results. The preliminary results indicated three possible energetic connections.

First, it appeared that a person's heart energy transmits to his own brain. Second, it appeared that one person's heart seems to exchange energy with the other person's brain. Third, it appeared that one person's heart transmitted to the other person's heart. These results were also reported in studies by McCraty at the Institute of HeartMath. It appears that we are all connected heart to brain and heart to heart.

Vagal Brake and Coherent Heart Rate Variability

What is the relationship between a strong and flexible vagal brake and coherent heart rate variability? The body of work done by the folks at the Institute of HeartMath and the body of work done by Dr. Porges and his colleagues both involve the ANS and the heart. Each uses different models and does different research. The HeartMath people use a mathematical model that evaluates coherence of the rhythm of heart rate variability, and they study how that coherence can be increased by positive, heart feelings. Porges describes the neuroanatomy of the ANS and the importance of the ventral vagal, or the vagal brake, in preventing sympathetic or fight/flight activation. His research employs a direct measure of vagal tone, which is the scientific name for the vagal brake.

Fight/flight feelings are not positive feelings. They result from a perceived threat to the integrity of the organism, and when they don't lead to action, the coherence of the rhythm of heart rate variability decreases. The HeartMath group and Porges' followers employ different methods to improve the quality of human life and human feeling. Generally speaking, both groups' objectives are the same —the growth of positive feelings in the heart and improvement in the quality of human life.

Forgiveness and the Heart

"Forgive us our trespasses, as we forgive those who trespass against us."
~ The Lord's Prayer

It seems inconceivable to write a book about healing the wounds of childhood without considering forgiveness. In the process of awakening the heart and increasing its coherence, letting go of the hurts and forgiving the perpetrators are essential. As we saw above, even minor states of negativity decrease the heart rate variability's coherence. There is more noise in the system. To feel really open, appreciative, grateful, truly peaceful, and loving necessitates forgiving those whom we have perceived as hurtful in any way—including our parents and also ourselves. Holding on to resentments, rancor, and perceived injustices limits our heart's ability to live, love, and know in the sense I described above. Holding on to resentments is like squeezing a sharp, flat rock and thinking you are hurting someone else.

How do we forgive? Isn't it naïve to think we can simply say, "I forgive you," to someone who has spent years hurting us? I agree; it is. Believe me, it takes work. Everything I have written in this book makes it easier to reach a point where we can forgive those who have deeply hurt us.

For example, as we begin to awaken the heart and develop our pre-frontal cortex, it becomes easier to understand the wounding in a different way. For example, for me, my crazy childhood provided my life's work; I have been able to be with so many wounded people and really get where they are. Further, I have been able to see my parents in their historical context and understand how they were passing down what they received (or didn't receive). In other words, growing our comprehension facilitates forgiveness. My parents didn't wake up in the morning thinking about how best they could screw up their son's life. They were simply struggling to survive and cope with the very limited resources they had. I am in no way excusing what they did; it was almost criminal. I am saying that my relationship to what they did has gone through quite a transformation.

Also, we usually need to be very firm in not allowing our thoughts to repetitively indulge the injustices. When someone has hurt us, we have a tendency to continue replaying the event in our minds—or to replay what we have done wrong over and over again. Often, we need help to forgive. It could be from a therapist, a minister, or just from your relationship to the Divine. However we do it, it is work that is worth doing.

The Intelligence of the Heart

There is one more issue I want to put forth—the intelligence of the heart. There is no way to complete this book without questioning the prevailing conviction that the brain is the seat of all intelligence, and that rational, analytical thinking is the diamond of intelligence. The more I delve into this subject, the more convinced I am that intelligence—as Mae-Wan Ho said above—is a function of the whole organism, and that the heart is as important a player as the brain. Assessing this in depth is beyond the scope of this book. However, here are some examples of what I consider brain intelligence without heart.

Let's look at politicians the world over. Many are from the finest universities and have so-called good intellects. But when they spend every waking hour on figuring out how their party can win and the other can lose, it is a manifestation of an absence of heart intelligence. The heart knows that we all win or we all lose. It is not self-serving to see the other as the enemy.

Here is another example. A recent *New York Times* article said that 17 percent of our Medicare budget is spent on the last six months of life. We consider death the enemy. How can that be? Only the inclusion of the heart can bring wisdom to this conversation, not only to save multibillions of dollars, but also to make death a more positive experience for the elderly.

Heart intelligence suggests that compassion and loving kindness should be front and center in our lives—in our homes, in our businesses, and in our policies. The heart recognizes the essential unity of all humanity and seeks solutions that are inclusive. The heart sees the absurdity of dichotomies such as pro-life versus pro-choice, and recognizes how both sides have important contributions to make to the conversation. The heart can hold the tension of opposites. The heart can say, "It is this *and* this."

The heart knows that to hold resentment, rancor, or hatred against any person or group is to inflict spiritually mortal wounds upon yourself (not to mention the injurious effects to your physical health). The heart can see the perfection in every moment in your life. Yes, I know without doubt that this wonderful moment I am experiencing as I write this page depended upon every moment that came before, and yes, that includes all of my childhood. It is the heart that can hold both the hideousness of my childhood and the perfection of it. The analytic mind cannot grasp this and will dismiss it. Its comprehension is not sufficient.

The heart recognizes that psychic phenomena exist, that astrology has merit, that certain intuitives can see and know in ways that boggle our conventional minds, and that what conventional science has offered as "reality" is a small slice of life, indeed (until perhaps very recently, that is). In short, awakening of the heart to its place in the center of the organism, and as a key player in full partnership with the brain, leads to a much greater comprehension of the nature of life on earth. Until this opening occurs, you are living in a cave while believing you are seeing the great, vast beyond, when what you are seeing, in fact, are the walls of the cave. The awakening of the heart will lead you into the great outdoors.

WHAT YOU CAN DO: PRACTICES

1. The quintessential practice to awaken and clear the heart is the practice of gratitude. Before sleep, or whenever you remember, take a few minutes to review your day and express thanks for all you have or have experienced. Don't overlook the small things: a neighbor's smile, your child's hug, the paper you completed. And, of course, don't forget the not-so-small things: your partner's love, your good health. But what if times are tough? Then the practice of gratitude is even more important. If you haven't noticed, negativity breeds negativity, and gratitude breeds more things to be grateful for.

2. Right up alongside gratitude in importance is the practice of appreciation. There is so much beauty in the world. Take a moment and let it in, whether it is a sunset, children playing, a rose, or a work of art. Pause, breathe, and absorb.

3. Think of someone or something you love unconditionally—a child, a pet, or a very special place in nature. Think of that person, pet, or thing while you also keep your attention on your heart. Notice the sensations and feelings in the area of your heart. Cultivate those feelings.

For more practices on the heart, go to www.heartmath.com.

1. Armour and Ardelli, *NeuroCardiology*, 1994.

2. Google will say between 60,000 and 100,000. I had believed that it was 25,000. Whichever it is, it's lots of miles.

3. Ho, Mae-Wan, *The Rainbow and the Worm: The Physics of Organisms,* World Scientific Publishing, 1998, p. 185.

4. See www.heartmath.com.

5. Ibid.

CHAPTER 13

YOUR BODY MATTERS: QUALITY OF TISSUES, STRUCTURE AND MOVEMENT

"The Body is the Shore and the Ocean of Being"
~ Sufi Saying

Many human beings want to mend, heal, or improve from their childhood circumstances. Few realize that those insults and impacts have affected them down to the level of their very tissues. Taking the concept of coherence into account, every part of you influences and is influenced by every other part—from the very water your body is composed of—all the way to your relationships, brain, nervous system, beliefs, and so on. All of you! Your whole being!

WHY I DIDN'T DIE

My past caught up to me. On October 10, 2001, in a hotel in Albuquerque, I had a severe heart attack. The pain was intense. For approximately forty minutes, I could neither lie down nor straighten myself up. It was as severe as any pain I had ever experienced. The sweat poured off my forehead, but the pain was all in my solar plexus. I didn't experience any pain in my chest or arm, so I—in my infinite wisdom—assumed I had somehow yanked my esophagus out of my diaphragm and decided to sweat it out. Finally, the pain subsided and I went to bed. The next morning, I felt a general sense of malaise but no pain, so I went about my business for the next two days in Albuquerque.

The trip back to Seattle was excruciating, but once home, I felt fine again and managed to teach a workshop that weekend with no discomfort. Convinced of my hypothesis that the intermittent pain I felt in my solar plexus was GI, I attempted to modify and lighten my diet. When after a month I was still experiencing pain daily, but on a seemingly random basis, I went to my physician. In fairness to him, the way I framed my story led him to order X-rays of my abdominal area.

It was a slow process to schedule two rounds of appointments for X-rays and for receiving the results, which were all negative for a GI problem. In those almost three months, I went on three airplane trips; in addition, I went snowshoeing in the mountains on three occasions. All three times, I walked for a hundred yards or so and then had to stop until the pain subsided. Even so, I just couldn't imagine that anything was wrong with my heart. I was only fifty-nine years old and had been living a rather healthy lifestyle for over twenty years.

Finally, I was out of hypotheses, and my third trip to San Francisco was awful. I consulted a cardiologist. He said, "I don't think we'll find anything wrong with your heart. You look too healthy." He ordered an echocardiogram and an angiogram and discovered that three major coronary arteries were almost entirely shut down and a blood clot was loitering in my left ventricle. Much of my left ventricle (that's the chamber that pumps blood to the whole body) looked like it might be gone (infarct, dead). With so little of my left ventricle functioning, it was astonishing that I was able to walk at all. Dr. Jim was incredulous. "I can't believe you walked in here. We call this pattern the 'widow-maker.' It kills men your age."

I had to wait a week to take a thallium scan to determine whether or not my left ventricle was mostly dead or just hibernating. It was a surrealistic week. There we were, praying for a triple by-pass. The alternative was a transplant. At last some good news: the thallium scan revealed that the ventricle was mostly hibernating, except for the apex. According to Dr. Jim, the apex of my heart was indeed infarct, never more to return to life. If you can imagine it, that was the good news!

When the clot dissolved, surgery was performed. Having had ample time to prepare—and I recommend preparing for surgery whenever you have the opportunity—the procedure went gracefully.

Three months later, after a second thallium scan, Dr. Jim called to say he needed another echo because the results of the scan suggested that the apex of my heart was no longer infarct, and he knew that couldn't be true. He was a very experienced and competent cardiologist; he just didn't make those kinds of errors, and everyone knows that cardiac tissue doesn't just regenerate.

"Impossible! I have never seen this in fifteen years of administering these tests," Dr. Jim's assistant confidently proclaimed just before turning on the echo. Five minutes later, his demeanor visibly altered, he turned sheepishly to me and said, "Man, you should go to Las Vegas. You are one lucky dude."

The questions are: how did I survive a serious heart attack for three months with no intervention? How did I present so well that the cardiologist predicted he wouldn't find anything wrong? How did I survive three round-trip flights and three snowshoe trips in two months with three of my coronary vessels almost completely closed and a blood clot in my ventricle, which was barely functioning? How did the apex of my heart, pronounced infarct by a competent cardiologist, with the agreement of an experienced assistant, return to normal?

I will offer three hypotheses, and you can choose the most likely. One, it was sheer luck. Weird things do happen. This was just one of them. Two, it was Divine intervention. It was not my time, and somebody up there liked me. Three, the level of organic coherence—fluidity, integration, and wholeness—I had attained was sufficient to overcome the disorganization that manifested as the symptoms I described. Personally, I prefer hypotheses two and three.

I had already done a great deal of personal work, which I will describe in Part Two. This included years of various types of psychotherapy, many sessions of Hellerwork Structural/Integration/Rolfing, years of practicing Continuum Movement, and much more. There is no doubt in my mind that I would not have survived otherwise.

It's Not Just in my Head

Realizing that my problems were not just in my head is what set the course of my entire adult and professional life. From 1964, when I first realized I needed help, until 1968, I assumed what I needed was psychological help. It was an obvious conclusion considering that my challenges were in the domain of self-esteem, deep shame, relational incompetence, and so forth. My assumption wasn't entirely incorrect; I did need a great deal of psychological help. However, it was not until I directly engaged my neuromuscular and connective tissues through body work and movement that the more profound changes I was hoping for began to come about. What was it about my body that so cried for help?

It was wound tight. I had very little breathing room. The lower part of my rib cage protruded and could never fully relax, meaning that my diaphragm never really let go to allow a full exhale. My chest had a sunken in look, as if I already was defeated by life. We've learned about the vagal brake and heart rate variability. Consider that the exhalation phase of respiration utilizes the parasympathetic system, and if the diaphragm does not fully release with exhalation, it affects the quality of the vagal brake and your heart rate variability. In other words, the exhalation phase of respiration affects the moment-to-moment quality of how you feel. The sense of a deep, easy relaxation cannot really happen as long as your rib basket cannot fully release down.

My neck was one of the most affected areas of my body. The tension was chronic and unbelievable in its intensity. As a consequence, I had difficulty feeling almost anything below my neck. You could say that I was, quite literally, cut off from myself. I have often said that in those days I knew only two sensations: pain and no pain. My eyes usually had a deeply pained look. My facial muscles were so taut that I conveyed little feeling in my face. I was tired almost all the time, and I had frequent migraine headaches.

One quality that was not immediately visible and obvious, but which highly characterized my tissues, was the quality of disconnection between my consciousness and my body. Think of a cat moving stealthily towards a prey, of how every motion seems to be intricately within the cat's awareness. That's what connection between the consciousness and the body looks like. I was disconnected. It was not that I looked freakish, by any means. It required a fairly trained eye to see the rather intense effects of those years of abuse, beatings, and constant humiliation. To that trained eye, however, the effects were brutal.

Today, in my early seventies, I am significantly more fluid, spacious, connected, and integrated in my body than I was when I was forty. In fact, I am a Continuum Teacher. I teach fluid movement, and many of my students are in their thirties and forties. Here I am, teaching them how to be and move fluidly in their bodies and lives. Of course, I am pleased by this fact, especially given where I began. However, there is an implication that is far more important. The average adult human body is far more constricted, compressed, and disconnected from consciousness than anyone can even imagine. What is normal, in the sense of "this is how most of us are," is not even close to what is possible and perhaps to what is essential to our nature, once we understand how we have been compromised as organisms.

I was given a gift in being so extremely dysfunctional psychophysically. I was compelled to search, to seek wholeness, to keep from suffering daily. What we consider normal aging; normal living with its aches and pains; normal use of drugs, legal and otherwise; normal use of alcohol; normal eating; normal hundreds of billions spent on health care; and normal relating and loving—these are normal, in a statistical sense only. These kinds of normal are far from optimal; and they are far, far removed from what is possible.

Quality of Tissues

What do I mean when I refer to the *quality* of the body's tissues? Earlier today, I was playing with my five-year-old granddaughter, demonstrating some of my fluid movements. I challenged her to do the same. She had no trouble. The fluidity of her tissues and their responsiveness to her intention were marvelous. As I keep saying, we are mostly water.

Your tissues ought to feel somewhat like a wet sponge: yielding, elastic, fluid, supple, responsive, receptive, vibrant, and capable of some strength in any direction. Ideally, you should be conscious enough throughout your body to feel its storehouse of sensations and capacities: its multi-textured layers; its myriad feeling tones; and its ability to dissolve, melt, merge, harness, and slow way down, as well as to move quickly with strength and intention. Add some cardiovascular tone, and you have what I consider true fitness. I consider today's model of fitness rather primitive. Clearly, it is much better than being a couch potato. However, you have the capacity to be so much more conscious, supple, fluid, awake, spacious, and alive throughout your entire body. You have so much more room for feeling, sensation, nuance, and texture than you can even begin to imagine. Furthermore, all of this relates to your sense of well-being, to your health, to your aging process, and to your capacity for deep intimate connection! The quality of your tissues is a significant aspect of your coherence, your wholeness.

Because this is clearly not something that is generally understood, let's look closely at what I mean by tissues.

Tissues

There are four types of tissues in the human body: muscle, epithelial, nerve, and connective.

Muscle tissue

There are three types of muscle tissue: skeletal, smooth, and cardiac. *Skeletal muscle* is a voluntary type of muscle tissue that is used in the contraction of skeletal parts. *Smooth muscle* is an involuntary type of muscle tissue found in the walls of internal organs and blood vessels. The *cardiac muscle* is involuntary in nature and is found only in the walls of the heart.

Epithelial tissue

Epithelial tissue covers the body surface and forms the lining for most internal cavities. The major functions of epithelial tissue include protection, secretion, absorption, and filtration. The skin is an organ made up of epithelial tissue, and it protects the body from dirt, dust, bacteria, and other microbes that may be harmful.

Nerve tissue

Nerve tissue is composed of specialized cells which receive stimuli and also conduct impulses to and from all parts of the body.

Connective tissue

Connective tissue is the most abundant and the most widely distributed of the tissues. It ranges in density from bone, which is the hardest—although it is approximately 15- to 20-percent water—all the way to blood. Yes, blood is considered a connective tissue. Most of the fluids in the body—blood, lymph, cerebral spinal fluid—are considered connective tissue. The connective tissue we are most interested in here is called fascia. (In the image on the following page, everything other than the bone, blood vessel and muscle fiber is fascia. However, the bone is covered by fascia, as is the blood vessel and muscle fiber.)

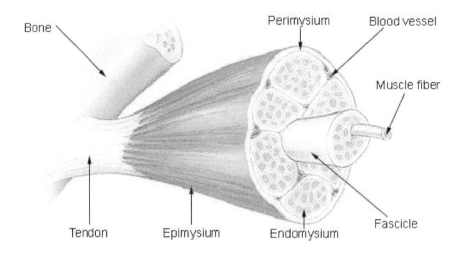

Bone

Perimysium   Blood vessel

Muscle fiber

Tendon   Epimysium   Endomysium   Fascicle

Fascia

Fascia forms a continuous web throughout the entire body. It is a fascinating tissue, and very little was known about it until recently. Just about everything in the human body is covered in fascia. It is found superficially under the skin, acting as a body stocking over the entire body. It slips over every muscle. A skeletal muscle is made up of muscle bundles, and each bundle is covered by fascia. Each bundle is made up of muscle cells or fibers, and each muscle cell is wrapped in fascia. It covers every organ of the body. In the brain, fascia is known as *meninges*; in the heart, as the *pericardium*; over bones, as *periosteum*.

The fascia that wraps the muscle fibers and muscle bundles comes together at the end of the muscle in what we call a tendon. The tendon is not connected directly to the bone, as many believe; rather, it is connected to the periosteum, the fascia of the bone. In certain places on the body, for example around the ankle joint, are bands of fascia known as *retinaculum*. In other places, across the top of the head for example, are sheets of fascia known as *aponeurosis*. Thus, ligaments, tendons, cartilage, superficial fascia, deep fascia, aponeurosis, septa, and retinaculum are all part of a continuous network throughout the entire body.

If it were possible to remove every other tissue and organ from the body and leave only the fascia, we would have a three-dimensional representation of the entire organism. The fascia forms a three-dimensional matrix of structural support, thus creating a unique environment for the functioning of body systems.

To envision the relationship of fascia to muscle, picture an orange. If you peel an orange, the white that surrounds the orange represents the superficial fascia. If you quarter an orange, you will see that the white interpenetrates the quarters. If you look at still smaller pieces, you will see tiny slivers of white mingled with the orange. These represent each muscle fiber, covered in a layer of fascia.

Composition of Fascia

Fascia is comprised of three components: *collagen*, which is the toughest of the three and is the supporting component. Within the collagen protein is an ordered network of water molecules; *elastin*, which is tissue that is elastic; and an *amorphous ground substance*, which is gelatinous. It transports metabolic material through the body and also acts like a cushion. Again, remember, this fascia tissue is everywhere. It not only covers every muscles and muscle cell, it covers every bone, nerve, organ, and cell in the body. And, fascia is very moist. It is wet.

Fascia forms a unitary matrix, so if you could take hold of it in some way and give it a little twist, the ramifications would resonate throughout the organism. To visualize this concept, think of a lovely, special sweater that fits you perfectly. Now, imagine a snag or pull in the material of the sweater that begins an unraveling process. The effects can gradually create a change in the shape of the entire sweater, causing it to lose its shape and integrity. It would no longer fit you in the same way. This is what happens with fascia. It is, indeed, a tissue that is present throughout the body and is affected by the events of your life, from conception to current time.

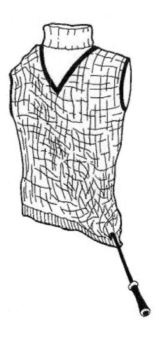

A PULL ANYWHERE AFFECTS THE WHOLE

Fascia has not been easy to study and research because it is pervasive and so interconnected that it is hard to divide it into discrete numbers of subunits, which could then be classified, described, and measured. For the most part, it has been presumed to be merely a structure that supports and divides. This is hardly so. Each cell in the body is connected to every other via this connective tissue, fascia.

Fascia and Communication

Water layers on the collagen fibers provide conduction pathways for rapid intercommunication throughout the body, enabling the organism to function as a coherent whole. Collagen is the principle protein; it makes up approximately 70 percent of all the proteins in connective tissues. The picture that emerges is of a vast network of high-speed processing that is taking place in the connective tissue system. Water is the critical element in this high-speed, instantaneous communication and coordination of the human body, and water is what allows for coherent functioning.

Another factor that supports this intercommunication is the patterned nature of collagen. Collagen is the principle protein of connective tissues. Listen to Mae-Wan Ho:

> Patterns of collagen fiber alignment are important for biological organization and function. These patterns affect, not only the mechanical properties of the connective tissues, but, through the network of associated structured *water,* also the electrical conductivity and detailed circuitry for intercommunication, on which the health and well-being of the individual depends.[1]

No longer does science believe that connective tissue serves only a mechanical supporting function. The complete new narrative has not yet become part of main stream science, but the science is there and what we see is that communication is a big part of the job of connective tissue.

To sum it up and quote Dr. Ho one more time:

> Quantum coherence is possible because of the 70% or so of water that makes up an organism. Quantum jazz is the music of the organism dancing life into being. It is played out by the whole organism, in every nerve and sinew, every muscle, every single cell, molecule, atom, and elementary particle.... Intercommunication is the key to quantum jazz. It is done to such sublime perfection that each molecule is effectively intercommunicating with every other, so each is as much in control as it is sensitive and responsive. And intercommunication is predominantly electronic and electromagnetic, thanks to liquid crystalline water....[2]

So, when I say that our tissues ought to feel somewhat like a wet sponge—yielding, elastic, fluid, supple, responsive, receptive, vibrant, and capable of some strength in any direction—I am referring not only

171

to our muscles, but to our connective tissues, as well. In fact, the two are impossible to separate. I will be speaking more about the neuromuscular aspect of our being in Part Two in the context of introducing the work of Dr. Thomas L. Hanna.

It is my belief that our fluid nature is what allows us human beings to resonate with each other. Our fluid nature is what allows us to experience exquisite connections that we can call love. Water is a highly resonant substance, and our hearts are at the center of our fluid system, so I believe it is our hearts and our fluidity that most allow for our ability to be in close harmony with one another.

From Tissues to Structure

The body is a physical structure, and as such, it obeys the laws of physics and architecture. The major structural components of the human body should be—ideally—in alignment with each other. The head should pretty much rest on top of the neck and shoulders, and not jut way out in front. Twists, displacements, and other misalignments have consequences, and those consequences are not merely physical. Why? Because coherence means that every aspect is influencing and being influenced by every other. Our physical structure affects and is affected by our personalities, our tissues, and our relationships. Our physical structure is just another part of the whole.

In Chapter 15, you will gain a much deeper understanding of these concepts and their importance for your well-being.

To Movement

The quality of your tissues and the quality of your structure are reflected in how you move. You can think of movement in two ways. One is functional: It is how you sit, stand, walk, bend, reach, or lie down. The other is how your tissues move. For example, how do your tissues move when you breathe? How responsive, receptive, fluid, and elastic are they? Both kinds of movement are important. For a thorough understanding of functional movement, see the works of Judith Aston,[3] Mary Bond,[4] or Dan Bienenfeld.[5] As regards how your tissues move, Chapter 16 examines this in depth.

Throughout this book, I have been saying that our childhood wounds affect the entire organism. I have stated that what must be addressed in the process of healing is the entire organism, the *whole living body.* We can no longer afford to overlook the structure of the body—its muscular system and its connective tissue and fluid systems. It is fabulous that scientists have included the brain and even the autonomic nervous system in their areas of investigation. Let's not stop there. There is another whole universe to explore.

WHAT YOU CAN DO: PRACTICES

1. This practice is vital and extremely challenging. Practice accepting your body. A hundred "Yes, buts" may come up, but just let them come and let them go. Yes, of course, you may prefer a smaller waistline or stronger arms or whatever, but even so, accept your body exactly as it is. I have worked with hundreds of individuals over the years, and the percentage of people who liked their bodies was very small, indeed, especially women. Our culture tortures women with unrealistic and unhealthy ideals. Realize that judging and criticizing your body will not change a thing. What it will do is make you disconnect further from your body. Doing something like moving, exercising, changing your eating patterns, or receiving bodywork is what will help. But the absolute best place to change anything is from a place of acceptance. Further, disliking an area of your body results in greater disconnection from that area.

2. Listen to your body. Learn to pay attention to your heart and to your guts. Learn to feel your legs and arms. You can easily incorporate body awareness into your walks. As you walk, let your awareness sense the movement of your arms and legs. Walk as if your mind were located inside your body. You can select areas such as your arms and legs, or you can tune into your back for a while. Certainly tune into your breath. Sense your breath as you are walking. I have been doing this practice for decades, and I still find new ways and places to tune into.

3. Practice softening your belly. A hard belly is a first-line defense against soft, tender feelings. It signals a decrease in coherence. Whenever you remember, allow your belly to soften as much as it can.

4. Practice the three-part breath. Take an easy breath, sensing a front-to-back movement between your pubic bone and your coccyx; i.e., from very low in your belly to the lowest part of your back. As your soft, easy breath continues, feel the lower part of your ribs expand laterally and widen. And finally, feel the very top of your ribs and clavicles expanding front to back. Many people tend to breathe high in their chests and find it difficult to feel any movement low in their bellies. Others breathe very low but can get almost no movement in their chests. Ideally, you should be able to feel all your tissues as they respond to your breath everywhere, including in your arms and legs.

There is no one, right way to breathe. Breathing is contextual. Different breathing is required in different situations. You breathe differently when you run than when you watch television or make love. But as your body becomes less and less constricted, as you breathe, you will be able to feel an easy movement in three places—low in your belly and in your lower back, in the lower part of your ribs all the way around, and at the top of your ribs and clavicles.

1. Ho, Mae-Wan, *The Rainbow and the Worm: The Physics of Organisms*, World Scientific Publishing, 1998, p. 190.

2. Ho, Mae-Wan, *Living Rainbow H2O*, World Scientific Publishing, pp. 4-5.

3. Aston, Judith, *Going Beyond Posture*, www.astonkinetics.com.

4. Bond, Mary, *The New Rules of Posture: How to Sit, Stand and Move in the Modern World*, Healing Arts Press, 2006.

5. Bienenfeld, Dan, *Align for Life*, (e-book) www.danbienenfeld.com.

PART TWO: RESOURCES FOR HEALING

INTRODUCTION

Was it Horace Greeley who said, "Go west, young man, go west?"

California called to me. It was where everything exciting was happening in the late 1960s and early 70s. It was giving birth to a whole new force in psychology, one that reached well beyond psychology's old boundaries. Humanistic psychology and existential psychology, fathered by the likes of Abraham Maslow, Sidney Jourard, Rollo May, Fritz Perls, and Virginia Satir, were described as a third force in the field. Its tenants felt revolutionary, because it called for an authentic encounter between client and therapist, for self-revelation on the part of both therapist and client, for the primacy of the relationship, and for a feeling connection. This was heady stuff for a boy from Port Chester who was just beginning to get inklings of what it might be like to feel something in my body besides pain and tension.

Alongside of the new psychology was the first sprouting of what has become the mushrooming field of Somatics. The body was reborn. The names Ida Rolf, Moshé Feldenkrais, Emilie Conrad, and Matthais Alexander were being heard. Their basic premise was that anyone interested in improving their well-being needed to address the body. Powerful change was in the wind, and I was drawn, like Gopis to the flute of Krishna. I had no choice but to follow. I had been touched!

I had been enrolled in a good, yet conventional, clinical psychology program. The human body was never mentioned. The entire gamut of difficulties I described earlier was considered psychological. I began to realize how deep the separation of mind and body went. By the end of my third year of graduate school, the program felt increasingly irrelevant to me. So, I listened to Ram Dass speak of spiritual awakening, I took LSD and perceived the awesome imperceptible, and I looked into a field of grass and saw a world of life teeming in shining brilliance. On occasion, with the help of marijuana, I even felt an emotional connection with another human being. I knew that something existed beyond anything I had ever known or imagined. It awakened in me a gnawing hunger for life and an awareness of just how far away from it I had been living.

Conviction grew in me that somehow we were all connected; that body and mind were intimately related; that there was infinitely more to reality than what I perceived in my everyday, dull consciousness, in a body that was almost always fatigued; that human beings were part of a great network of life, forming an unfathomably rich web of interconnections. I saw how social structures and institutions too often served to reinforce my sense of separation and isolation. From then until this day, I have been planted in three worlds: the body and movement, psychology, and relationships.

I begin Part Two by sharing an overview of my professional journey. From 1970 until 2010, forty years, I studied a variety of systems. I will mention most of them (the ones I can remember) and go into some depth with several. Part Two is a compendium of resources. It gives a view of the "whole organism" through the eyes of several visionaries, each with his/her own perspective on what the body is, what psychotherapy is, and what healing is about. It is my firm belief that no one process or therapy can offer a panacea. Further, the greater the wounding, the more intelligent it would be to avail yourself of several.

As I describe some of the teachings, therapies, and understandings I encountered, I will include my own experiences. The therapies and teachings I used in my own journey are available today, yet, most people I encounter have not heard of many, if not most, of them. When it comes to the somatic therapies, the vast majority of people are truly clueless to their existence. So much is available to make your life richer, to enhance your comprehension, to further your coherence, and to make love and vitality more possible. I will take you into my experience of various therapies so you can understand how they work and know what to expect as you proceed to healing and wholeness.

Body Therapies

Soon after I left graduate school, I came upon the work of Wilhelm Reich, who was a student of Sigmund Freud. After working with people for a long time, Reich concluded that, if significant personality changes were to be made, changes must be made in the body. Intuitively, given how I had realized the condition of my body, I sensed this to be true. So, off I went in search of a Reichian therapist. I worked with him for three years and then entered into a training program with him. In Chapter 14, we will explore Reichian Therapy.

While I was experiencing and studying Reichian Therapy, I discovered the work of Ida P. Rolf. She, too, believed that changing the body was the path towards growth. Being a triple Taurus, however, she simply applied her knuckles, fingertips, and elbows and directly changed the body with skillful force. I was enchanted. She worked with the connective tissue system of the body, primarily fascia. Fascia is a tissue that covers every muscle, every muscle cell, and every bone, fiber, and organ. In Chapter 15, we will explore it in depth.

Of course, once I had begun the inquiry into my body, it was natural to explore how it moves. My good fortune led me to the empress of human movement, Emilie Conrad. She called her work Continuum Movement. If you want an image of how she moved, picture an octopus-like creature who has no bones and can change shape. If you think I am greatly exaggerating, I invite you to go to You Tube and look up Emilie Conrad, Fluid Movement. A fundamental premise of Continuum Movement is this: given the fact that we are at least 70 percent water, the natural movements of the body are wave motions, including spirals, curves, and arcs. Further, the impacts of life cause constrictions, tensions, and compressions of our body that devitalize the water within, making it stagnant. This is when I became fascinated with water, which comprises so much of what and who we are. We will visit this topic in Chapter 16.

Next, I sought out Dr. Peter Levine, one of the world's leading experts on what he calls shock trauma, or in the language of this book, *a severe impact*. A shock trauma occurs when an impact is so overwhelming that your biological defenses of fight/flight are overwhelmed. Of course, having experienced dozens of such shocks, I was keenly interested in his perspective, and off I went to be trained and to receive a year or more of personal sessions. We will explore Peter's work in Chapter 18.

Dr. Thomas Hanna, arguably the foremost philosopher of the somatic movement, was another important influence. He came later in my career and added a neuromuscular perspective to my thinking. Tom argued that the impacts and insults of life create a type of amnesia—a loss of the ability to fully contract and fully relax our muscles. As we will see, this has many serious consequences. We will look at Tom's teachings in Chapter 17.

Psychotherapies

In the psychotherapeutic arena, I encountered many who offered me new understandings and new pieces of myself. In the 1970s, I worked with students of Fritz Perls, the founder of Gestalt Therapy. Gestalt was quite confrontational in those days; fortunately, most of my teachers had the ability to be kind and gentle as well as confrontational. Such lessons served me well. As you can imagine, this healthy style of interaction was nowhere to be seen in my family. Gestalt is not as popular today as it was in the 1970s, and I do not devote a chapter to it. However, there are still some very good Gestalt therapists in the world today, and they can be found online.

Later, I encountered the work of Bruce Ecker, who taught that symptoms such as anxiety had meaning within a broader context and should not simply be eradicated. He said anxiety symptoms were coherent within a bigger picture. For example, your anxiety may be a way of avoiding your vulnerability, so it makes sense that the solution is not to get rid of your anxiety, but to find a better way of dealing with your vulnerability. Again, I have not devoted a chapter to Bruce's work. He is located in the Oakland area and can be found online. He now calls his work Coherence Therapy.

In 2004, I came upon the work of Dr. Diana Fosha. I believe her work will make an enormous impact on the field of psychotherapy for decades to come. She brings a depth of humanity and intimacy into the work, within a rigorous, theoretical framework. When I first met her at a conference, I realized I had never met anyone who had both sides of their brain firing to the extent that she did. I even flew from Seattle to New York several times to receive sessions and to begin her training program. Accelerated Experiential Dynamic Psychotherapy (AEDP) is an approach to psychotherapy that I believe can be of enormous value to almost all of us. It isn't about curing pathology; it's about living to one's fullest, and especially learning to let love in. An AEDP therapist offers love in abundance (in the form of acknowledgement, appreciation, affirmation, acceptance, and so forth); then, she helps the client learn how to receive it. I describe Dr. Fosha's approach in Chapter 19.

Although I have not dedicated a chapter to it, I studied an elegant approach to treating couples. It is called Emotionally Focused Couple's Therapy by Dr. Susan Johnson. It eliminates the blame game about who is right and who is wrong by identifying the distress a couple presents as a dance they learned in which each plays a part. The dance has three levels. The one the couple is expressing is surface level. Usually, one partner is angry and blaming, and the other partner is sullen and withdrawn. The dance has several variations, but common to them all is that neither partner is in touch with a deeper layer of feeling beneath what he or she is presenting. There is an even deeper layer, and that is the layer of needs. It is the job of the therapist to help the couple enter into and relate from the two deeper layers.

In Chapter 20, I present the work of four individuals: Werner Erhard, Dr. Hal Stone and his wife, Dr. Sidra Stone, and Dr. W. Brugh Joy. Werner Erhard was an individual who had a significant impact on my life. He was the founder of the Erhard Seminar Trainings (EST), whose work continues to be taught today as the Landmark Forum. Although Werner is no long part of the organization and the content has changed, his influence can be seen and felt. It was a controversial program, but I personally witnessed countless people derive great value from their participation—me included.

Hal Stone is a Jungian analyst who, with his wife Sidra, developed a system called the Psychology of Selves, along with the Voice Dialogue method to facilitate awareness of your various selves. It is an intriguing approach to uncovering unknown dimensions of Self and balancing the different aspects of your personality. Hal and Sidra were awesome teachers; they combined wisdom, humor, and a perspicacious ability to ferret out just the right piece to focus on and bring to their client's awareness. Their work greatly expanded my vision of myself and my world.

Another whose work would probably be considered spiritual is William Brugh Joy. Brugh, as he was known, was a medical doctor who left medicine to begin teaching what it means to live from the heart. Until meeting Brugh, I was a former Catholic turned agnostic turned atheist. What I received from Brugh was a powerful experience that God is Love; and from that moment forward, I was interested in spiritual teachings.

Each individual or work I described above had a positive influence on my life. I feel so fortunate and grateful to have met and studied with them and received their work. Now let's look at some of these systems in more depth.

CHAPTER 14

Dissolving Body Armor: Wilhelm Reich

"As long as you do not live totally in the body, you do not live totally in the Self."
~ B.K.S. Iyengar

From Madman to Prophet

Why am I beginning the Resources part of this book by telling you about a psychiatrist who worked in the early/mid-twentieth century, who was considered crazy and was ostracized by his peers? First, because developments in the fields of psychology, energy psychology, trauma and somatics, have transformed Reich's preachings from those of a madman to those of a prophet. Simply stated, Reich was the first Western medical doctor to see the importance of the body in the study of mental health.

Second, therapies around the world have descended from Reich and are popular in some areas today. Third, my journey into "the whole organism" started with my study of Reich's work. Fourth, I believe we should all know where in Western psychology the interest in the body began. For some people at some time in their lives, these approaches may be exactly what are needed.

When I walked into a psychiatrist's office in 1964, I believed psychotherapy would fix me. A few years later, I realized that "fixing" was a whole-organism project. This change in perspective began with my introduction to the work of Wilhelm Reich. Sadly, it is an extremely rare student in psychology who becomes acquainted with Reich's work. I believe this stems from the adamant desire to keep the body and the so-called "mind" located in different parts of the campus.

Reich was a medical doctor and a sexologist when he became a student of Freud. In my years of undergraduate and graduate psychology, not one of my professors mentioned his name. Yet, his influence has been vast and far-reaching. His thinking went so far afield from the psychology of his day that I consider him a true visionary.

Reich's Contributions1

One of Reich's major contributions to the psychoanalytic field was his work in describing what he called "character structures," or patterns of protective mechanisms composed of consistent attitudes and behaviors that served to protect the person from painful feelings. This understanding of character or personality patterns was a huge breakthrough in the field, and Reich's status soared. The idea that an individual's character, that is, the *how* of his mannerisms, could have a protective function was easily palatable to Reich's contemporaries. These were emotional, attitudinal, and behavioral patterns well within the domain of psychoanalysis—the talking therapy. However, the more Reich ventured into the body, the more ostracized he became professionally. And then, with his next step, he ushered in the demise of his reputation. It was a giant step, indeed!

Reich claimed that the character of the individual was functionally identical to the structure of his body. This means that observing an individual's body would enable the therapist to know the nature of his character and the patterns of his resistance. Chronic tension patterns and chronic personality mannerisms have the same function. They are protective and block the free flow of energy. Chronic muscle tension binds sexual energy, it binds anxiety, and it binds anger. Further, to resolve the conflicts from which the individual suffers, the tension patterns in the body must be released. These tension patterns were mechanisms of coping with the conflicts that were at the root of the disturbance. For example, the association of sexual pleasure with moral guilt could result in both chronic bodily tension patterns and character patterns that bind and inhibit the free flow of sexual or life energy. Reich was pointing towards and describing the *organism as a whole*. The conflicts and inhibitions are not simply psychic. *They are structured into the body, as well!* This came to be called *body armor.*

I have taken workshops with descendants of Wilhelm Reich. I have watched these therapists stand individuals up in front of a group and, looking at their mostly unclothed bodies, describe their childhoods and their major issues and challenges. As a beginner in the area of the body, I was amazed when the individuals corroborated the therapists' readings.

The Reichian Orgasm

Reich believed that if an individual could not experience a full, whole-body release in orgasm, the undischarged energy would organize itself as symptoms or disturbances. This ability Reich believed to be the hallmark of good health. He believed that an individual should be able to build a very strong charge throughout the whole body during the sexual arousal process, then, in orgasm, release the entire charge. Healthy orgasm should be an almost cosmic experience, in which the individual loses the sense of himself as a separate being. From Reich's point of view, when a person achieved this, then he was healthy.

Components of Reichian Therapy

The therapy Reich developed involved four components.

- Deep breathing. Different kinds of breathing exercises are used in this therapy. A primary purpose is to build a charge of energy in the body. As the charge builds, the therapist notes where the individual is constricting his body and not allowing the charge to move through.

- Expressive movement exercises. Pounding a bed with your fists or kicking it with your legs while verbally expressing something like, "No! No!" There are a couple of objectives here. One is to move the energy where it is not moving well. The other is to incorporate into the individual an expression that has been stifled in his personality.

• Massage of areas of the body that contract as the client intensifies breathing. The obvious objective is to free up those areas.

• Psychological analysis. Reich was a psychoanalyst and believed in the method. Today, there are still some traditional Reichian therapists in the world, but they are far and few between. The off-shoots of Reich are far more common, and their methods of doing psychological work vary a great deal.

Three of the primary descendants of Reich whose work is available in many countries are Alexander Lowen, John Pierrakos, and Eva Pierrakos.

Dr. Alexander Lowen was a student of Reich's. He founded a system he called Bioenergetics. Lowen included exercises that were designed to move energy and to build and release "charge" from the body. A typical Bioenergetics exercise might include having a client stretch backwards over a stool with his arms up over his head. This would create quite a stretch on the back, and the therapist might intervene with some manual massage to facilitate release of muscle tension. Another example is to have a client stand with his fists in his lower back and bend over backwards while uttering a guttural sound. Like his mentor Reich, Lowen believed that emotions locked into the musculature were at the root of psychological issues, and it was the therapist's job to unearth and help release them. We are sexual beings, and we are social beings. If our sexual drives are overpowered by restrictive taboos, the result is body armor and chronic tensions.

Dr. John Pierrakos was a long-term associate of Alexander

Lowen. Eventually, as is often the case with gifted collaborators, he began his own system, which he called Core Energetics. Whereas Lowen was concerned with the physical, mental, and emotional levels of the patient, Pierrakos added a spiritual dimension. His vision of the human being was broader than was his mentor's. Pierrakos' wife, Eva also began her own system, which she called Pathworks. A Google search can locate practitioners of Bioenergetics, Core Energetics, and Pathworks in a number of different countries. Wilhelm Reich directly influenced all three.

Looking back to the 1970s and 80s when I was immersed in different therapies and seminars, it isn't easy to say what I received from which process. However, during those early years of my personal work, I can say I grew in a number of different ways. I learned to tolerate more excitement in my body without flying off the walls.

I had stopped crying somewhere around my fifteenth year. Momma could no longer make me cry. Fifteen more years passed before I shed another tear. What a blessed relief it was to regain that ability. Perhaps most importantly, little by little, my level of self-acceptance increased.

Wilhelm Reich was a prolific writer. He authored at least eleven books. He argued passionately that both mechanistic thinking and mystical thinking keep humans from knowing their real freedom as biological creatures. He argued that rigid bodies produce rigid thinking and that fascism was the ultimate expression of that rigidity. He argued that adolescents should be allowed their sexuality, and that cancer was caused by stasis of this biological energy. He built devices to harness that energy and experimented with treating cancer patients. The Federal Food and Drug Administration became involved and issued an injunction. Reich refused to go to court. He argued that he should be tried in the court of science. He was convicted of contempt of court, and in 1957 died in a federal penitentiary in Lewisburg, Pennsylvania.

1. For a thorough consideration of the work of Wilhelm Reich, see *Wilhelm Reich: Selected Writings*, and *The Function of the Orgasm* by W. Reich.

Note: Another system that uses the breath to transform consciousness is Stan Grof's *Holotropic Breathwork*. I have not experienced it but many have told me they found it quite valuable.

CHAPTER 15

GRAVITY WILL ALWAYS WIN,
UNLESS YOU ARE WELL STACKED:
IDA P. ROLF AND STRUCTURAL INTEGRATION

"Even if you live to be a hundred, it's really a very short time.
So why not spend it undergoing the process of evolution
of opening your mind and heart, connecting with your true nature—rather
than getting better and better at fixing, grasping, freezing, closing down?"
~ Pema Chödron

The writings of Wilhelm Reich flowed as heady wine into the psyche of a young man so constricted and disconnected from his physical form as I was. It offered the promise of salvation, of releasing all those rings of armor, and of allowing the flow of energy and the fullness of sexuality. My therapist, Alan Darbonne, had the patience of Job. In session after session for months upon months, he guided as I breathed until my limbs began to tingle and directed me in expressive activities, such as pounding, pushing, or kicking the bed upon which I lie.

One day, I read a magazine article written by Sam Keane, titled, "Sing the Body Electric." It was about the work of Dr. Ida P. Rolf. Immediately, I knew that Structural Integration was for me. My own compressed and collapsed body convinced me of the correctness of Reich's assertion that if you are going to change your personality, you must change your physical structure. And what better way to do exactly that than to take your two hands and plunge into the tissues and change them. This is exactly what Ida Rolf did—with her own two hands, she reshaped the human structure.

By 1971, my own experience made it obvious to me that extensive impacts and insults warp the body as well as the psych. So, when I first read about the work of Dr. Rolf, I was immediately enchanted. Ida Rolf was a triple Taurus, and no astrology buff would be surprised to learn that she was a very direct and sometimes forceful person. From her perspective, if you wanted to change the body, well, then, get your hands in there and do it! It required courage, vision, and a profound knowledge of human anatomy to manually enter deeply enough to release, lengthen, and soften tissues from the surface all the way to the bones. Structural Integration, as she called her work, is a remarkable approach to the human body, one that has yet to be fully appreciated. Yet, for those who know and have had the good fortune to experience Structural Integration, they know it is a gift to human kind. It is a dimension of healing that cannot be overlooked. *It addresses the coherence of the structure as a whole.*

Structural Integration

In order to understand and appreciate the import and benefits of Structural Integration,[1] you need to grasp several concepts. The body is a physical structure, and its major components—such as the head, shoulders, chest, spine, pelvis, and extremities—have a spatial relationship to each other. When I refer to structure, I am referring to the spatial relationship of the various parts of the body. For example, where is the pelvis in relationship to the feet when an individual is standing up straight? Where is the pelvis in relationship to the shoulders? The practice of Structural Integration requires the skill to see these relationships and know which tissues have shortened or tightened to create the patterns observed. The relationships of the various parts have implications for the functioning and movement of the body. And as we have seen from Reich, chronic tension in the body, i.e., excessive constriction and holding, also have implications for our psychological or emotional well-being.

Now, let's look at these various physical structures—your head, neck, shoulders, spine, arms, legs, and so forth—in the context of coherence. I am defining coherence as a state in which both individual autonomy and global cohesion are maximized. Let's take the example of the shoulder of the human body. How could it be described in terms of local freedom and global cohesion? The shoulder girdle has four joints.[2]

Now, to raise your arm smoothly above your head involves not only the freedom of those four joints, but also movement between the ribs, and movement of the spine. In other words, for your shoulder to be coherent, you need the joints of the shoulder girdle, ribs, and spine to do what they were designed to do—move freely and in a coordinated fashion. And this is true for all the joints of the body. Ideally, movement is a dance of fluid freedom and coordination.

Structural Relationships: Don't Fix the Door, Fix the Foundation

Structural relationships are determined by the length of the soft tissues—muscle and connective tissues. When the length of the tissues that flex and extend a particular joint are at their optimal length, we can say they are in balance. Let's simplify for the sake of clarity. The biceps muscles—and their fascia—flex the elbow joint; they shorten the angle between the bones of the upper and lower arm. The triceps muscles extend the elbow joint; they increase the angle, straightening out the arm. If the biceps have shortened from their optimal length relative to the triceps, the elbow joint will be chronically flexed. Both sets of tissues will be tighter than is optimal. By design, they have an optimal length and should contract fully and extend fully.

Here are some words from Dr. Rolf:

Rolfing seeks to enhance function by changing structure...we see that bones are held in place by soft tissue. If a muscle is chronically short, it will pull the attached bone out of balance. When one part is in trouble, the body as a whole gets out of balance. In a static structure, such as a house, for example, if a door doesn't swing true or close properly, it really isn't enough to rehang the door. In order to balance the door permanently, it would be better to look to the symmetry of the foundation. Structures must be balanced as a whole—this is as true of living structures as it is of houses and bridges. [3]

Nature Designed the Human Body to be Vertical

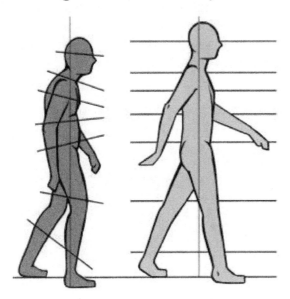

The direction of human evolution is towards the vertical. It was Dr. Rolf who first called attention to the fact that each of us lives and breathes in a field of gravity and that our physical relationship to gravity matters. To Ida Rolf's mind, gravitational energy, the field of the earth, is a source of nourishment that may reinforce and augment the field of the body. However, in order for this to happen freely and easily, the body must be in an unhindered relationship with gravity—it must be well stacked (pun intended). That means it must be truly vertical, in a fluid alignment with gravitational forces.

To the degree that the human body is not well aligned within the field of gravity, we can safely conclude that the body is holding excessive amounts of tension and strain. If, for example, the head is held well forward of the shoulders, which is extremely common, then the weight of the head is "falling" into the middle of the chest and will create tension in the ribs and chest muscles, prohibiting an easy and full inhalation and exhalation in respiration. Further, the muscles in the back of the neck chronically have to work overtime to compensate for the head falling forward. They will chronically "hold on." Remember, chronic tension in the body serves as a feedback loop to the limbic system, reinforcing its hypersensitivity. And that is only one of the negative effects of chronic tension, which affects our health, our mobility, our sense of who we are, and our capacity for intimate connections. Chronic tension is, literally, a weight on our hearts, and renders them just a little less available for connection.

For many years, I have observed how little children, ages three to four, sit. I have been impressed at the vertical thrust in their little bodies. Their heads reach for the sky and are aligned over their chests, which sit well balanced over their pelvises. We were born to become vertical, and it matters how well we achieve and maintain that verticality. It matters for our mobility. It matters to our psychology. And it matters to our health.

So, what is it that keeps us from reaching our full length? What keeps us from occupying the fullness of our being? It is not only in the vertical dimension that we do not reach our full physical potential. It is also in the front-to-back and side-to-side dimensions. We can, literally and physically, be more filled out, and I am not referring to weight or muscle building; I am referring to a quality of fullness in the tissues.

Why is it that most humans get shorter as they grow older? Why do their rib cages sink subtly towards their pelvis, their heads fall slightly more forward, and their mobility decline? For most of us, the question doesn't even cross our minds. Is it simply normal aging? Is gravity literally pulling us down? Does it have to be this way? Structural Integration says no, it doesn't have to be this way.

What we see when we look at any human body is its genetic expression in interaction with the effects of impacts, chronic insults, learned habits, nutrition, exercise, and the overall quality of the environment in which that body was reared. Obviously, genetic factors influence how we age; however, for most of us, how we age relates to how we deal with the effects of the impacts and insults that have accumulated throughout a lifetime, and more generally, it relates to how we care for ourselves. Remember, impacts can be both physical and psychological. A breach birth, a serious fall off a high chair, an accident, and yes even surgery can create definite and substantial effects on how the physical body coheres and how it is aligned and balanced within the field of gravity.

Let's take a look at a very simple impact that most people wouldn't consider worth mentioning in a narrative of their life. A young boy falls from a tree and displaces his coccyx, his tail bone. In addition, he experiences a slight twist in his sacrum. Yes, in the moment, it was an intense experience, but after a good cry and some parental comforting, this little boy goes about the business of his childhood. Now, the little twist in his sacrum and the lateral displacement of his coccyx, over time, will affect his entire body. Since the muscles of his pelvic floor attach to his coccyx, they will be pulled and create a tension situation. The placement of the rest of his spine will be altered because his sacrum is its foundation. His structural integrity has been compromised, and this will create chronic tension with all its implications, including possibly an effect on the boy's sense of self. This is a simple demonstration of how a body's structure can be impacted even without the contribution of any other psychosocial life conditions.

Obviously, our structures are affected by the myriad wounds we receive. When a child is told a thousand times not to express in a particular way, she will learn to obey that injunction by holding the muscles of that expression. For example, typical body movements accompany assertion. There is a certain freedom of movement in the arms, shoulders, chest, and facial expressions, as well. If a child is not allowed to assert in relation to a parent, she will learn to hold herself in a way that keeps the expression of assertiveness from occurring. Over time, that holding will become automatic and structured into the body

Good self-care includes so much more than simply eating healthy foods and exercising the body. For excellent self-care, you need to understand what areas of your organism have been affected and how those effects are limiting your enjoyment of life, impacting your well-being, affecting your health and aging process, and challenging your ability to enjoy love connections. We have looked at the effects of your wounding on your psyche, on your model of self, and on your attachment styles. We looked at how these wounds affected an area of the prefrontal cortex and at how they affect our autonomic nervous system. Now, with Dr. Rolf, we arrive at a mind-blowing understanding of the interconnectedness of the whole body and its potential for improved coherence.

International Medical Research on Fascia and a New Image of the Body

Since 2007, there have been three International Medical Research Conferences on the subject of fascia, and the data is fascinating.[4] The old image of the body was based on Newtonian physics, and it was mechanical, a conception of movement based on muscles, bones, and joints. But the picture is changing! A new image of the body is emerging. One fascinating video presented in the conference involved a tiny camera inserted under the skin. The title was "Strolling Under the Skin." And though it would be impossible to do justice in words to what was shown, I can say with certainty that any Newtonian understanding of how the movements of the body function can be gently laid to rest. The wet webbing of fascia is ubiquitous and very much involved in our movements.

Muscles rarely transmit their full force via tendons onto the skeleton. They distribute a large portion of their force onto sheets of fascia. These sheets can extend to several joints and to several other muscles. It would not be simple to say which muscles participate in a particular movement. Here is an image that might make it more meaningful. Rather than thinking of the 600-plus muscles in the human body, visualize it as one muscle poured into 600-plus pockets of fascia. Everything is connected. The more coherent the body, the more likely it is that every one of those muscles and fascia will respond to a movement in any other of those muscles. The body is whole; the idea of segments is man-made.

Hellerwork Structural Integration

"As the body is the hologram of the being, so Hellerwork is a process of realizing that being in the flesh."
Joseph Heller[4]

One variant of Dr. Rolf's approach is called Hellerwork Structural Integration. For twenty years in the 1980s and 90s, Hellerwork Structural Integration was a large part of my professional practice.

Joseph Heller was president of the Rolf Institute back in the middle 1970s. A successful practitioner who was very much in demand in Santa Monica, Joseph began his work day at seven a.m. and finished at seven p.m. He was very much in demand. What made him so popular was that, in addition to having highly skilled hands, he always worked with the person and not just with the person's body. His attitude was that his work was about people, not just bodies. Therefore, it was natural when he decided to leave the Rolf Institute in 1978 to open his own school that his emphasis from the beginning was to attend to the person, and not just the body. The work itself was just as he had learned from Dr. Rolf; however, by focusing on the person, a different quality of experience was created. Further, it reinforced the correct idea that body and person cannot be separated.

Practitioners of Hellerwork are concerned with how the body expresses its psychology. In Joseph's words: "As Reich, Lowen, Feldenkrais, and others have recognized, people are always perfectly self-expressive through their bodies, both consciously and unconsciously, advertising their attitudes and beliefs in their postures and movements."[5] Hellerwork Structural Integration is done in eleven sessions, and a different theme was developed for each session to help the client understand that her body reflected her life and to provide a starting point for dialogue within the session. For example, in the first session of the series, much of the work focuses on the area of the chest and diaphragm. A typical result is greater ease of breathing. Thus, the theme given to this session is "Inspiration."

Dialogue is an aspect of Hellerwork, and the theme often provides the catalyst for a meaningful conversation between client and practitioner. The direction of the dialogue is not pre-set; it might be about relationships, self-esteem, confidence, and so forth. However, by beginning with the theme of Inspiration, the client not only gets a physical experience of more ease in breathing, but also an understanding that the breath is related to feeling inspired in life.

Themes for the other sessions include: "Standing on Your Own Two Feet" for the session in which the legs and feet are addressed. As the sides, arms, and shoulder girdle are being released, the theme of "Reaching Out" may begin the dialogue. We have looked at the importance of the fight/flight mechanism. The arms and legs are vital to the activities of fight/flight. The feet and legs ground us in relation to the earth, and the arms ground us in relation to people and things. This is the kind of information clients learn during the Hellerwork series.

"Control and Surrender" is the theme associated with the pelvic floor, which is the area of the body where self-control is first addressed. It is also the area of the body where we learn to surrender to deep pleasure in the process of orgasm. The theme associated with work in the abdominal region is "The Guts." Our language provides clues to that theme. We say that a person is "gutsy" or that we relied on our "gut feelings." In each session of the series, as different aspects of the body are attended to, a new understanding or experience can be brought into conscious awareness.

Since the whole person is the focus in Hellerwork, it also became the guiding principle in how Hellerwork Structural Integration was taught. It was not just the passing on of skills; the student was central. The Hellerwork Training is about helping each student learn more about herself, learn how to be present, and learn more about how to be in relationship with her clients.

The Vibrational Field of the Teacher

What is it that makes Hellerwork Education, Hellerwork Education? It is the "space" that the teacher creates through her *being* and *skills.* The space refers to the vibrational field that is created in any relationship. In the Hellerwork classroom, the trainer creates it by:

1. Recognizing the importance of maintaining a safe atmosphere for learning

2. Remaining centered, open, and attentive

3. Maintaining an energetic link to each individual and to the group as a whole

4. Carrying both a personal and impersonal energetic. This refers to an attitude that is both quite personal and friendly and quite impersonal and in charge.

5. Giving non-judgmental feedback

6. Knowing how to encourage student's self-disclosure and participation

7. Seeking to nurture student's strengths

8. Moving fluidly from academic presentation to personal process and back again

9. Not fearing the unknown and being willing to engage with whatever arises and use it for the class's benefit

10. Carrying the quality of authority without being authoritarian

11. Having firm, but flexible limits, expressed in words and actions

When I am asked how Hellerwork Structural Integration differs from others schools of Structural Integration, I can say that we were the first to emphasize working with a person, and not just a body. It makes a difference in the quality of experience, and it makes a statement that we cannot separate the body from the person. I know that some other schools of Structural Integration have begun to recognize the importance of the client/practitioner relationship, and for this, I am profoundly happy.

I want to insert a caveat as I conclude this discussion of the work of Dr. Ida P. Rolf. Many people have told me that they did a ten-session series of SI bodywork. Most say it was good, and that was that. Why has it not become an ongoing part of their health regimen? In the early days of the work, when the only school was the Rolf Institute, practitioners told their clients to get ten sessions, or maybe fourteen if they wanted to include an advanced series of four sessions. Before I was trained, I asked Dr. Rolf why her practitioners did this. I added that I had already had over forty sessions and that my body was continuing to improve. She responded, "Of course, your body is going to continue to get better, but there are 250,000,000 million people in this country and only 200 Rolfers." I took a deep breath and thanked her for her honesty.

As of today, I have had over 350 Structural Integration sessions and I have no plans to discontinue. Uncannily, my posture continues to improve at the age of seventy-one. How do you want your posture to look when you're seventy? And, remember, we are talking about coherence!

As you may recall from my personal story of my high school experience, I had given up. A blatant expression of having given up showed in how I carried myself. Along with everything else I have described about how my body looked and felt. I also wore a droopy, hang-dog expression. Amazingly, my chest began to fill out and my head lifted up, and my physical form no longer felt like that defeated punk kid from New York. A quality of dignity emerged in how I carried myself, and that quality informed my sense of myself. As my shape morphed from that of a defeated, discouraged, and beaten-down individual, my experience of myself was also changing dramatically. Even today when I receive a "tune up," I feel myself as a fuller being at the end of the session. There is no way I can quantify and compare the effects of the various therapies and processes I experienced; however, I can say unequivocally that Structural Integration ranks among the most profound.

My oldest client was Rudolph Schaefer, a man who was a huge force in bringing Eastern art, such as flower arranging, to the West. He was *ninety-nine years old* when we began, and I worked on him twice a month for two years. "St. John," he would say, "this is the best thing I do for myself."

In my opinion, it is simply silly to grow into old age without this work being part of your health regimen. For many of the reasons we have already explored, those fascial tissues can get so hard over the years that no amount of yoga, stretching, or exercise can restore their natural textures and the body's coherence.

1. There are several schools of Structural Integration, including the Guild for Structural Integration, Rolfing Structural Integration, Hellerwork Structural Integration, and Kinesis Myofascial Integration. Although different in flavor, all are branches off the tree of Dr. Rolf's insights and techniques.

2. The shoulder girdle itself, consisting of the shoulder blade and collarbone; the scapulothoracic joint for the shoulder blade's movement in relation to the upper ribs; the sternoclavicular joint, where the collarbone (clavicle) meets the breastbone (sternum); the glenohumeral joint (the true shoulder joint), where the upper arm comes into the girdle; the acromioclavicular joint, where the clavicle meets an extension of the shoulder blade (the acromion).

3. Ida Rolf, *Rolfing and Physical Reality*, Healing Arts Press, 1978.

4. Findley, Thomas, "Fascia Research from a Clinician/Scientist's Perspective," *International Journal of Therapeutic Massage and Bodywork,* Vol. 4, No. 4, 2011.

4. Joseph Heller in personal communication.

5. Joseph Heller, *Bodywise*, Jeremy P. Tarcher, Inc., 1986, p. 83.

CHAPTER 16

To Become Like Water
Is to Become Your Self:
Emilie Conrad and Continuum Movement

"Nothing in the world is as soft and as yielding as water. Yet, for dissolving the hard and inflexible, nothing can surpass it. The soft overcomes the hard; the gentle overcomes the rigid."
~ Lao Tzu.

"Oh, for a life of sensations rather than thoughts."
~ John Keats

Uncanny Fluidity

Never in my life had I seen such fluidity of movement. It was 1983, and at the time, Susan Harper[1] was the only other person authorized by Emilie Conrad to teach Continuum Movement. The way she moved seemed outside the range of what human beings are capable of doing. Her spine moved in waves and with apparently total freedom throughout all the many joints of the vertebrae. But her back movement wasn't only at the joints. What truly amazed me was the movement of the tissue under her skin. I felt like a complete klutz. How did anyone connect so deeply with themselves as to get the tissues to move like that? It was more than I could conceive. It would be many years before I began my study of Continuum in earnest.

From 1995, I have considered Continuum Movement my meditation and movement practice. There is evidence in the literature that mindfulness practices (as well as good relational psychotherapy or just a good close relationship) can grow structures in the brain. I consider Continuum Movement a mindfulness practice that can enhance not only the brain, but also tissues throughout the body, as well.

Given what we have learned about water, it is not far-fetched to believe that the quality of the water in our cells and tissues influences our vibrancy, our vitality, and our sense of aliveness. As I see it, the quality of water in our bodies correlates with the quality of our tissues, cells, fibers, muscles, connective tissue, and so forth. In turn, the quality of our tissues correlates with the quality of our structure—and to how the major components of our structure relate to one another. Each level influences and is influenced by every other level. Mae-Wan Ho tells us this is how it is at the subatomic and molecular levels and both macroscopically and microscopically. As she puts it:

> The ideal coherent whole, I suggest, is also the ideal of health. The coherent organism is a unity of brain and body, heart and mind, an undivided bundle of intellect and passion, flesh, blood and sinew that lives life to the full, freely and spontaneously, attuned not just to the immediate environment, but the universe at large.[2]

Emilie Conrad

For almost fifty years, Emilie Conrad, the founder and primary developer of Continuum Movement (along for many years with Susan Harper), said that the key to health and well-being lies in our body's water.[3] Further, through the use of sounds, mindful attention, and extremely slow and subtle movements, we can learn to participate with the fluid level of the body's movement. It was Emilie Conrad who developed a movement path that addresses the organism as muscle, as fascia, as sensation and feeling, as expression, *and as fluid.*

We Are Nourished by Life Itself

Every now and again a visionary sees a truth so simple and yet so profound that it will generate waves of change for decades, if not centuries, to come. Emilie Conrad's contribution is that we are all connected to the fluid system of the planet on which we live. By fluid system, she is referring to the 326 cubic miles of water that bathe this planet—the water of the oceans, lakes, and rivers. She is referring to the water of the clouds that nourishes our trees and plants. She is referring to the water in our bodies, the blood and lymph, and the tears and interstitial fluids—the 70 to 80 percent water that I have been referring to. And she is saying that all of that fluid comprises one continuous system. Not only are we part of this fluid sphere, but our connection to this biosphere is a primary source of nourishment, analogous to our umbilical connection before birth. *We can be nourished by life itself.* To the degree that our bodies are sufficiently open, sufficiently fluid, and sufficiently coherent, then life itself is a source of nourishment. It is a primary connection, which renders us just a little less dependent on other sources of nourishment. The fluid system is the medium through which we are connected to the web of life—not as a concept, but as a living reality. Seen through the lenses of conventional biology and chemistry, these assertions may appear outlandish. However, after looking at Mae-Wan Ho's work, Emilie's words seem prophetic. The wounds of life—as well as an insufficient comprehension of who we are in these bodies and what we need—have many serious consequences. *Among them is the severance of this connection to the universal nourishment that continually offers the possibility for delight at being alive in these bodies.* Children can feel supreme delight just running around the living room or jumping on a welcoming lap. They need so little to feel delight and joy. If reared in a relatively safe environment, and if their needs have been reasonably met, young children are still quite fluid in their tissues.

Water, like children, loves to move. When water is forced to move along a straight path, it gives away energy. Water prefers waves, spirals, swirls, and spins. When water encounters an obstacle, its forward movement is stopped, and it curls inward, forming a spiral. In this way, it gathers energy. The vortices in water interact with each other, and water always arrives at its destination with more energy than when it started out.[4] In this way, water is a teacher in Continuum Movement as the student learns to move in tiny, subtle spirals, and small and large waves. Everything in your body, every organ, muscle, and cell, is surrounded by water and to some extent comprised of water. Become like water, and you become yourself.

Let's go directly to some words of Emilie Conrad.

Technically speaking, our bodies are not exactly ours. What we call a body is an open-ended expression of an ongoing universal process that is in constant flux, arranging, re-arranging, and experimenting as new formations come into existence. The continuum of life on land takes place with the galaxy and humans alike…. The fluid presence in our bodies is our fundamental environment; we are the moving water brought to land…. When we see a newborn, essentially we are looking at the movement of water made flesh…. We are seeing a fluid system meeting the electro-magnetic field of the Earth, where an elegant exchange begins to take place. [5]

Water's Magic

Water carries within it the vibration of everything that is placed in it.[6] It is the ultimate example of receptivity. Water is perhaps the most resilient, adaptable substance on the planet. It can harden into ice and disappear into vapor. It is strong enough to gradually dissolve rock. In fact, each drop of rain forms an almost perfect sphere whose surface tension is strong enough to blast microscopic bits out of any landscape. It is an essential substance. One more thing about water is that it absorbs energy from light and converts it to different types of energy, such as optical, electrical, mechanical, and chemical energy.[7]

Water is the medium between heaven and earth. Water is transparent to light. When you become like water, you become transparent, adaptable, resilient, and strong. You become quite receptive, and being receptive means you can allow love in. This is what I mean when I say that to become like water is to become yourself—your true self, who is strong, adaptable, resilient, receptive, responsive, transparent, and fully capable of loving and absorbing love!

If water is the means, medium, and message of Continuum Movement, the octopus is its best representative here on earth. If you want to get a real feeling for what a student of Continuum Movement is striving for, watch a video of an octopus. Its shape-shifting adaptability, strength and fluidity are what every serious student of Continuum Movement strives to emulate.

We have seen how wounds of life affect our psyche. How they shape what we believe to be true about ourselves and others, how they influence our ability to bond and sustain intimate relationships, how they affect our brain, our nervous system, our physical structure and the muscles, fascia, and fluids of our body. Repeatedly, I have argued that it is the organism as a whole that must be understood and addressed. Given that we are so highly fluid, it just makes simple sense that an approach that recognizes and addresses us as fluid creatures will have far-reaching implications. If we don't address this level, we will continue to get stuck in our defensive circuitry. If we work just at the psychological level, too much of our organism is not attended to, and the inevitable result will be limitations in the growth we can attain. Of course, working on the psychological and relational levels will influence our muscles, fascia, and fluids, but not nearly as much as addressing them directly.

In Continuum Movement, we make sounds for the purpose of penetrating tissues and stimulating fluids. If you stand in front of a big gong and bang it, the sounds are intensely palpable. They vibrate tissues. The kinds of sounds made in Continuum Movement are often vowel-like sounds such as O or E. These sounds are directed into different areas of the body. Ultimately, the sound should be sufficient to generate movement of tissue. Initially, the student may attempt to consciously make such movements, going slower than you can even imagine. After a while, the student is listening for the movements that want to happen. It is a dance between intention and attention. In a sense, the very essence of Continuum Movement is learning to merge your consciousness with the deepest layers of your body. In doing so, your tissues are enriched by the increasing vibrancy of their fluids.

To accomplish this, you must slow way down to a level that can be challenging to those of us with our iPads and cell phones, multitasking as we eat, drive, and text. For some, it seems impossible. Yet, when you slow way down, that's when you are able to enter into depths of your body that you previously could not have imagined. By slowing way down, you can energize the fluids, and slowly over time you feel yourself becoming more sensual, which is simply another way of saying that you are becoming more alive.

The Body is Movement

From a Continuum Movement perspective, the body *is* movement. You don't "do" movement; you learn to participate with, enrich, and enhance the movements that you are. Included in the movements that you are, are links to your ancestral heritage, so it is natural for those ancestral movements to arise in your consciousness. You can literally feel your primordial self arising. You are connected to a greater life sphere; it is a universal connection. All too often, human suffering comes from having a much too limited sense of self. The value of these movement experiences broadens and enriches your sense of who you are.

Continuum Movement is a secular process, and yet it has a powerful transpersonal dimension. It offers a tangible, realistic, and intelligent way to understand a basic premise of transpersonal psychology and of many spiritual traditions: namely, that we are all connected. We are connected via the water that is most of what we are, and by the water that surrounds us and in which we dwell. As we engage this work, we gradually enhance our capacity for fluid resonance. Resonance carries information. It is how we can tune in to another in a very deep, whole-body way.

Fluid Movement is the Movement of Love

Resonance allows two people to vibrate in each other's presence. As bodies become more fluid and more resonant, they can transmit and receive, simultaneously, a force that is delicious to experience. Again, we can call this love. It can be in a sexual context, and it can also be in a loving context that isn't sexual, at all.

Let's hear it in Emilie Conrad's own words:

> It took me many years to recognize that the undulating fluid that I felt in my body is the movement of love. Looking back, it seems so obvious—that the undulating waves of primordial motion are the movements of love. Not emotional love but an encompassing atmosphere of love—a love that has its own destiny. [8]

As you progress in your Continuum Movement practice, your undulations become increasingly subtler. They become waves within waves, ripples changing speed, direction, and size. You continue to let go of the "me" and its rigid limits and begin to sense whispers of your origin. Occasionally, there is a sense of surrender to the Divine in an almost ecstatic yielding to the sublime. Your basic connection to this resonant field becomes more available. This field is the ultimate healer, the perfect mother/father. It reminds you that you are not alone. This is a felt presence, not a conceptual presence, and it is always available. It is always already here to comfort you and love you, and it never leaves you. What could compare?

For a list of Continuum Teachers worldwide, check www. continuummovement.com/teachers. If there is not a teacher in your area, or if you can't find a convenient workshop to attend, there are many movement disciplines that can help foster coherence. Yoga, Authentic Movement, Somatic Movement, Feldenkrais, and BodyMind

Centering are among those you can choose from. Google makes it easy. Start soon.

1. For more information about Susan Harper, who is among the finest teachers I have ever met, see www.continuummontage.com.

2. Ho, Mae-Wan, *Living Rainbow H2O*, World Scientific Press, pp. 4-5.

3. Conrad, Emilie, *Life on Land: The Story of Continuum*, North Atlantic Press, pp. 290-291.

4. Pangman, M.J. and Evans, Melanie, *Dancing with Water: The New Science of Water,* pp. 2-3.

5. Conrad, Emilie, *Life on Land: The Story of Continuum*, North Atlantic Press, pp. 290-291.

6. See Pollack, Gerald, *The Fourth Phase of Water*, Ebner and Sons, 2013, for a complete discussion of this phenomenon.

7. Ibid., p. 119.

8. Conrad, Emilie, *Life on Land: The Story of Continuum*, North Atlantic Press, pp. 320-321.

CHAPTER 17

YOUR BODY FROM THE INSIDE:
SOMATICS AND PHILOSOPHER THOMAS HANNA

"The Human Body is not an instrument to be used, but a realm of one's being to be experienced, enriched and thereby educated"
~ Thomas L. Hanna

Speed Kills

Until this point, I have talked about the wounds and injuries of childhood as being the primary source of our diminished coherence. Another source of diminished wholeness and freedom is the tendency in our culture to live in overdrive. This is very much related to an insufficient comprehension of what it means to be embodied. The combination of the heavy value we place on achievement and production, and technology that keeps us ever "online" has resulted in a population that is losing the ability to really let go and let down. In the context of the work of Thomas L. Hanna, we will understand how this contributes to chronic tension, chronic pain, and a lessening of our coherence.

Dr. Thomas L. Hanna began his career as a philosopher and served as chairman of the department of philosophy at the University of Florida. Themes that ran through his philosophical writings[1] included: What does it mean to be human? What does it mean to be free? What does it mean to be embodied? What is the relationship between freedom in the body and social repression? How is tyranny exercised? To my knowledge, no one has elucidated the importance of freedom in the body and what I have been calling the "quality of tissues" with such depth and clarity as Tom Hanna.

In the previous chapter, we saw how Continuum Movement focuses on the sensations of the body, and Tom Hanna couldn't agree more! At the heart of Tom's theory is the critical importance of awakening the whole sensing-feeling body. Because of the need to tame and control a harsh environment, the human being had to develop and privilege the rational mind—fair enough. Now, however, we have built an altar to it and exalt it far beyond its current usefulness. It's time to bring the organism into balance. It's time to privilege the whole feeling body.

My body was in need of serious restoration. By any criteria, my level of disconnection would have been judged as serious, indeed. The work of Tom Hanna was one more discipline that helped me reintegrate. As with the work of Moshe Feldenkrais, there are two components to what Tom called Hanna Somatic Education: a hands-on component and a classroom component, the latter consisting of movement exercises.[2] Let's take a look at how Tom put it together.

Soma vs. Body: Experience of the Body from the Inside

When we look at a human being from the outside, whether he is walking, sitting or lying on an operating table, what we see is a body.

Anatomists, physiologists, and physicians have studied the human body intensively. The data they have accumulated is immense, impressive, and has benefited mankind enormously. However, it is not complete, nor can it ever be complete until we recognize that we are observing the organism from just one side, the outside looking in.

When a human being looks from the inside, he feels something quite different. This is perhaps Thomas Hanna's most important contribution to the field of human understanding. In order to facilitate this crucial distinction between being outside and looking in, and feeling from the inside, he chose the term *soma* to name the living body *as it is experienced from the inside*.

Body is a third-person view. *The* body. A *thing*. Pronouns in our language refer to *I*, a first person reference; *you*, a second-person reference; and, *it*, a third-person reference. The body is referred to in the third person as an *it*.

Soma, from the Greek *living body*, refers to sensations, feelings, movements, and intentions. Hanna was emphatic that any attempt to understand the human being without understanding this somatic view must be incomplete. Science and medicine, so committed to its third-person, objective view, are incomplete and doomed to suffer inadequate and insufficient results. They must realize that the human body must also be studied *from the inside*. This is the somatic perspective. Quoting Hanna:

> The great calamity of the human sciences is that we have, as it were, ganged up on ourselves. Only one person can see himself or herself as a first-person somatic being, but millions of people can see that person as a third-person bodily being. Consequently, these millions can join together and observe, measure, and diagram the objective body of the human person. That is the easy and obvious way taken by sciences. [3]

But what is obvious and easy is not always complete and effective.

Sensory-motor Amnesia: The Loss of an Ability We Forget We Had

*"The most suppressive forces are the ones
no one knows are at work."*
~ Ken Anbendar

For Tom Hanna, how we age is the most obvious consequence of the gross neglect of the first-person, *I* side of the body. The myths of aging, as he referred to them, are that we believe it's normal to lose mobility, become increasingly more rigid, and beset with aches and pains. We can study the third-person body from now until eternity, but until we include the somatic perspective, we will miss the mark, because we will miss the condition that underlies the majority of problems associated with aging. He called that underlying condition *sensory-motor amnesia* (SMA). There are some 640 skeletal muscles in the human body; and SMA is a chronic contraction of many if not most of those muscles. Optimally, skeletal muscles operate under the control of the cerebral cortex, which means they're under voluntary control and can be contracted or relaxed at will. Sensory Motor Amnesia is the loss of voluntary control of our musculature, which results in chronic tension. It means not being able to fully contract or fully relax a given muscle.

As we have seen, the brain can be viewed as having three major parts: the reptilian brain, the mid-brain or limbic system, and the cerebral cortex, which is the most recent part of our brain. However, as a result of impacts and insults, sustained stress, abuse, speed, etc., the locus of control of many muscles shifts from the higher cortex to the lower centers of the brain. Once this has happened, you cannot consciously will those muscles to relax, because the cortex isn't receiving the sensory input necessary for relaxation to occur. Muscle action occurs in a feedback loop between sensory and motor neurons. Without the sensory input, the cortex loses that control and the muscles remain contracted.

Remember, chronic tension serves as a feedback loop to the limbic system, maintaining it in a state of hypersensitivity, which means that it sets off the fight/flight response at a lower threshold or is unable to turn it off, which is another negative consequence of what Hanna called sensory-motor amnesia, or chronic tension. Further, we don't know that we have lost this ability.

This morning, my wife and I were walking in the park. In front of us were two young adults with their dog. The contrast in how they moved was striking—free and flowing movements throughout the dog's body and very little movement flowing in the two humans. We have lost ability, and we don't know it.

Reflexes That Organize Patterns of Muscle Tension

Based on his clinical work and understanding of neurophysiology, Hanna described two basic reflexes that organize patterns of muscle tension: *the red light reflex* and the *green light reflex*. He calls the accumulative effects of these two reflexes the *senile vise grip*.

The red light reflex

The red light reflex is a startle or withdrawal response. For example, if you are walking down the street and suddenly hear a loud explosion or the sound of gunfire, in milliseconds, your body will move into a protective posture. The muscles of your jaw will contract, followed immediately by the muscles around your eyes and brow. Your shoulder muscles contract, elevating your shoulders as your head juts forward. Your abdominal muscles contract, bringing your chest down and your head farther forward as your diaphragm contracts, obstructing your breathing. Your pelvic floor tightens, and your knees point inward as your ankles roll inward.

Obviously, just as the stress response is adaptive and necessary for survival, this reflexive action is a means of protection. When the muscles can relax and return to their normal state after the danger passes, there is no problem. When this reflex becomes habitual, as for example, when a child is frightened repeatedly, the muscles cannot return to a relaxed state and sensory-motor amnesia kicks in.

The green light reflex—Speed kills

The green light reflex is another way through which tension accumulates and coherence diminishes. The green light reflex is the opposite of the red light reflex. Hanna sees it as a consequence of modern living, in which we are guided by alarm clocks, schedules, calendars, quotas, coffee, and deadlines. It is the tendency in our culture to live in overdrive. Essentially, the green light reflex is a "Let's go!" reflex; it contracts the large extensor muscles of the back. Whereas the red light reflex is protective and curls the body forward, the green light reflex is assertive and prods us to go. As it contracts the extensors of the back, it lifts the chest forward. Both sets of movements are adaptive and essential, but when habituated, they cause sensory motor amnesia and its ensuing problems. It is clear that individuals who have suffered a great deal of fear tend to have a red light reflex posture, whereas individuals who are assertive and "out there" tend to have a green light reflex posture.

The senile vise grip

In aging, most people reveal a combination of both red light and green light reflexes. The fear and withdrawal reflex *and* the "Let's go" reflex are revealed in rotations and distortions of posture. Both are present, and we call the results "the challenges of aging." Once you know what to look for, the evidence is everywhere. Most individuals do not grow old in an agile, vibrant body. The forward-thrust heads, the elevated or pulled-back shoulders, the sunken or pushed out chests, the ribs compressed into the pelvis, the dense, rigid legs, the very tight backs with exaggerated lumbar curves or flattened lower backs with no lumbar curves—all broadcast habituated reflexes and announce the accumulated effects of our wounding, of living in overdrive, chronic stress, and poor movement habits. The muscles cannot fully relax, we cannot reach our full potential, and we will not age with grace and fluidity. This is what Tom Hanna saw about how our bodies change the way they do. His solution called for somatic education.

Somatic Education

Hanna Somatic Education brings consciousness to our muscles and frees our movements. Based initially on the work of Feldenkrais, Hanna created a clinical-educational approach to help people who are in pain and teach people to live with more freedom. Like Feldenkrais, Hanna offered both a one-on-one experience with a trained practitioner and group-movement lessons with a teacher. Since muscles require sensory feedback in order to function, he built the work around sensory awareness. Heightening sensory awareness increases a muscle's ability to release. What has been outside of our control returns once again.

The field of Somatics has developed over the last half century through a process of inquiry into how consciousness inhabits the living body. Today, the field of Somatic Education has a growing international organization called the International Somatic Movement Education and Therapy Association (or ISMETA), which includes a wide variety of somatic disciplines. Tom Hanna was not the founder of the organization and was probably never a member. However, the body of work he left behind makes him indubitably its preeminent philosopher.

Some things I got from meeting and studying with Tom Hanna— in addition to a looser lower back for which I was eternally grateful— is what I would like you to get. *The quality of our tissues is important to the quality of our lives.* Ida Rolf focused on the fascia, a ubiquitous tissue, Reich on emotions and the muscles, Emilie on the body's fluids, and Tom on the muscles and the brain. For me, he rounded out an understanding of what it means to be alive in these bodies, an understanding that we must address our bodies in more than one way to restore our full humanity and potential.

Although Tom Hanna focused on graceful and pain-free aging, his work and thoughts had bearing on how we live our lives. In her lovely book, *Daring Greatly: How the Courage to be Vulnerable Transforms the Way We Live, Love, Parent and Lead*, Dr. Brené Brown states that the courage to be vulnerable is what brings purpose and meaning to our lives. She talks about the importance of whole-hearted engagement in all areas of our lives, as well as the importance of being willing to be uncertain, take risks, and cultivate compassion, relaxation, rest, authenticity, and many other great qualities. However, like most psychologists writing about how to improve the quality of our lives, she assumes that we can decide from our will to make a change in the deepest layers of our personality and behavior without changing the quality of our bodies.

Once you understand the insights of Tom Hanna, Ida Rolf, Moshe Feldenkrais, Emilie Conrad, and many others in the field of Somatics, it is clear why the hundreds of thousands of books written on self-improvement have not resulted in hundreds of millions of people living whole-heartedly and enjoying fabulous intimate relationships and good health. If these authors haven't been convincing enough, then the work of Dr. Peter Levine should provide that last ounce of convincing. It's to his work we will go next.

RESOURCES

The Novato Institute for Somatic Education

Also google Feldenkrais or Functional Integration or Awareness Through Movement

1. See *The Body of Life* (1980), *The End of Tyranny: An Essay on the Possibility of America* (1976) and *Bodies in Revolt: A Primer in Somatic Thinking* (1970) to appreciate the depth and importance of Hanna's philosophical writings.

2.   Hanna, T., Somatics: *Reawakening the Mind's Control of Movement, Flexibility and Health*, Perseus Books, 1988.

3.   Ibid., p. 20.

CHAPTER 18

HEALING OVERWHELMING IMPACTS:
DR. PETER LEVINE'S SOMATIC EXPERIENCING

"...Your deepest presence is in every small
contracting and expanding.
The two as beautifully balanced and coordinated as birdwings."
~ Rumi

Throughout this book, I have referred to the whole organism or the whole human being, including relationship skills and capacities, belief structures, identities (or one's sense of self), physical structure, movement of structure and tissues, and even the very water that comprises 70 percent or so of our bodies. Each of the visionaries I have chronicled contributed to an aspect of understanding that whole. Peter Levine has made an enormous contribution to our understanding of what happens to the body—particularly the autonomic nervous system—when an individual is overwhelmed by fear and helplessness.

Reich was a psychoanalyst, not a Somatic practitioner; nevertheless, his contribution was seminal to understanding that healing must consider the body as well as the psyche if we intend to reach our full potential. In classroom talks, I heard Peter Levine say he has attempted to stand on the shoulders of Wilhelm Reich. Both Reich and Levine understood that the autonomic nervous system was significantly compromised when there was significant stasis in the structure. Reich attempted to release the body and defensive patterns while restoring autonomic equilibrium via high-intensity breathing and explosive expressions or catharsis. Levine did just the opposite. He realized that the best way to restore the autonomic nervous system's functioning when human beings are highly traumatized is to work with a very small amount of excitement and very small releases. Peter's discharges were homeopathic in size compared to Reich's.

In order to understand Levine's contribution to the importance of treating the living body as a whole, let's examine a hypothetical situation and a fictional character. Rob is an extraordinarily healthy being, having had an excellent upbringing that included much love and care. Impacts and insults were minimal. Then, one day, let's say, he suffered a massive trauma. He was mugged, beaten, and tossed in front of an oncoming vehicle. When the ambulance arrived, the EMTs were highly functional; they treated him efficiently but like an object, as they had no comprehension of the psychophysiological effects of trauma. Through the consummate skill of the medical staff and the wizardry of modern medical technology, Rob lives. However, the intensity of this impact *could* usher in a full-blown, post-traumatic stress disorder (PTSD), even though, previously, Rob had been robust in every sense of the word. (Without doubt, this high-quality upbringing makes it much less likely that Rob would develop PTSD.)

If an individual like Rob is not given the proper care and allowed time to "discharge" the shock, he could have symptoms and difficulties for the rest of his life. As Dr. Levine explains,

> The nervous system compensates for being in a state of self-perpetuating arousal by setting off a chain of adaptations that eventually bind and organize the energy into 'symptoms', such as: hyperarousal, constriction, dissociation (including denial), feelings of helplessness, hypervigilance, hyperactivity, exaggerated emotional and startle responses, nightmares, mood swings, reduced ability to deal with stress, difficulty sleeping. [1]

A variety of symptoms can occur over time, but this example gives you an idea of the long-term effects of serious trauma. This single high-impact incident, uncomplicated by an early history of serious impacts and insults, is the kind that is best treated by the Levine system.[2]

Throughout his study, Dr. Levine looked to animals in the wild for inspiration and to make sense of the symptoms presented by traumatized individuals. He observed that these animals often were subject to near-death experiences. Strangely, however, if they escaped death, they did not suffer PTSD. Why? Dr. Levine wondered. And why do humans who endure similar fates so often develop PTSD symptoms? To understand the answers to these questions, we must return to the *polyvagal model* of the ANS and review what occurs when there is a high-impact traumatic reaction.

In Chapter 11, we saw how social engagement is the first line of defense against stress. The ability to feel and deal, to self-assert, to ask for support, to share one's vulnerabilities, and to interpersonally care for self are all stress-protective, which means that, at the level of the nervous system, it is the ventral vagal complex that mediates these activities. When the mechanisms mediated by the ventral vagal system are compromised, our next line of defense is the sympathetic nervous system with its fight/flight mechanisms.[3] This is where we go to protect ourselves.

In the kind of high-impact events that are described throughout Dr. Levine's writings, the sympathetic nervous system and the fight/flight mechanism are overwhelmed. The organism can neither marshal the resources to fight nor to run away. Peter Levine describes what takes place. First, there is a sudden halt in activity, an arrest, characterized by extreme vigilance and scanning to orient for the danger. Next is an attempt to escape. If this is not possible, there is an attempt to fight. But if neither flight nor fight is possible, all that remains is to freeze, to become scared stiff and/or collapse. Let's use Peter's words to describe exactly what he calls a trauma. "Trauma occurs when we are intensely frightened and are either physically restrained or perceive that we are trapped. We freeze in paralysis and/or collapse in overwhelming helplessness."[4]

As we saw in Chapter 11, the freeze response is mediated by the dorsal vagal complex and involves the viscera to a great degree and the heart to some degree. In preparing to fight or flee and not being able to, all the muscular tissues tighten and remain tight. In addition, with freeze, the guts and organs also tighten. The animal in us is preparing to be captured or eaten, so going numb makes very good sense. There are several reasons for this defense. In the wild, there is a chance that the predator will conclude the prey is already dead and not want to eat "dead meat." Or the predator might get careless and allow the prey an opportunity to escape. At the very least, the prey won't feel the pain of becoming lunch. Nature, in its mercy, has designed a mechanism by which the prey can dissociate, "not be there," for his final fate. This is an act of dissociation in which our consciousness leaves our tissues.

However extreme this example of dissociation may be, this mechanism nevertheless is used in less extreme situations. Many human beings walk the earth in a partial state of numbness, unaware that their essential nature is fluid, sensual, and erotic.[5] Our essential nature is life flowing. However, just one impact of extreme intensity or thousands of much lesser intensity will strip us of our birthright to be the vibrant, awake, loving, sensual, erotic beings that nature intended.

How many millions of individuals have suffered an impact of this degree? Many types of events can result in such a traumatic reaction. Rapes, muggings and beatings, automobile accidents, falls, birth traumas, war traumas, and even surgery can cause this reaction. How many millions of individuals walk around never having resolved the impacts they may have knowingly or unknowingly received? They walk around in a state of contraction with both their sympathetic and parasympathetic systems stuck in high gear.

When an animal in the wild survives a "freeze" state, it shakes, vibrates, and quivers. Little by little, it thereby discharges the impacted energy; all of the fight/flight energy that has accumulated is gradually released. The animal is then free to go back to peacefully munching grass. The experience is resolved. We humans rarely allow this natural process to take place. We pick ourselves up, dust ourselves off, and start all over again. If we are assisted by well-meaning friends or an EMT team, we are likely encouraged to lie still, calm down, and not shake. Recovery is interrupted. I am speaking here of high-impact traumas, but what about the impacts and insults that I have referred to throughout the book? If their effects are not resolved *through the tissues of the body*, they accumulate. Over time, undischarged energy forms the foundation for a myriad of physical and emotional symptoms.

We are designed to be self-regulating and to *digest* experience. With a regulated, resilient system comes the experience of "I can," of being able to handle life. There is a sense of having options, of feeling connected to ourselves and able to enjoy life and deeply relax. High-impact trauma and an accumulation of life's wounds interfere with the best of what life offers.

Levine's Method for Treating Trauma

In addition to bringing forth a psychobiological understanding of what happens when an individual is subject to a high-impact traumatic event, Peter Levine has also developed a method for its treatment.

Below is an outline of the SE protocol to offer a flavor of this work. A sharp contrast to the cathartic approach of Reich and his descendants is apparent. Dealing with a nervous system that has been overwhelmed, Levine brilliantly realized that to attempt cathartic interventions would only exacerbate the situation and "re-traumatize" the individual.

It is important to remember that SE is not employed in a rigid, sequential, unidirectional manner. Although it is a protocol with nine steps, the steps are intuitively applied to meet the needs of the client. Usually, they are repeated several times, always allowing the client time to process each step as the healing process unfolds.[6]

1. Develop safety

As with any therapy, developing safety is paramount. The more traumatized you are, the greater your need for safety. The therapist must present a calm, stable presence and hold an energetic field that can serve as a container for the client.

2. Support the client in exploring and accepting her body sensations

Second, the therapist supports you in exploring and accepting your body sensations. Many individuals present with a very limited repertoire in the feeling sense of themselves. The greater the intensity and frequency of impacts and insults you have experienced, the less access you are likely to have to your sensations. The therapist must proceed with care to prevent you from being overwhelmed by sensation. Entering into the realm of sensation is often fraught. The skill the therapist needs involves finding and noting each small, positive shift in your affect and any and all indications of a bright moment in your experience or memory. These bright moments will be resources for you, helping you know that sensation is not all scary or bad. As you gain confidence that you can enter this terrain and still be okay, that you can manage the experience, you will likely become increasingly more willing to stay with difficult, uncomfortable sensations. The therapist won't allow you to stay with them for long until she knows you have learned to access your own resources as needed.

3. Pendulate and contain

Whereas trauma is about being stuck in pain, pendulation is about mimicking the rhythms of nature, the rhythms of expansion and contraction. So now, the therapist gradually moves back and forth from a positive or resourced place to the sensations associated with trauma. Gently, artfully, the therapist directs your awareness from a place that feels okay to one that doesn't. It is a slow, back-and-forth process.

4. Titration

With pendulation, we enter the fourth step of the process, which is closely related to it, and that is titration. Usually, intense explosive emotions like terror and rage are associated with traumatic events. Entering a field of emotional landmines, the therapist works to prevent explosions. Instead, the work is to help you learn to digest very small bits of energy at a time, which is why the term titration is used. You are learning self-regulation. In chemistry, titration is a process in which small amounts of a substance are mixed with another substance to produce a small effect, a fizzle rather than an explosion.

5. Restore active biological defenses

In a traumatic event, the movements involved in the activities of fighting or running away—as well as the impulse—are truncated or completely impeded. The energy generated for those activities is vast, and it implodes into the body. It is in this stage of the work that the therapist looks for minute body movements that have even the mere suggestion of running or fighting and slowly works to facilitate your ability to feel the urge and feel these tiny movements. Numerous times, clients have felt the urge to run, to feel their legs as if in motion. The result is often a discharge of energy that is experienced as tingling, vibrating, or trembling sensations in the legs.

In this step you are beginning to regain essential biological defenses you lost as a consequence of severe impact. Along with that loss, you likely had experienced a profound sense of helplessness. When you most needed to run or to fight, you were unable get away or even to move. You are empowered as the channels for those activities are restored. Once again, you can take care of yourself. You can move! You know you have survived!

6. Uncouple fear from the immobility

The sixth step is vitally important and is at the very core of healing high-intensity trauma. As we have seen, when fight/flight is overwhelmed, the only remaining option is to freeze. In the wild, when an animal enters "freeze," it will, when the predator has gone, begin to vibrate, at first slowly and then intensely. Vibrating will end the immobility. The animal will be able to run or to fight another day.

In humans, however, this doesn't happen so cleanly for a variety of reasons, one being that most humans have a large accumulation of insults and impacts; for another, humans have lost contact with their instinctual nature. Shaking may feel weak or even silly. Whatever the reasons, humans rarely fully release the impact of those traumas. It is not uncommon for the immobility or freeze to remain deeply held in the body, often for the remainder of life. It is a frightening and exhausting way to feel and to live.

Ironically, it can be equally frightening to exit this immobility. There is tremendous rage associated with immobility, and bottled-up rage is terrifying. It requires skill on the part of the therapist to negotiate these states with patience and dexterity. As the active defensive responses are slowly restored and fear is slowly diminished, you can enter into the immobility and have a direct experience of it. It, too, is titrated so that the rage associated with it can be slowly discharged without terrifying catharsis. Traumatized people often have tremendous shame for feeling immobilized and paralyzed and thus unable to act well in their own behalf. When the fear has been reduced sufficiently, you can, by entering into the immobility, exit it, slowly gaining more and more access to your sensations.

7. Discharge energy

The seventh step is the discharge of the energy that has been held in the hyperarousal state. A great deal of energy implodes in your body when you receive a high-intensity impact. When all the mobilization that goes into readiness to fight or to run is turned and held inside, that energy must be discharged to restore a state of equilibrium. An SE therapist is always looking for and encouraging discharge of energy at a pace you can handle. Changes in skin temperature or color, for example, can be indications of your nervous system discharging. The therapist must become expert at reading your body cues.

8. Restore self-regulation and equilibrium

A good feeling comes with the resolution of a serious traumatic event. You feel that you can trust something inside yourself. It is a sense that disturbing events don't have to be crippling, that they can be experienced and released. As your self-regulation improves, it is important to bring these changes to your awareness. As your awareness grows, you and your therapist can enter the ninth step.

9. Engage the here and now

Being able to engage the here and now, to bring presence and flow to an activity, is a hallmark of good health. An inevitable consequence of serious, impactful trauma *or* an accumulation of insults and impacts is loss of the ability to be fully present. Unresolved, high-intensity trauma, as well as the accumulation of thousands of smaller wounds, can seriously diminish full participation and enjoyment of all areas of life. Therefore, as you begin to reclaim yourself, more of you is available to live and love.

The above protocol offers just a flavor of Peter Levine's work. Somatic Experiencing filled out my understanding of what it takes to heal the wounds of childhood. With SE and the previous four chapters, I hope I have filled out for you a new picture of the body and its well-being. In a sense, I have shown you five different perspectives on the body and healing that I believe are all-important. These are the body and unexpressed emotion, the physical structure of the body, the neuromuscular system and its reflexes, the fluids and tissues of the body and movement, and the effects of impacts on the autonomic nervous system.

You may not have undergone any significant, high-impact traumatic experiences in your entire lifetime; or you may have but don't know, such as a seriously traumatic birth. Nevertheless, I have almost never met an individual who didn't have room to improve all of those capacities that are seriously affected by a traumatic experience. We can all become more resilient, adaptable, capable of deeper and more satisfying intimate connections, more fluid, more receptive and responsive and so forth.

I have engaged all that I have described in this book, and I am grateful that I continue to feel the benefits. I have said that there is one ability in which we can all improve, and that is learning to let love in. So, let's go next to Diana Fosha and AEDP. In so many ways, AEDP is about learning to let love in.

RESOURCES: Somatic Experiencing Trauma Institute, www. traumahealing.com.

1. Levine, Peter, *Waking the Tiger*, North Atlantic Books, p. 145.

2. In the more typical situation of an individual with a moderate to severe history of impacts and insults who shows up after a high-impact event, Levine's method is best used in the context of a relational psychotherapy, in my opinion.

3. I refer the reader back to Chapter 11 for a review of the polyvagal model of the autonomic nervous system.

4. Levine, Peter, *In an Unspoken Voice*, North Atlantic Books, 2010, p. 48.

5. When I use the word *erotic*, I do not mean it in the way the word is commonly used. I am speaking of a highly relational, pleasurable connection to life itself.

6. See Levine, Peter, *In an Unspoken Voice*, for a beautifully detailed explanation of the process.

CHAPTER 19

LETTING LOVE IN:
DIANA FOSHA AND ACCELERATED EXPERIENTIAL DYNAMIC PSYCHOTHERAPY

"Everything flowers from within of self blessing;
Though sometimes it is necessary to reteach a thing of its loveliness,
To put a hand on the brow of the flower
and retell it in words and in touch,
'You are lovely'
Until it flowers again from within, of self-blessing"
~ Galaway Kinnell

It wasn't many decades ago that only so-called crazy people went to a psychotherapist. There had to be "something wrong with you" to even consider such an intrepid act. Even today, when millions upon millions of individuals and couples regularly visit a therapist's office, a faint hint of blame still exists. From my perspective, albeit biased, finding and working with a good therapist is an act of great intelligence. Let me state from the outset that you don't need to be depressed or suffering from intense anxiety or have an addiction to receive a great deal of benefit from a course of AEDP or any good relationally oriented therapy. Of course if you are experiencing those things, all the more important to find a good therapist. In any event, it can be an enriching experience, and help you enjoy close relationships even more.

All human beings need good relationships in order to thrive. But here is the Gordian Knot: In order to have good relationships as an adult, it helps a great deal if your parents were able to be present with you, empathize with you, attune to you emotionally, and everything else I presented in Chapter 4. Think back to how children have been treated for centuries, and it is easy to understand why we see human beings who are challenged by relationships everywhere we look. A therapist who has done her work and is capable of engaging in a good relationship while imparting skills to her client is a treasure to be held in the highest esteem.

I want to emphasize that you can have the most vibrant of human tissues and the most aligned physical structure, but that does not, by itself, guarantee you the ability to form great, intimate relationships. It supports your capacity to do so, but you must take one more step and learn how to utilize and apply your capacities with the people who mean the most to you. But what if you have never had a real experience of being seen, understood, and met with emotional connection? What if you received only a little bit of attuned caring love or empathy? What if you never learned to soothe yourself instead of reflexively slashing back when your feelings are bruised? For me this is where a psychotherapist can help and guide you. A relationship with an older, wiser other can be so helpful.

For me, the decision to look in the Yellow Pages for a psychotherapist saved my life. I was twenty years old, in the Air Force, and drinking myself silly. After awakening in the back seat of my car at five a.m., bleeding from my throat due to outrageously excessive drinking and hollering, I knew I needed help. The type of therapy I received in those early years is best described as psychodynamically oriented therapy, which meant the therapist listened to me talk about my problems and attempted to provide meaning within a framework first established by Freud.

On one hand, very little change occurred in the work; however, one single comment by my therapist, Dr. Lou, made all the difference in the world. The dialogue went like this:

"I want to major in psychology, but what would I do with a bachelor's in psych.?"

"Get your Ph.D."

"But, I barely went to high school."

"You can do it."

Wow! If this Harvard-trained M.D. psychiatrist thought I could do it, then....

This conversation took place in 1964. In 1967, I began a doctoral program at the University of Kansas in clinical psychology. Dr. Lou was right. I could do it. He was able to see and hold a higher view of me than I was. This is one of many gifts a therapist can offer.

From 1964 to 2008, I experienced and studied a variety of different approaches to psychotherapy. All contributed to who I am today both personally and professionally. I have listed them at the end of this chapter. If you are interested, you can look them up.

Of all the psychotherapies I experienced and studied, the most humanly relational one I encountered is called Accelerated Experiential Dynamic Psychotherapy (AEDP).[1] Dr. Diana Fosha is the founder of this approach to psychotherapy. It is elegant, effective, and very relational. What makes this approach so beautiful is that it explicitly and without shyness states that therapy is about growth and transformation, and not merely about treating symptoms. It is about helping people to live their lives fully, to engage in life, to work, and to love. AEDP isn't content with symptom alleviation and stress reduction; it aims higher—towards thriving, flourishing, and resilient functioning.

Further, AEDP explicitly aims to provide those ingredients that so many human beings did not receive in their first primary relationships. As we saw in Chapter 4, as an infant and young child, we require a good dose of an adult's presence, someone who can be there emotionally, who can welcome us into the world and delight in our being. We need someone who can attune to our feelings states and meet us there; we need someone who can support our deeply ingrained motivation to grow and fully inhabit our true selves. We need someone who has the capacity to empathize, to feel what we feel and support our emotional explorations and development. To the degree that these basic needs are not met, we suffer and don't develop the capacities to engage others in an open-hearted, whole-hearted, undefended way.

AEDP Explicitly Provides What Was Missing

From the very first moment, AEDP therapy seeks to provide what was missing. Almost all schools of psychotherapy emphasize to some extent the importance of the therapist offering unconditional positive regard, empathy, and warmth. This is more front and center for some approaches; others keep it more in the background. In all my years in the field, I have never encountered a psychotherapy that so actively extends warmth, support, acknowledgement, and affirmation as AEDP does. The typical client enters therapy accustomed to living within the confines of the protective structures he created in childhood to minimize the pain of not having his essential needs met (or worse); but they are now a source of pain. The love, resonance, and good vibrations of others have a hard time penetrating and touching their heart. I cannot emphasize this enough. Based on many years of experience, I have come to believe that the lack of love that reaches the human heart is a root cause of so much human suffering. It is a lonely way to live.

So, the AEDP therapist generously and profusely offers loving words and feelings. She may meet the client with empathic prizing, such as, "I'm just so amazed at the courage you showed in standing up to your father. That couldn't have been easy." Each time the therapist makes a comment like this, she observes carefully the reactions of her patient. Usually, she will notice that the client deflects, blocks, or minimizes the care that was just extended. As we have seen, letting love in is an almost universal challenge. Gently and with care, the therapist helps her client become aware that he is not letting in the good stuff. Thus, the profusion of validations and affirmations—sincerely offered—not only provide a climate of real safety, making it much easier for the patient to soften his protective structures, but they also make it quickly clear just how the patient goes about keeping at bay what he most craves.

A beautiful moment during such therapy is when the client lets the therapist touch his heart. It is a special moment for both therapist and client. Something new has occurred. The client feels seen and valued; he begins to recognize he is genuinely loveable. I have witnessed anxiety disappear from a client's daily life as the recognition of his worth grows, session by session. As his protective structures melt, he discovers his worth and lovability, but more than that, his deep, inner strength and a sense of mastery in his life.

Transformance

Dr. Diana Fosha coined a term, *transformance*,[2] to refer to the motivational drive towards wholeness, coherence, contribution, and connection. From the very first session of therapy, the therapist looks for the manifestations of transformance, however subtle they may be. For example, a client describes his awful feelings, and the therapist acknowledges his courage in sharing them with another human being. Throughout the AEDP process, the therapist strives to recognize every moment in which the client's fundamental drive to wholeness shows up.

This approach is different from those that focus on the problem, seeking better ways to think and act or seeking to work through all the negativity and arrive at what's positive. Fosha's approach is to build the positive first. Eventually, those highly distressing and incomplete feeling experiences will surface and be addressed from a positive base; in AEDP language, "self-at-best" deals with "self-at-worst."

When individuals who have not experienced a successful intimate love relationship come in for therapy, the work is to help them feel safe enough to let their protective mechanisms down and disclose their vulnerabilities and their tenderness, as well as access their strengths and assertiveness. The work helps them learn to receive and accept authentic praise, affirmations, and acknowledgments from others—to let love in.

Here is an extreme example of how difficult it can be to take in and absorb what we most long for. As a child of six or seven, I recall kicking my grandmother if she tried to hug me. I craved affection, but I was simply incapable of letting it in. The pain associated with not receiving what you need, and especially the pain associated with receiving the awful stuff you don't need, makes it hard to accept love when it is offered.

Many years later, in my personal AEDP therapy, I found it enormously helpful to have the depths of my experience felt and seen by another, and to have my strength validated. I was able to take it in. The experience of being deeply seen is a fundamental need. Many of us live with that longing. Yet, fulfilling it often requires not only someone willing to see, but also willing to help process the pain so closely related to being seen.

The following dynamic is common in couples I see for therapy. One partner complains bitterly and frequently about the lack of care and affection from her spouse. Of course, she has picked a partner who is challenged when it comes to giving emotionally. If, in treatment, her spouse begins to come forward, invariably she is challenged in receiving. This is why, from the beginning of therapy, AEDP works to facilitate the patient's ability to receive love and care.

A beautiful feature of AEDP is the therapist's willingness to verbalize her own feeling experience. Many approaches shy away from this out of fear of blurring boundaries. Yet, what the client needs most, what he has never had, is a real, genuine relationship experience in which he is prized and cared for. For example, the therapist might express her fondness for the patient or the pain she feels in seeing how difficult something is for the patient. Whatever the expression, she then explores how the client was affected by it. Recall how important it is for an infant to have the moment to moment engagement with mother, communicating through facial expressions via the heart and via the right brain. The absence of such attunement insults the organism. When the AEDP therapist offers it open-heartedly and plentifully, it invariably evokes conflicting responses. When it does and the client is able to consciously see them; the opening has begun.

Some of the most poignant moments I have experienced while doing AEDP are when I simply say something like, "I am so sorry that happened to you." When such an expression is honest and sincere, the client can feel that someone really is there and experiencing their feelings with them. The therapist might help the client verbalize these relational moments, for example:

"What do you see when you look at me right now?"

The client might say, "Kindness."

"How does it feel to see me looking at you with kindness on my face?"

In traditional psychotherapy, the therapist is usually more passive. She doesn't judge and is kind and understanding, so over time the client will likely feel close to his therapist. In AEDP, however, the therapist actively and immediately works to establish an intimate relationship with the client. (That's why it is called *Accelerated* Experiential Dynamic Psychotherapy.) The therapist establishes a good, intimate relationship with someone who doesn't yet have the skills to establish a good, intimate relationship. In the process, the therapist points out the client's every small success. A new and secure and successful relationship is established. In this context, the old emotional wounds are brought forth and worked through in the light of the field that has been established.

Undoing Aloneness

There is another ongoing goal in the work of AEPD. When shame, guilt, and fear block our access to our deepest feelings and resources, we invariably feel very alone. It is exactly our inability to access and process these inhibitors that keep us stuck. Thus, a central objective of AEDP is to undo the painful sense of aloneness that our clients live with. In many different ways, the message expressed is, "I am here with you. Can you feel me here with you?" The client's growing sense that he is not alone is part of the healing process. By having another who can witness, hear, understand, attune to, and empathize, the client can work through the things that hurt and develop a sense of mastery in the process.

In AEDP, the client learns to participate in a shared experience, gets validation for his responses, and sees someone who is present with him and communicating nonverbally with a focus on feeling. For example, the therapist might reflect, "Your tone just changed, and I had an uneasy feeling you were moving away." The client is strongly encouraged to articulate what he notices about the therapist's nonverbal communication and how it makes him feel. Although it's been quite a few years, I can still feel my AEDP therapist's presence as a force of solace and support.

I want to mention two more features of AEDP. First, it pays exquisite attention to the body. The therapist knows whether or not she is on track by observing and tracking markers in the body. Changes in skin color, facial expression, sighs, shifts in breathing, changes in head position, changes in posture, tone of voice, and many more are signs illuminating the therapist's way. This requires the therapist to remain exquisitely attuned to the moment-to-moment changes in the client's body. It is not too dissimilar from a mother gazing into her infant's eyes and responding to the minute changes of feeling and expression revealed.

A simple exchange I had with a client just yesterday will serve as an example. After I expressed how moved I was by what she had just revealed, I noticed a deep sigh.

"I noticed a deep sigh," I said. "I wonder what you were experiencing."

She responded, "It felt like I had just released something I have been carrying for a long time."

Processing and Meta-processing

Another of Dr. Fosha's brilliant therapeutic innovations is to alternate between processing and meta-processing. In essence, meta-processing is a reflection upon the experience just completed. We want clients to take home their experiences, to integrate them, and reflecting on them with the therapist helps them do that. Their mutual reflection then may become a take-off point for another round of experiencing. For example:

"How was it for you to see the delight on my face when you asserted so powerfully?"

Patient, "It was great. I've never had anyone pleased when I came across like that."

If the therapist notices some expression that suggests a small part of the client for whom it wasn't so great, she asks about that, ushering in another round of experience.

From my perspective, AEDP is the most caring, relational, and outright loving therapy out there. At the same time, it is deeply rooted in neuroscience, relational psychology, and psychodynamic theory. The first time I heard Dr. Fosha speak, I thought I had never met anyone who embodies both sides of her brain in such a thorough and fluid way. I knew I needed to experience and study her work. Professionally, AEDP has influenced my work more than any other system. Not only has my work become more effective, but it has become much more enjoyable to do. Working in this way gives back to me as much as I give. Of course, it is very powerful for a client to see that his therapist is deeply moved by his expression.

Personally, AEDP clarified for me my challenges in letting love in and greatly enhanced my capacity to do so. As I said before, it takes more than preparing your body, and even more than changing your beliefs. It is important to experience being given to and dealing with the emotional habits and tendencies that block our receiving. AEDP trainings are being held for therapists in different parts of our country and in different parts of the world. I urge you to check out this approach. Your life will be richer for it.

RESOURCES

AEDP Institute Institute

If you are unable to find an AEDP trained therapist, here are some other resources:

Hakomi Therapy, Dr. Ron Kurtz

Complex Integration of Multiple Brain Systems (CIMBS), Dr. Albert Sheldon and Beatriz Wyn-Stanley

Gestalt Therapy, Fritz Perls

Emotionally Focused Couple's Therapy, Dr. Susan Johnson

Coherence Therapy (formerly, Depth-Oriented Brief Therapy), Bruce Ecker

1.   Fosha, Diana, *The Transforming Power of Affect*, Basic Books, 2000.

2.   Fosha, Diana, *AEDP: Transformance in Action*, Excerpted and modified from Fosha (in press). In K. J. Schneider (Ed.), "Existential-Integrative Psychotherapy: Guideposts to the Core of Practice," Routledge.

CHAPTER 20

EST, VOICE DIALOGUE, AND BRUGH JOY'S HEART CONSCIOUSNESS

"There is some kind of a sweet innocence in being human—in not having to be just happy or just sad—in the nature of being able to be both broken and whole at the same time."
~ C. JoyBell C.

Werner Erhard and the EST Training

It was January of 1974, and my friend Joe Heller was excited to tell me about a two-weekend seminar he had just completed called EST, which stands for Erhard Seminar Trainings. He was vague in describing its value except to say I would learn to wake up without an alarm clock. Why in the world would I want to learn to awaken without an alarm? That baffled me. Nevertheless, I trusted Joe and decided to attend a no-cost guest seminar. I had been out of graduate school for almost four years and was convinced I had found the real growth stuff. Anything that wasn't Gestalt therapy, Reichian therapy, or Rolf's Structural Integration was suspect. And, of course, all practitioners of these modalities dressed like leftovers from the flower children's movement.

Just imagine my eye-rolling hubris when suit-and-tie-clad Werner Erhard, looking more like a car salesman than a seminar leader, strode down the aisle of the auditorium and began exhorting his audience to acknowledge that their lives didn't work. Highly skeptical but intrigued, I handed over my deposit and enrolled in the next seminar. It's been over forty years since that day, and I still regard the EST training as among the most valuable experiences of my life.

Werner Erhard became a controversial figure. Many people objected to what they considered the pushy approach to marketing. Many believed the organization had cultish qualities and took advantage of its mostly volunteer staff. Many people objected to and feared the boot-camp approach they used in the seminar. I can certainly understand the objections. EST was unlike anything I had experienced; yet, I am filled with gratitude that it existed.[1]

My trainer, Randy McNamara, had all the qualities of a Marine drill sergeant, including a scar on his cheek that really made him look the part. His voice roared as he called out the "games" people play; the ways we aren't sincere; how we don't say what we mean; and, most of all, how we don't do what we say. Over the four days, most of the hundred or so participants had an opportunity to engage directly with Randy, and by the time each sat down, he had learned something new and profound about himself. Never had I seen such skillful facilitation. Randy never stopped until the ring of truth sounded.

I received several immense benefits from the Erhard Seminar. First, I became open to possibilities other than Gestalt therapy, Reichian therapy, and Structural Integration. Why, it turned out that even men in suits could offer me a great deal! What was important, I learned, was my experience, and I was in charge of my experience. The seminar was the beginning of a significant turnaround. I also learned the importance of integrity. I had grown up on the perimeter of the mafia; integrity was not a high value in my household. At EST, I learned how important it was to do what I said I was going to do, to keep my promises, commitments, and agreements. How else would anyone trust me? I learned how important our choice of words is. Listen to people speak and you will notice that their words are often replete with blame and carry an air of victimization or helplessness. How we speak, both to others and to ourselves, plays a huge role in shaping our lives. Words carry vibrations.

I also learned how afraid I was to simply be with another human being. There I was, a psychologist, and I had the jargon down pretty well. Yet, to be with another, without façade, was terrifying. Through various exercises, Randy showed us how afraid we were to just "be with" other people. I had no idea! Today, being with people in an open-hearted way is what I cherish and teach.

EST wasn't psychotherapy. However, it was a process that shifted the course of my life. It spawned many offshoots, which varied in quality, and it influenced the culture in a big way. Not infrequently, I hear expressions on TV or read passages in articles about how we should live that have their roots in EST. One of Werner's favorite quotes goes something like this: "When you tell all of the bad things you've been withholding, and when you tell all of the good things you've been withholding, what is left is, 'I love you.' You don't have to go looking for love; it is where you come from."

Hal Stone and Sidra Stone: The Psychology of Selves and Voice Dialogue

I think I said this before, but somebody up there likes me. When a boy grows up bullied by his mother—intimidated, threatened, beaten, and humiliated—he more than ever needs a father to be there for him. When the father is passive, withdrawn, hostile, and humiliating, that leaves a great gap in a person's psyche. Pain and inadequacy live where confidence and competence should be. It is not a very good way to go through life. Somehow, that's not how it was meant to be for me, because, over and over again, I encountered strong and loving men. From each, I took something into me that filled the void.

Hal Stone was one of those men.[2] Rugged and ruddy, he looks more like a Greek sea captain than a Jungian analyst. At the center of his teaching is the importance of owning and supporting your vulnerability. It may have been harder to hear that message had it come from someone who looked less masculine than Hal.

The Psychology of Selves

Hal and his wife Sidra began developing what they call the

Psychology of Selves and the Voice Dialogue method in the mid-70s. Their aim wasn't to develop another school of psychotherapy, but a system of awakening consciousness. Simply stated, we humans are much more than we take ourselves to be. We limit ourselves by identifying rather rigidly with the constellation of beliefs and attitudes that constitute our sense of who we are and who we are not.

Hal and Sidra use a metaphor to describe this process. If a young lion cub gets lost in a storm and is taken in by a herd of goats, over time, he assumes he is a goat and even "baahs" like a goat. The cub becomes a full-grown lion, but he still believes and acts like a goat because that is all he knows. One day, an old lion comes along and sees what is happening. He takes the misguided lion by the scruff of the neck and places him in front of a pool of water. The young lion sees what he is, and with the help of the old lion, he learns how to roar. The awakening process has begun.

Now, let's look at Hal and Sidra's concept of "selves," or "parts." We have seen that we are fluid creatures who have the capability to shift in a variety of ways to meet novel conditions or necessities. In other words, we are more than we think we are. For example, in the boardroom, you can be decisive, unequivocal, and analytical. In the bedroom, you can be a passionately sexual, playful, and sensual creature; you can be dominant, loving, hot, submissive, tender, sweet, caring, fierce, or even another fantasy character altogether. You can be practical, rational, and empirical; or, you can be intuitive and mystical. You can be vulnerable, playful, and innocent, or any combination of these. For instance, an individual might identify with the rational, serious, and practical part of him and leave little room for a part of him that is intuitive, playful, and romantic. It isn't as if he should be the other way, but ideally, *he could access and engage those qualities when the situation called for them.* Rational, serious, and practical might not be the qualities he would want in a romance or while enjoying his children. In essence, the system looks at the selves or parts each of us identify with most as well as those we disown or haven't yet developed.

In order to skillfully facilitate the emergence of these undeveloped aspects of self, the facilitator needs not only skill and compassion but the ability to access these parts in herself. The "vulnerable child" is an aspect of self that is precious and contributes enormously to our ability to experience genuine intimacy in our lives. Yet, the wounds of childhood often leave this part buried under a mound of protectiveness. That protectiveness can take the form of a controlling personality or an over-intellectualized or critical "self." In fact, the individual who is fiercely critical of self and others is usually one whose vulnerable self was deeply wounded. In this situation, the facilitator would first establish rapport with the critical self and reflect her understanding that this self has good intentions, namely, to protect the individual from pain. Then, she would gently invite the vulnerable self into dialogue with the intention of opening space for this precious aspect of the individual to emerge.

The work of the Voice Dialogue Method is to bring into consciousness those parts of us that have been disowned, or insufficiently developed. At the same time it strives to reduce the influence of those parts that have been over-developed. Examples of parts that tend to be over-developed are the Pusher, (think Tom Hanna's green light reflex), the Critic, the Pleaser, the Controller, or the Rebel. Parts that tend to be disowned or underdeveloped are the Vulnerable Child, as we said above, the Power self, the Lover, the part that doesn't give damn about what anyone thinks, and so forth.

Voice Dialogue is the name of the method Hal and Sidra have given to the work of facilitating awareness of the many aspects of self. In Freudian theory, a major component of personality is the so-called Super-ego. It's the part that carries the injunctions and rules. Hal and Sidra have elaborated the concept to include the Inner Critic, The Perfectionist, The Pusher, The Controller, and The Pleaser. The words are self-evident, and most of us have one or more of them as heavyweight aspects of our make-up.

The Energetic Aspect of Selves

Becoming aware that different aspects have different energetic qualities is a beautiful feature of the Voice Dialogue process. For example, the facilitator may then ask to speak to a part of the individual, who has been submerged by the Inner Critic, let's say the Vulnerable Child. This part will have a very different feeling tone, a different vibratory quality, than the Inner Critic. This is what Hal and Sidra Stone refer to as *energetics*, and it involves attunement to the emotional body of an individual. It is a felt sense of the part.

To get a full sense of human possibility, the Hal and Sidra turned to Greek and Roman mythology to describe aspects of self. For example, Aphrodite, the Goddess of Love, might be a part the facilitator asks to speak to after speaking to Inner Critic. Again, this is not just a mental conversation. The facilitator uses her own Aphrodite quality to evoke the same feeling tone in the client. If this part in the individual has not developed, he essentially gives birth to this new dimension of self with the facilitator as midwife.

The Voice Dialogue method awakens the ability to "hold the tension of opposites;" Hal and Sidra Stone consider embracing "*And*" consciousness a hallmark of maturity. If an evangelical minister could only acknowledge how good it would feel to sleep with someone he met at a party *And* that it is against his moral values, he could hold that tension without letting it snap and get him caught at the local brothel.

We can become aware of and embrace selves we have previously disowned. When we do, we won't have to find other people to hold our projections. The hatred directed towards certain groups is an example of abhorring an aspect of self; and, instead of owning it, projecting it onto another and hating it in them. Obvious examples are the sexually promiscuous and homosexuals. Whether we agree with their values is not the issue. If there is hatred, that indicates a projection. As Hal and Sidra Stone put it, it is time to embrace our selves.[3] As we do, we become more coherent and better capable of loving self and others.

Selves and Movement

Now, here is an example of the relationship between selves and movement. Back in the early 1990s, Diane and I were directing a Hellerwork Structural Integration Training. In the final week of the training, we introduced the Psychology of Selves system. We introduced this system so that our students would have the opportunity to engage more of who they are and also to supply them with conceptual tools to facilitate their understanding of their clients.

After introducing the system academically, we did the following ritual. Sequentially, each student spent time in the "hot seat," while the class, led by the teachers, identified how the student presented himself in the world. What was his or her primary identity, or sub-personality, to use Hal and Sidra's language? One student, a man named Harry, had been a construction worker prior to becoming a student in the Hellerwork Training. On first appraisal, he could be a bit intimidating. He had a thick, black beard and very dark hair. His shoulders were broad and, despite a full series of structural body work, they were not exactly what I would call fluid. He usually wore blue jeans and flannel shirts and jean jackets, giving the overall impression of a man's man. He looked tough, rugged, outdoorsy, rigid, remote, emotionally unavailable, and super-masculine. These were some of the adjectives the class used to describe him.

Next in the process, the class was to pick a set of qualities that represented an opposite of those Harry presented in his day-to-day life. After some deliberation and experimentation, the class agreed: The perfect opposite was a flamboyant, gay interior decorator we named Armando. To our surprise, Harry agreed to play the role. Everyone in the class was given their opposite character to play. They were given the afternoon off to go to town, find costumes, and come to dinner as their new characters. We would have dinner in character and a dance afterwards, also in character.

There was no contesting the winner of the best male actor that evening. Harry, as Armando, had shaved his beard, cut his hair, and found colorful and expressive clothing. He entered the dining hall wearing a bright-pink sarong and jewelry and carried a very strong feminine affect. He never once came out of character the entire evening. We were impressed and awed. What was even more stunning and equally edifying was that, when he danced as Armando, *Harry's shoulder girdle moved with a fluidity and grace we had never before seen in him.* Harry's image of himself, who he took himself to be, did not include moving with ease and grace. Yet, when he adopted Armando, he could!

Identity limits movement, feeling, and being. The next day, he came to class as Harry, and it was interesting to note that his shoulder girdle appeared as it usually did, only perhaps a little bit softer. However, the change in Harry's life over the ensuing years has been nothing short of amazing. He is a congruently gentler man, and he gives ample attention to the artistic side of himself.

William Brugh Joy, M.D.: Heart Consciousness

Once again, it was my good friend Joe Heller who suggested I consider taking a ten-day retreat with a man named Brugh Joy.[4] As with EST, his description of features and benefits was vague. "It's about love," was all he said. I was just about to open a private practice, so I thought, "Why not? A little more love in my practice can't hurt." Repeatedly in my life, when I sensed the possibility of growth, I was in. Rarely have I been disappointed, and my experience at Brugh Joy's retreat was far from disappointing.

As a child, I was a devout Catholic, but by the time I was in college, I considered myself an agnostic. Too much of what the Church believed didn't make sense, and too often the Church officials weren't walking the talk. My agnosticism yielded to atheism by the time I was a graduate student. And even though EST had broadened my vision beyond Wilhelm Reich, Ida Rolf, and Fritz Perls, spirituality had found no home in my heart. That is, not until those ten days with Brugh Joy.

Brugh employed the Hindu chakra system to make sense of how

people live their lives. His view is that most humans on earth live in the lower three chakras, concerned with survival, sex, and power. All the games get played out within the context of the first three chakras: accumulation of wealth, machinations of politics, relationship dramas and conflicts, feelings and perspectives of victimization, games of who is right and who is wrong. Brugh's mission was to move us to the fourth—the heart chakra. The heart level begins true spiritual life, and for most humans back in 1976, it was a giant leap.

It certainly was for me. At the time, I was in my second marriage. The entire relationship lasted only five years, but in those years I had taken a new direction in relationship—I was attempting to be authentic and monogamous.

The retreat began in a gentle fashion: meditation, dream interpretations, lectures, and walks. The work deepened as the group coalesced. On the afternoon of the third day, I received an unexpected visit from my wife. She came to inform me that she wanted to explore an open marriage and—oh, by the way—she had already commenced. She had driven two-plus hours to inform me in person, took about five minutes in conversation, and drove another two-plus hours back home. I was in shock.

Slowly, pain and rage began to surface. In our evening session, Brugh turned all his attention—and the attention of the group—to me. He was empathic and deeply understanding. As upset as I was, I was also beautifully held. Even my own therapist and Reichian teacher, Allan Darbonne, was a member of the group. Finally, a deep calm came over me and I slept. The next morning, Brugh dropped a bombshell.

With the fierce compassion and clarity of a true Zen master, he opened morning circle by saying it was time to choose. It was time for the group to let go of issues of the first three chakras and enter a new dimension—the heart. We had until evening to make a choice. If we chose to leave, we would receive a refund and a friendly send-off, but it was time to make a choice.

What! How could I possibly let go of my emotional turmoil? I had just been betrayed. There could be no way in hell anyone could let go of it and ascend to higher ground.

Brugh was not going to budge. We had until the evening circle.

I was a basket case that day. I must have bounced off every wall of the retreat center, metaphorically speaking. I don't remember when it happened or how it happened. All I remember was a profound moment of clarity that descended throughout my being. *Yes, I could!* I knew it. I got it. I could transcend the drama of my relationship. Along with this clarity came peace that seemed completely out of place in my heart, given the circumstances. But there it was! And along with this peace was an even stranger quality of love. It wasn't love of any particular person, place, or thing. Love entered me from somewhere outside of me, but I could feel it within. I made my choice; I was in.

And what a ride it was! The experience I just described may have lasted an hour, and then the pain, sorrow, and rage returned. But they too lasted for only brief intervals. At times, the peace and love returned, and at other times, different types of unusual experiences occurred. One evening, just as I lay down to sleep, I truly left my body; I was on the ceiling, looking down at myself. Greatly excited, I wanted to call to Brugh and tell him; then, suddenly, I was afraid, and in the next instant was back inside my form. I have not had such an experience since.

Most importantly, I had the experience of looking into my future and seeing that it was bright. I learned a major lesson from those ten days. An experience such as I had with my wife might be awfully painful, but there is another dimension to engage. It might be summarized as: "God knows what He is doing. Pay attention." Yes, it was terribly painful and enraging, but in the retreat environment and with Brugh's assistance, I did not get lost in the pain and rage. I did not become a victim of her infidelity. Soon, I could see the perfection in the experience and the perfection in ending that marriage soon after. She and I came to that conclusion at the same time. We parted as tender friends. We had served our purpose with each other.

My days as an atheist were over. I couldn't give an intellectual discourse on the nature of God, but I can unequivocally assert that love in this grander sense is pretty close. I learned that to grow spiritually, we have to let go of all sense of victimization. This is such an important point; it can take years for some folks to get it. Yes, she was unfaithful, and that act caused a lot of pain. And in that pain lay a great gift.

Yes, my parents were brutal; had some of their actions occurred today and been reported, I probably would have been taken away. And, of course, I suffered a great deal at their hands. Yet, the enormous gift I received is what this whole book is about. Hopefully, many others will learn to live a better life as a result. From my practice and teaching, many already have.

To transcend the lower three chakras does not mean to repress or deny. I felt my pain and rage intensely; only I didn't make up stories so I could erect alters to their presence. In that holy environment, I was able to keep opening to a higher perspective and walk on higher ground.

In those ten days, Brugh also taught us to center in our hearts and learn to feel the energy from our hearts as it travels down through our hands. He described it as the energy of love and a powerful healing energy. Keep in mind that Brugh Joy began his career as a highly respected medical doctor—he was the Director of Medical Education at Good Samaritan Hospital in Los Angeles—and came to realize that many, many medical issues are rooted in spiritual malaise.

The retreat awakened my appetite for spiritual knowledge. From that retreat in 1976 to this day, I have sustained an interest in understanding authentic spiritual life. My conclusions after thirty-eight years are rather simple. A spiritual path is authentic if it challenges its adherents to live with more peace and love in their hearts and greater clarity in their consciousness. It is a true path if its adherents grow into loving their neighbors (of all colors, genders, sexual preferences, and religions) as they love themselves. It is a true path if they really can learn to love themselves. It is true if it facilitates our connection with nature, given we are part of nature itself. God has been given many attributes, such as love, peace, light, and justice. In my opinion, a spiritual path is true if it facilitates its followers to embody those very aspects to the best of their ability.

RESOURCES

The Landmark Forum—EST, Werner Erhard's creation, became the Landmark Forum and is still active in many cities across the country.

Voice Dialogue—There are many Voice Dialogue practitioners around the world. Hal and Sidra Stone's website is a great starting place for your search: www.voicedialogueinternational.com.

Although there are no Brugh Joy practitioners, his influence in the Hellerwork Structural Integration community is strong. Contact Joseph Heller in Mt. Shasta, California, for more information.

1. EST is still active today under a new name, The Landmark Forum. I don't know how much it has changed since 1974, but I do know several people who have taken the program, and all have been inspired by the results.

2. As were Joseph Heller, Allan Darbonne—my Reichian therapist and teacher—Werner Erhard, and Brugh Joy.

3. See Hal and Sidra Stone's, Embracing Ourselves; *Embracing Each Other*; and *Partnering* for a thorough exposition of their work.

4. The author of *Joy's Way,* Brugh (William Brugh Joy) was the medical director at Good Samaritan Hospital in LA. An illness catalyzed his spiritual journey, and in the mid-1970s, a good number of psychotherapists and body workers were on the waiting list to attend one of his residential retreats.

CHAPTER 21

PERSPECTIVES ON LOVE

"Our heart knows what our mind has forgotten—it knows the sacred that is within all that exists, and through a depth of feeling we can once again experience this connection, this belonging."
~ Llewellyn Vaughan-Lee

Over many years I have learned that no matter how poorly you begin or how disadvantaged you may have been, you can change course and continually enrich your life. In some cases, the magnitude of the changes required is formidable and daunting. Certainly, mine were. Definitely, a commitment is required, and it is much easier to make once you know it's possible, and have some idea of how to go about it. Further, most of us have suffered significant wounding simply because of where we humans are as a species. Our ignorance of our fluid nature is another insult that contributes to the societal conditions that allow impacts and insults to occur in the first place. In reading this book, you have seen how the wounds of life, the speed of life, and the ignorance of our culture conspire to rob us of our potential. You have learned how all those impacts and insults affect you at every place in your being. Most important, you have understood that no matter how bad the wounds were, the knowledge and resources are now increasingly available to transform your life for the better.

You have also seen the critical importance of love as a nourishing force in your life; we all need it in copious amounts. There are different ways to think about love. Love can be defined as a deep, caring bond between two people that includes respect, affection, and an appropriate level of commitment. The love of a mother for her child, the love of a husband and wife, the love between dear friends are examples.

However, it is essential to note that this understanding of love *may or may not include an abundance of love connections.*

Love can be described as those moments of exquisite connection between two (or more) people. These are precious moments and are extremely nourishing. When they began to occur in my marriage, my wife and I knew we had arrived at something quite special. Increasingly often in my life, in my private practice, and in my teaching, I look to cultivate these moments. Whenever they occur, I feel energized and enriched. Exquisite connections are possible whenever two or more are together. These connections require a strong sense of safety and a shared positive emotion, and usually eye-to-eye contact. From our very beginnings in infancy, these connections are crucial for our health and well-being.

Love also can be defined as a manifestation of the Divine, a spiritual presence that is always ready to nourish us if only we can open to it. In this sense, love is a given of nature. As we have seen, the fluid stream to which we are connected may be the medium of Divine love.

Too many human beings walk the earth believing that love is scarce; that there is just not enough to sustain them. But love is as abundant as air and water. Divine love requires only that we open to its presence. You may feel this in nature, or you may feel it in prayer or meditation. I have certainly felt it in my Continuum explorations. Further, as we learn to walk on higher ground, we begin to see Divine love through each moment of our lives, no matter what the challenges.

Let us go forward and live with more harmony, peace, and balance. Let us value coherence. Let us treasure exquisite connections and positive relationships. Let us go for a more authentic, whole-hearted, and engaged life. I urge you forward—for yourself, for all those with whom you are in relationship, and for this world in which we live.

ABOUT THE AUTHOR

Don St John, Ph.D., is a psychotherapist, somatic-relational teacher, coach, public speaker, and author. He is an authorized Continuum Movement teacher and Hellerwork Structural Integration practitioner and trainer. He has taught and given presentations in the US, Canada, New Zealand, and Brazil.

Dr. St John studied Gestalt Therapy at the LA Gestalt Therapy Institute and Neo-Reichian therapy with Drs. Allan Darbonne and Jack Lee Rosenberg; the Psychology of Selves and Voice Dialogue Method with Drs. Hal and Sidra Stone; Hakomi with Dr. Ron Kurtz; Coherence Therapy with Dr. Bruce Ecker; AEDP with Dr. Diana Fosha; and CIMS with Dr. Albert Sheldon and Beatriz Winstanley. He has taken immersion courses and core training in Dr. Sue Johnson's Emotionally-Focused Couple's Therapy. He is certified in Somatic Experiencing, the work of Dr. Peter Levine. He has also studied cranio-sacral therapy and for twenty years has been studying and practicing Continuum Movement developed by Emilie Conrad and Susan Harper.

Don brings two general qualifications to the authorship of *Healing the Wounds of Childhood*. The first, and perhaps most important, is that he has traveled the territory he describes, and he has accomplished an arguably miraculous level of personal change in one lifetime. As a psychotherapist, he works in a style that requires deep empathy and attunement with his patients. It is a level of emotional presence that he could not even have understood or imagined when he began his healing journey. As a Continuum Movement teacher, he teaches fluid movement. Again, this would have been unimaginable to him three decades ago. Thus, he has clearly walked what he talks.

His second general qualification is that he has been immersed in both the psychotherapeutic and somatic therapy worlds for the past forty-seven years. His roots were in traditional clinical psychology, but early on, he realized from his own experience that the body must be included. Thus began his journey in both the psychotherapeutic and somatic realms.

Don's doctoral dissertation, written at the Western Institute for Social Research, focused on the consequences of and recovery from relational maltreatment in early childhood. He lives in Salt Lake City with his wife of thirty years, Diane, co-founder of Paths of Connection. They have been teaching together for twenty-five years.

BIBLIOGRAPHY

Childre, Doc and Cryer Bruce. *From Chaos to Coherence*. Boulder Creek, Ca: Planetary, 2004.

Conrad, Emilie. *Life on Land: The Story of Continuum: The World-Renowned Self-Discovery and Movement Method*. Berkeley: North Atlantic Books, 2007.

Ecker Bruce and Hulley Laurel. *Depth Oriented Brief Therapy*. San Francisco: Jossey-Bass, 1996.

Everly, George and Lating, Jeffrey. *A Clinical Guide to the Treatment of the Human Stress Response*. New York: Kluwer Academic/Plenum Publishers, 2002.

Fogel, Alan. *The Psychophysiology of Self Awareness: Rediscovering the Lost Art of Body Sense*. New York: W. W. Norton, 2009.

Fosha, Diana. *The Transforming Power of Affect*. New York: Basic Books, 2002.

Fredrickson, Barbara. *Love 2.0: Creating Happiness and Health in Moments of Connection*. New York: Plume, 2013.

Gilligan, Stephen. *The Courage to Love: Principles and Practices of Self-Relations Psychotherapy*. New York: W.W. Norton, 1997.

Hanna, Thomas. *The Body of Life*. New York, Alfred A Knopf, Inc. 1979.

Hanna, Thomas. *Somatics*. Cambridge: Perseus Books, 1988.

Hanson, Rick. *Buddha's Brain*. Oakland, Ca: New Harbinger Publications, 2009.

Hanson, Rick. *Hardwiring Happiness*. New York: Harmony Books, 2013.

Heller, Joseph. *Bodywise: Regaining Your Natural Flexibility and Vitality for Maximum Well-Being*. Los Angeles: Jeremy P. Tarcher,

Inc. 1986.

Ho, Mae-Wan. *The Rainbow and the Worm: The Physics of Organisms*. River Edge, N.J.: World Scientific Publishing, 1998.

Ho, Mae-Wan. *Living Rainbow H2O*. Hackensack, N.J.: World Scientific Publishing, 2012.

Holdrege, Craig, ed. *The Dynamic Heart and Circulation*. Fair Oaks, Ca.: The Association of Waldorf Schools of North America, 2002

Johnson, Susan. *The Practice of Emotionally Focused Marital Therapy: Creating Connection*. Philadelphia: Brunner/Mazel, Inc., 1996.

Kaufman, Gershen. *Shame: The Power of Caring*. Cambridge: Schenkman Books, 1980.

Kaufman, Gershen. *The Psychology of Shame: Theory and Treatment of Shame Based Syndromes*. New York: Springer Publishing Co., 1996.

Koob, Andrew. *The Root of Thought: Unlocking Glia, the Brain Cell That Will Help Us Sharpen Our Wits, Heal Injury, and Treat Brain Disease*. Upper Saddle River, New Jersey: Pearson Education Inc. 2009.

Levine, Peter. *Waking the Tiger*. Berkeley: North Atlantic Books, 1997.

Levine, Peter. *In An Unspoken Voice: How the Body Releases Trauma and Restores Goodness*. Berkeley: North Atlantic Books, 2010.

Levoy, Gregg. *Callings: Finding and Following an Authentic Life*. New York: Three Rivers Press, 1997.

Loehr, Jim and Schwartz, Tony. *The Power of Full Engagement*. New York: Simon and Schuster, 2003.

McEwen, Bruce. *The End of Stress As We Know It*. Washington, D. C: Joseph Henry Press, 2002.

Nathanson, Donald. *Shame and Pride: Affect, Sex, and the Birth of the Self*. New York: W. W. Norton, 1992.

Ornish Dean. *Love and Survival: The Scientific Basis for the Healing Power of Intimacy*. New York: Harper Collins, 1998.

Pearsall, Paul. *The Heart's Code*. New York: Broadway Books, 1998.

Pert, Candace. *The Molecules of Emotion*. New York: Scribner, 1997.

Pollack, Gerald. *The Fourth Phase of Water*. Seattle: Ebner and Sons Publishers, 2013.

Porges, Stephen. *The Polyvagal Theory: Neurophysiological Foundations of Emotions, Attachment, Communication and Self-Regulation*. New York: W. W. Norton. 2011.

Reich, Wilhelm. *The Function of the Orgasm*. Meridian Books, 1927.

Reich, Wilhelm. *Selected Writings*. New York: Farrar, Straus and Giroux, 1951.

Richo, David. *How To Be An Adult in Relationships*. Boston: Shambhala Publications, 2002.

Rolf, Ida P. *Rolfing: The Integration of Human Structures*. New York: Harper and Row, 1977.

Schore, Allan N. *Affect Regulation and the Origin of the Self*. Hillsdale: Lawrence Erlbaum Associates, 1994.

Schultz, Louis and Feitis, Rosemary. *The Endless Web: Fascial anatomy and physical reality*. Berkeley: North Atlantic Books, 1996.

Siegel, Dan. *The Developing Mind: Toward a Neurobiology of Interpersonal Relation*. New York: The Guilford Press, 1999.

Siegel, Dan. *The Mindful Brain*. New York: W. W. Norton and Company, 2007.

Solomon, Marion F. and Siegel, Daniel J. ed. *Healing Trauma*. New York: W. W. Norton, 2003.

Schwenk, Theodor. *Sensitive Chaos: The Creation of Flowing Forms in Water and Air*. London: Rudolph Steiner Press, 1965.

Stone, Hal and Stone, Sidra. *Embracing Our Selves.* Marina del Rey, Ca: Devorss & Co., 1985.

Stone, Hal and Stone, Sidra. *Partnering: A New Kind of Relationship: How to Love Each Other Without Losing Yourselves*. Novato, Ca: New World Library, 2000.

Stone, Hal and Stone, Sidra. *The Fireside Chats with Hal and Sidra Stone*. Albion, Ca: Delos, Inc. 2011.

Todd, Mabel Elsworth. *The Thinking Body.* Brooklyn, N.Y: Dance Horizons, 1972.

Van Der Kolk, Bessel. *The Body Keeps the Score.* New York: The Penguin Group, 2014.

Van Der Kolk, Bessel, McFarlane, Alexander and Weisaeth, L. *Traumatic Stress: The effects of overwhelming experience on mind, body and society*. New York: The Guilford Press, 1996.

Wirth, Fredrick. *Prenatal Parenting*. New York: Harper Collins, 2001.

For information about our work or to set up lectures, workshops or in-person or telephone appointments, please visit www. pathsofconnection.com or email me at don@st-jon.com

Printed in Great Britain
by Amazon

69856190R10159